# Memories of a High Flyer

## The downs and ups of a U-2 pilot

### By

### Colonel Art Saboski (US Air Force, Retired)

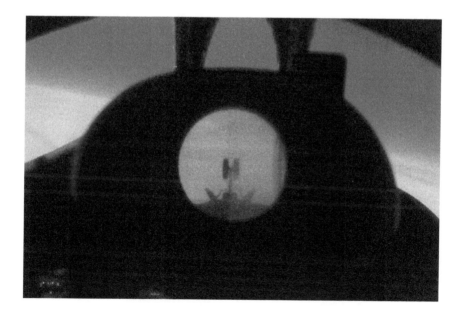

2

# Contents

*Intro*        *10*

*Prologue: an Aviator's Life*   *13*

*Kid Stuff*       *15*

The Earliest Years .................................................. 15
Four Years Wasted ................................................. 20
Post-Graduation ..................................................... 21
West by Southwest ................................................ 22

*Wings*       *25*

Pilot Training .......................................................... 25
Ground Training ..................................................... 26
On the Flight Line ................................................. 28
Arizona .................................................................... 31
The Germans ........................................................... 33
The Good Captain Wallace .................................. 35
From Tweet to Talon ............................................ 36
Flying the Talon ..................................................... 38
Hazardous Duty ..................................................... 41
The Real Meaning of It All .................................. 42
The Next Assignment ........................................... 45
Graduation ............................................................. 47

*The Phantom*  *49*

Survival School ....................................................... 49
Imprisonment ......................................................... 51
Tucson, Then to the High Desert of California ....... 52
The Fastest Guy on Earth? .................................... 55

*Young Pilot in War*    *60*

Da Nang, RVN ......................................................... 60
Flying the Phantom in Combat ............................ 62
Homer ...................................................................... 66

Stuff Happens ........................................................ 66
Fred's Accident ..................................................... 67
Flyin' With Chuck .................................................. 68
Denny Chambers, POW ......................................... 70
Strange Circumstances ..........................................71
Hawaii—on Business............................................. 74
Back to Da Nang .................................................. 78
From Da Nang to Delta......................................... 79

# The Bird Dog   82

Little Binh Thuy................................................... 82
Nha Trang and the Korean Army........................... 83
Complacency......................................................... 83
Working with Grunts ............................................ 85
A Bunch of Cuties................................................. 86
Nha Trang ........................................................... 87
Dumb Mistake...................................................... 88
My Encounter with the Press................................. 88
We Go Camping ................................................... 90
We Go Camping, Again......................................... 92
Why I Hate Helicopters ........................................ 93
Kimchi in Self Defense.......................................... 94
Living With the ROK Army.................................... 96
The Aussies ......................................................... 97
How Far Will It Go?.............................................. 98
R&R..................................................................... 99
Tet .....................................................................101
Tet Isn't Quite Finished ...................................... 102
End of Tour ........................................................ 104
The Last Time I Saw Charlie................................. 105

# Big Spring   106

Back Home.......................................................... 106
It's Academic....................................................... 108
A Student Meets Larry.......................................... 109
Ex-Student Byrne.................................................110
The Spin ............................................................. 112
Incentive Flights ................................................. 113

Social Life in Big Spring.......................................... 114

# Wichita Falls  117

Back to Vietnam? ................................................. 117
Mister Coulibali .................................................. 119
Academic Chief ................................................... 120

# The Dragon Lady  122

A New Career ........................................................123
A Tricky Airplane to Fly............................................125
... and Even Trickier to Land.......................................127
The Pressure Suit...................................................129
Chamber of Horrors................................................. 131
Take the T-Bird.....................................................132
Taxi, Please .......................................................135
Initial Qualification...............................................135
The Pleasures of Flying High ...................................... 140
Too Tall in the Saddle ............................................ 140
Flying the Dragon Lady .............................................142
The Dangers of Flying High ........................................ 144
What's for Dinner?..................................................145
Intake and Exhaust .................................................147
ALSS and Beyond.................................................... 151
How High Did You Fly? ..............................................154
Other Missions......................................................154
Time Passes.........................................................155
Nuclear Sampling ...................................................159

# California, Here We Come  163

England in Winter................................................... 164
It's Nice to Be Alone.............................................. 168
A Visit to Japan................................................... 169
Up in the Air With No Place to Go...................................173
Tragedy ............................................................177
Showdown............................................................178

# The Pentagon, Phase I    182

Sailing, Sailing ..................................................... 183
It's the White House Calling ................................185
Rear Admiral Fuller ..............................................187
Change of Life ......................................................187

# Olive Harvest  189

The Joke's on Me ................................................192
My Change of Life ...............................................195
Back to Cyprus .................................................... 196
The Way We Were ............................................... 198
British Friends ....................................................203
The Last Time I Saw Cyprus ..............................204

# In the States Again 206

Back to Beale.....................................................207

# The Pentagon, Phase II   210

# Then to Omaha      214

The SAC Senior ...................................................214
Nuclear Deterrence..............................................216
60 Minutes vs. America .......................................217

# England        219

The Mission........................................................221
The Organizations...............................................222
Day One..............................................................224
Superb People .................................................... 225
Dale ................................................................... 225
Our Home on Base.............................................. 227
The 17th At Work ............................................... 229
Nostalgia ........................................................... 233
Pride and Sadness.............................................. 237
An Accident Isn't All It's Cracked Up to Be .......... 237

Other Happenings................................................240
More Stuff ........................................................242
Time to Leave....................................................243

# In One Career, Out the Other 246

What Comes Next?............................................246
Civilian Life......................................................247

# From Air Force to Airline     250

Domicile Chief Pilot..........................................251
The Crash.........................................................254
We Move to Nashville .......................................256
New Job in Nashville ........................................258
Promotion Denied, Sort of . . . ..........................260
No More Lawyers!.............................................260
The Merger.......................................................262
The First Consolidated Bid ...............................262
Manager of Crew Resources .............................264
Enough, Already ..............................................265
Bill's Advice.....................................................268

# Two Careers Down, One to Go     269

On the Road Again............................................269
Welcome to Prescott, Arizona...........................270
Embry-Riddle ..................................................270
Ron..................................................................271
Teaching Again ...............................................272
Have a Heart ...................................................274
Talk, All Talk....................................................275
My "Fini" Flight ...............................................276

# I'm Almost Done     279

Retirement Number Three ................................279
Old Pilots, Old Instructors, Old Men..................280
Pure Politics....................................................282
Too Much Travel...............................................283
Old Hobbies, New Interests..............................283

Some of Us Get Old ............................................. 285
What Does It All Mean? ....................................... 286
Frosting on the Cake ........................................... 288
The View from Above ........................................... 292

## Acknowledgements     294

# *Intro*

I'm writing this to no one in particular. Memoirs are often intended for friends and family, but mine are somewhat depleted now—time has thinned my blood line to a trickle, and flying escapades and war have knocked off many friends prematurely. So I've compiled these memories just to capture and record the salient aspects of my life. For posterity, I suppose. I don't know who might read it, and I have no expectations.

I'm aware my life has been quite different from most. Most people live very pedestrian lives, where events generally occur as expected with some regularity and predictability and at a measured pace—and where altitude doesn't matter. Most people don't contend with much added risk in their daily lives, either.

My life wasn't that way.

This book is a crossover between autobiography and memoirs. Call it what you want. While I don't completely ignore the earliest and latest stages of my life, I don't dwell on life's "bookends," either. Frankly, kids are just kids, and they're all pretty much alike despite what their parents think. My childhood just isn't an important matter. Likewise, there's not a lot going on in my latter years that doesn't involve a bathroom in some way, so I didn't write much about that, either. There's simply not much meat left in the entrails of life.

But for those interested, there's a lot of aviation stuff sandwiched in the middle. If aviation doesn't appeal to you, stop and read something else. When a career pilot recounts his memories you can be sure he'll talk about flying until it's snooze time.

I didn't write about airplanes as much as I wrote about the people who fly them. Much of what I've written describes other pilots I've known. It takes a particular kind of character to push high-

10

performance aircraft to their limits—sometimes off-the-wall, unrestrained character. The flying business is populated with such people. This book is as much about many of them as it is about me.

I tried to avoid writing a plodding chronology of sonorous personal stuff. I'm not interested in droll chronology and I wouldn't expect anyone else to be. I've written stories and anecdotes that together recollect my life, my views, and interesting people.

I like history. History can be tedious, but it can be vibrant, too. Flying isn't tedious unless you screw up badly and make it that way. This book isn't about that kind of flying. If you like tedium, take the bus. Take an Airbus.

Any pilot—or conscientious citizen—worth his salt knows what a U-2 is. You don't have to be an aviation buff to know that the U-2 "Dragon Lady," called the "spy plane" by the press, played a big part in modern history. The U-2 has flown higher and longer above the heads of the world for more years than any other aircraft, by far. For over 50 years the exploits of the U-2 have provided fodder for books, movies, and TV programs of both fiction and fact. My role in the U-2 story involved seventeen of those years.

Eileen (my bride) said I should write it all down. I thought I had other things to do in retirement more deserving of my time—mow the lawn, play some golf, snore, etc.—but I finally relented.

For those who haven't sat in an airplane cockpit the aviation lexicon I use in these pages may be a little challenging, so I softened the lingo somewhat, avoiding overuse of acronyms as much as possible and explaining terminology where necessary. If there's something you don't understand, just read on. Maybe you'll get it later. Maybe you won't.

I considered including a glossary but that seemed too pedantic. Scholarly history buffs may kick off their shoes and read in leisure. This isn't a study; it's casual reading and there's no exam afterwards.

Eileen's sharp elbow in my ribs tells me it's time to get started before all is forgotten or my life reaches terminus. So before I lapse

11

into the shrinking stage of life where my brain begins to resemble a walnut—and before I begin to freely intermingle fiction with facts as old people do—I'll reminisce my story.

Here goes . . .

# Prologue: an Aviator's Life

When I reflect on my 43 years in professional aviation boredom sure doesn't come to mind. I've held an array of positions that had me travelling throughout much of the world, experiencing challenging events and circumstances that most people would never encounter.

One benefit of the aviator's life is that you never have to dig deeply to recall extraordinary episodes. If I had done nothing else but fly the U-2, I'd have enough interesting tales to last a lifetime of storytelling.

For 17 years I flew, operated, and commanded units of the U-2 "spy plane" of international renown. Almost everything we did was classified at very high levels. Many of those annals have only recently been declassified. In this book I relate an "inside story"—some personal experiences and everyday encounters that never made it into the numerous publications written about the infamous "Dragon Lady."

Flying and the aviator's life were a perfect fit for me. Along the way I apparently developed an adventurous spirit and independent tendencies. I've never thought of myself as a thrill-seeker, and taking inordinate risks for no real purpose wasn't my calling. But I was certainly no wallflower, either. I'd rather put my foot in the water than sit on the shore. I've had numerous close calls, but those were incidental to commitments I had made or responsibilities I held, not for seeking a blood-rush. I've taken acceptable risks—including mortal ones—when I felt duty and best judgment called me to do so.

Early in my flying career I discovered that piloting high-performance aircraft and putting them through their paces were immensely satisfying. Accomplishing difficult aerial missions provided me lasting feelings of accomplishment, and in that sense I rate military aviation far superior to most civilian flying. As time passed and the intrinsic thrills of piloting airplanes diminished, I found continuing satisfaction elsewhere in aviation, in leading its organizations and people.

I've had three distinct aviation careers, and I retired from each: Air Force officer and pilot; airline pilot and manager; and aeronautical university professor. In that last career line I enjoyed the sublime satisfaction of "passing my baton" to young and upcoming aviation students. In fact, three of my students went on to join the Air Force and fly the U-2 as I did—most extraordinary considering the relatively few people on earth who have ever flown the airplane. It doesn't get much better than that.

# *Kid Stuff*

The Earliest Years

I'm writing mostly about my aviation life, so I won't re-hash my childhood for long except to relate how I fortuitously stumbled my way into a profession of piloting and other aviation pursuits.

I didn't have a flying background. That is, no one among family or friends had flown or had any aviation knowledge. There's no particular reason I should gravitate toward flying except a boy's early fascination with airplanes. Sure, I collected model airplanes as a kid, but I also had model ships, too. I might as well have joined the Navy, for that matter. In fact, there was probably a greater likelihood that I'd become a swabbie since as a boy my family and I lived on a private island.

Living in Pittsfield, Massachusetts, we were somewhat of an ordinary family in most ways. Long after my parents have gone I appreciate how fortunate I was to have them. We were a small family. My brother, Tom, was born five years ahead of me.

My grandparents had all emigrated from Poland in the early 20th Century. They fled war-ravaged Poland for America's freedoms and promise, and they embraced this country. They admonished my parents not to teach my brother and me the Polish language because they fervently wanted us boys to be raised us as good Americans speaking only English. American patriotism had primacy in our immigrant family.

Mom and Dad had been high school friends and neighbors in their small hometown in upstate New York. After graduation they left the town, went separate ways, found each other again and married. Mom graduated from prestigious Mount Sinai nursing school in New York

15

City as class valedictorian. Dad grew up hard scrabble on the family farm and simply persevered to better jobs and success.

Dad was very resourceful. During The Depression he held down three jobs while also playing minor league baseball and basketball. He apprenticed with Stanley Electric Company (a.k.a. General Electric Company) while holding down a daytime foundry job and also working as a musician in speakeasy orchestras at night. Dad played five different instruments, and friends said he played them all well.

The Depression times were tough, and work was hard if you could get it. While Dad was playing semi-pro basketball he made extra bucks by going a few rounds with a professional boxer during halftimes before returning to the court to finish the game. I can't imagine any athlete doing that today.

After Dad and Mom married and started our family, Dad quit playing music. Mom worked as a practical nurse and Dad spent long days at General Electric as a machinist.

Mom was Secretary of the Pittsfield Women's Club. The club owned an island on a lake outside of Pittsfield. Francis Island was about two acres with a two-story house, a remnant from when a causeway once connected it to the mainland. The club needed a caretaker for the island during summers, and Mom and Dad volunteered. Our family of four plus the dog spent several summers living alone on the island. There was no plumbing or electricity, just kerosene lamps, a wood stove, a fresh water pump, fireplace, and a lovely one-hole outhouse.

I was quite young, and the two-acre island seemed big to me. It was a boy's perfect adventure place.

From my earliest years Dad and Mom gave me responsibility and trust. Even when quite small I was allowed to take the rowboat out alone. Later I'd run the motorboat, too. I loved the water, and in later life sailing became a major recreation for me.

We lived without conveniences, and our life on the island taught me independence and gave me much confidence. I found I could be quite content alone with my curiosities and explorations.

At General Electric Dad was promoted to foreman. Soon after came a managerial opportunity—in North Carolina. GE was building a new manufacturing plant in Hickory, located in the foothills of the Appalachian Mountains. The job of Manager of Facilities was Dad's if we'd move. It was a difficult choice—separation from family, friends, and home—but we did it. Dad commuted to Hickory from Pittsfield for quite some time until we could join him. We built a house—quite simple, but adequate. For months while it was being constructed our family lived in a tent in the foothills of the Blue Ridge Mountains.

I learned important lessons with our move. One came from Dad's determination to seize opportunities that came along—or to create his own. The other lessons came from relocating to an entirely different culture and learning how to adapt. Seizing opportunities and relocating when necessary would describe my entire working career.

I entered Hickory's schools in the 9th grade. My first year was quite a trial. I was well-prepared academically by Massachusetts schools, but the Southern culture was a shock to all of us.

We were Yankee, Catholic, and Polish. Anyone who thinks the Civil War is over needs to experience being the vanguard family of a Yankee invasion. The Old Southern culture simply didn't know what to do with us. The South of western Carolina was a stratified society of class distinctions. Although we were a blue collar family and didn't have much money, Dad's new management position thrust us into the southern upper class where we really didn't belong.

Our religion was an issue, too. Southern communities were wrapped around their churches, all protestant. Catholics were a novelty, at best. When I was doing summer roadwork along the Blue Ridge Parkway, another teenage worker said his preacher told the congregation that the Pope's hat (his mitre) was shaped to hide the devil's horns under it. He asked if that was true. I said it was.

17

There was no cloaking our accents or our strange last name, either. Our name decried us as foreigners, but much worse, our accents proclaimed we were Yankees. At high school football games Dixie was sung while the Confederate flag flew and everyone stood. If someone by chance remembered, the national anthem followed. Some stood for that, too.

We just gutted it out. There were numerous disappointing and embarrassing moments, and the social atmosphere was particularly hard on Mom. The small community center had some duckpin bowling lanes. When Mom organized a ladies bowling group there, the Mayor approached and told her, "Our ladies don't bowl, Mrs. Saboski."

The Southern attitude in those days revealed considerable distrust—even enmity—toward northerners. Our family had to learn Southern ways and change. This was also the segregationist South, and I had a tough time accepting that one.

Years passed. We adapted, and I did well in school and made good friends. I learned a lot about how history shaped deep Southern culture. I began to understand it more and to appreciate it, too.

There's currently much controversy over flying the Confederate flag and displaying civil war statuary. I might have held a different opinion if I hadn't lived in the South for many years. Now I understand the intrinsic meaning of those icons which runs deep into the psyche of Southern families, still healing from the scars of America's most horrible war.

Older brother Tom was off to college during the school months, and I found independent activities to busy myself at home. The piano lessons Mom and Dad arm-twisted me to take had taken hold, and I played the piano in our basement. From then on, playing the piano and creating music would become an important part of my entire life. I joined a dance band with some classmates and played a few gigs at local parties. When our band played on stage at the high school, I was the emcee. My teachers gave me the lead role in the senior class play, and I also gave some other performances on stage to the class assembly.

Our Catholic church was quite small, and it had an old organ that resembled a relic from the Middle Ages. It was an organ without an organist, sitting unused in the loft. Dad and Mom prevailed upon me to play for our services, and I'd stop by the church after school to practice.

Our congregation began to expand as more General Electric families moved into the area. With the newly renovated, expanded church came a new organ, and it had foot pedals. My organist occupation suddenly became more complex. I was quite certain that feet were meant for walking, running, or kicking a ball of some sort— not music. Mine sure weren't meant for playing the organ, as I found out. The new organ already had three keyboards, so why were foot pedals even necessary? Learning to play foot pedals would require far more time than I was prepared to donate, and I was in a quandary.

Then a true miracle happened—a real organist moved into the congregation, and I was finally off the hook. As I stood beneath the loft contentedly listening to the new organist play during Sunday morning mass, I leaned against one of the support columns. The column was already occupied by a wasp that resented my intrusion and stung me. Fortunately I stifled a yell that would surely have punctuated the service.

I took the event as a profound religious omen: I had been displaced from my brief sojourn as church organist and punished by one of God's creatures for basking in gratitude. In succeeding years I began to disaffect from church and religion, and I'm pretty sure that wasp had something to do with it.

I got a taste of both flying and military life when I joined the Civil Air Patrol in high school. I flew for the first time in a Piper Cub. I soaked up whatever aviation knowledge I could glean and enthusiastically studied flying manuals Dad got from a family friend who had flown in the War.

My first exposure to the Air Force was when the CAP cadets were flown on an Air Force C-45 to a week's encampment at Turner Air Force Base in Georgia. On the flight going there I got to sit in the

19

cockpit and put my hands on the controls. After returning to Hickory I was promoted to cadet captain and appointed as squadron commander. I was hooked.

## Four Years Wasted

I had a lot of growing up to do before I ever came near an airplane again.

I headed off to college at the University of North Carolina in Chapel Hill. I performed miserably and barely graduated with my B.S. in Business Administration. I had excelled in high school, contested for a Fulbright scholarship, and gained advanced placement in college entrance exams. But I was a year younger than my classmates and sorely lacking in maturity and discipline. Rooming in the jock dormitory with two sophomore football players didn't help my freshman study habits, either. My grades plummeted my first two years, and I spent my last two pulling them up.

In my sophomore year I moved into another dorm with two new roommates. One night as we studied one roommate became frustrated and decided to spice up his evening by dropping a cherry bomb out the window. The dorm advisor lived directly below and quickly figured out where it came from. Soon there was a knock on our door. My roommate was frantic because he was on scholarship and would be kicked out of school. For some reason I took the rap for him. I was kicked out of the dorm and took up temporary residence at the Theta Chi fraternity house. My grades were already hurting and that episode sure didn't make things better. I was sliding downhill.

Most of what I gleaned from those undergraduate years came from outside the classroom, just growing up. In my junior and senior years there were some brighter academic moments, but I still had a lot of maturing to do. Although I fell short in my studies, I actually began to enjoy the learning experience. My favorite courses were Business Law, Logic, and Statistics. Those dull subjects shouldn't appeal to a kid who was scraping by academically. But in statistics a very tough professor gave me a "B" course grade; the rest of the class got Cs or below. I was beginning to come around.

I moved out of the frat house into an off-campus apartment with two other guys and miraculously graduated with a 'C' average. I had sorely disappointed myself and my parents.

## Post-Graduation

There weren't a lot of prestigious jobs waiting for someone with such a mediocre college transcript. I moved to Fayetteville, NC, to work as an assistant manager at a department store. Not my cup of tea. I was disappointed in myself for wasting my undergraduate years and now had no particular direction to my life or work. I was also facing the draft.

I must have been gaining some maturity and beginning to think more adult-like, because I began to ponder my circumstances. I weighed my current life, my prospects, and the likelihood of being drafted into the Army and decided to resolve matters differently. Recalling my Civil Air Patrol experience, I decided to join the Air Force. I drove to the Air Force base at Goldsboro and took entrance tests to qualify as an officer. I was never confident in my eyesight, so I elected to test for the navigator career field with its less-stringent vision requirements. The officer administering the qualification exams asked why I wasn't testing to be a pilot, and I explained my vision doubts. He said, "Take the pilot exam. We'll tell you if your eyesight is good enough."

I passed the aptitude tests for pilot. After the written testing I took the physical exam. The very last step was the optical exam. I sat in the waiting room anxiously awaiting the results. I was elated when the optometrist stepped out and blithely said, "Congratulations, pilot."

I was ecstatic. I stepped outside, intending to drive down to the flight line and look at airplanes. When I hit the parking lot and got a face-full of sun, I realized my eyes were still dilated from the eye exam and I couldn't see. Squinting blindly, I somehow made it to the flight line, but stare as I might, the sun was too much for me to see the airplanes except as a blur. It took a half hour for me to get my vision back. That was okay—I just stood there, basking in my thoughts of becoming an Air Force pilot.


## West by Southwest

My first step into the Air Force was to attend Officer Training School and get my commission. OTS isn't always available; its existence depends on whether the Air Force Academy and Air Force ROTC can meet the demand for officers. But it was open for me in 1965 during the ramp-up to the Vietnam War, and the demand for officers and pilots was climbing.

So I was headed for San Antonio and three months of OTS. As I got aboard the Air Force transport plane an officer told me that I was in charge of the other recruits on board. I was bewildered. I had never been placed "in charge" of anyone except some CAP cadets and some hens on a friend's chicken farm. I was the only officer candidate on board and wasn't prepared for this—my first taste of officer responsibilities.

We flew west and south out of North Carolina, across the Mississippi—a milestone for me. I saw for the first time the flat, sparsely populated lands west of the great river, and they looked inviting.

OTS was grueling, instilling physical and mental discipline in a very stark and harsh way: fundamental basic training. OTS was admittedly a crash course to obtain an officer commission, but for that reason it was also very concentrated and very unforgiving.

We got little sleep and lots of punishment. I was chewed hard for being a quarter inch off in making my military bed. Why? To teach "attention to detail"—a phrase I heard over and over again. We were being systematically molded into something other than raw recruits.

22

It sounds trite to say this, but in every boy there's a man. With some boys they just have dig deep and drag it out of you.

There's nothing nice about basic training, but I embraced the spirit of it all and was glad to be where I was. Everything was new, different, and demanding. Ahead of me was pilot training, my ultimate goal, and basic was a step toward that goal. It meant finding something I really wanted to be doing—a remarkable change from my college days and assistant manager job.

Twenty-five years later as a colonel and ROTC commander, I ran the southwest region's summer camp for a couple of hundred cadets using those very same facilities where I had attended OTS long ago.

Not everyone made it through OTS. It was very intense. There were failures and drop-outs, and I saw more than one cadet reduced to tears. I learned that rigorous personal discipline was necessary and not everyone had it. Some of my classmates couldn't endure the harsh treatment. Like all military basic training, OTS challenged us all—mentally, physically, and emotionally. The training involved every waking moment, everything we did. We got very little sleep.

I accepted the challenge and tried my best. There was no doubt that the school was changing me. At first it was daunting. OTS tore at every cadet's fabric, breaking us down into raw meat. But step by step it built us up into better, stronger men. Three months of OTS gave me a much needed and rewarding boost to my direction in life. I was ready for more.

When graduation and commissioning came, we assembled in an auditorium to receive our assignments. The first announcements were for the pilot training bases. The top graduates were given their choice among the seven pilot training bases, all scattered throughout the southern and southwestern US. As the base names and available slots were read aloud, we were polled by class standing to stand and declare our choice.

There was only one base I really wanted—Williams Air Force Base near Phoenix, Arizona. The talk among us, however, was that "Willy" had the highest wash-out rate of all. I feared being washed out, but the prospects of living in Arizona attracted me. When my name was called, there was just one remaining slot at "Willy," and I took it. It was another good choice—my life-long love affair with Arizona and the southwest had begun.

# *Wings*

## Pilot Training

Williams AFB was typical of the seven pilot training bases of the Air Training Command. The flying training wing was the base's principle organization, consisting of two training squadrons and other squadrons for support, supply, and maintenance. In Air Force parlance, a "wing" can either be part of an airplane or the large, principal organization that occupies and dominates an Air Force base. "Wings" are also the insignia worn on the uniform that designate a military pilot.

In those days the cost of making an Air Force pilot was a cool million bucks. Pilot training lasted 55 weeks, divided into the Primary Phase and the Basic Phase. The Primary training aircraft was the Cessna-built, twin engine T-37 "Tweet," a medium-performance jet with side-by-side seating. After half of the year, those who passed all flying check rides and academic testing passed on to the Basic Phase, flying the supersonic T-38 Talon.

The Air Force had recently decided to start its pilot trainees directly into jets, so the "Tweet" was the first aircraft I flew. It was incredibly noisy. The cockpit was only a few feet away from the engine intakes, and its engines made a high-pitched scream that destroyed eardrums. My progressive hearing loss began with flying the "Tweet."

Workdays were divided: mornings attending academic classes and afternoons at our flight line squadron building, adjacent to where the aircraft were parked. Each week we'd swap the morning and afternoon activities with our twin sister squadron, which remained on the opposite schedule from ours for the entire year until we graduated together.

25

I had never worked so hard. Days began very early and afternoons were long, often leading into night flying. We sometimes worked into the weekends flying day-night, out-and-back, and cross-country navigation flights to other destinations. We were given two weeks off during the Christmas season when the entire wing's training shut down; otherwise, there were no breaks. The Air Force doesn't take time off for national holidays like civilians do.

## Ground Training

Classroom academics were in an academic building apart from the flight line. We studied aerodynamics, aircraft systems, physiology of flight, flight instruments, meteorology, and navigation. We spent hours in aircraft simulators, rehearsing procedures and instrument flying. Our physical training classes consisted of track and field, sports, and combatives—hand-to-hand combat. We went to the firing range and trained how to fire hand weapons. In marksmanship we qualified to shoot a .45 automatic, the standard sidearm for officers at that time. But we were training for combat, not just plugging targets, so we trained how to shoot around barriers, prone position, rapid fire, etc. I earned an Expert Marksmanship award in the process.

Lurking near the flight line was an ominous contraption that towered above nearby buildings. It was called the "Boom Bucket." The Boom Bucket was an ejection seat mounted on a near-vertical, 80-foot rail. It was outfitted with a 35mm cannon charge beneath the seat. One day we lined up for our one and only ride in the Boom Bucket. Taking turns, we strapped into the ejection seat and were instructed to use the correct posture—spine alignment, etc. Then the student pulled up the arming handles and squeezed the trigger. The cannon charge exploded, sending seat and student shooting up the rail. My back was sore for days afterward, but I set the class record at 68 feet.

We spent time in the altitude chamber learning the physiological effects of flying and training to operate aircraft oxygen systems. The altitude chamber is a massive, thick metal structure with plexiglass portholes built to handle the strains of changing atmospheric

26

pressure. Throughout my Air Force flying career I spent lots of time in altitude chambers after that. And I learned a new word: "flatus."

We received a few days of classroom instruction on aviation physiology before we and our instructors entered the chamber wearing oxygen masks and helmets. After the door banged shut we listened to the ominous, echoing sounds as huge pumps evacuated air from inside the chamber.

The instructors placed us in pairs, facing each other. One student turned off his oxygen supply and conducted a simple task, like dealing a deck of cards or counting, while the other observed the effects of oxygen deprivation and nitrogen narcosis on his buddy. Fingernails and lips turned blue as the student gradually lost cognizance and memory, feeling a tingling sensation in his fingertips. Before the student lost consciousness, the instructor turned the oxygen back on, and when he recovered they discussed the learning experience.

It was an important lesson to teach us the consequences of an oxygen supply failure and to be able to recognize the onset of our personal symptoms. In real life over the years, I know of numerous circumstances of in flight oxygen loss.

We also learned about parachutes and parachuting. We learned how to eject or bail out, how to deploy and steer the parachute, how to fall and roll when contacting the ground and to gather the parachute afterward.

We were taught about spatial disorientation. Most humans walk, pedal, or drive in two dimensions, but pilots must contend with three dimensions. Unfortunately Mother Nature didn't anticipate humans would fly and didn't provide us bodies designed to cope with three-dimensional contortions.

We were placed in a rotating chair, blindfolded, and then spun around while rotating our heads downward. When the chair stopped turning, the blindfold was removed and we stood up. Some people experience instant nausea when sensations disagree with what they see. Pilots train to learn that their senses may be completely deceived by the motions of an airplane or when the pilot moves his head up,

27

down, or sideways too rapidly. Like oxygen deprivation, spatial disorientation can be dangerous.

I know of a pilot in Vietnam who crashed and died that way. Returning from a night strike mission, he likely confused stars with lights on the ground causing him to think down was up. He told his wingman he was having orientation problems, then drove his aircraft straight into the ground.

## On the Flight Line

During the other half of a day when we weren't in academic or other ground training, students reported to their squadron building located at the flight line with the aircraft parked outside. Each student class was grouped as a "flight" within the training squadron. I was in Class 66H, reflecting the year and sequence I was expected to graduate. For the Primary Phase flying the T-37, I was in John Black Flight. After six months, when we advanced to fly the T-38 in the Basic Phase, we moved into Gombey Flight. I'm sure there was plenty of history behind those names, but I was too focused on the present to learn about them.

Each student was assigned to an instructor pilot—the "IP." My IP in the T-37 was Captain Harlen Adams, a former B-47 bomber pilot. Within the flight room each IP and his students sat around a table. On one wall of the flight room was a large scheduling board that told us which students were scheduled to fly and depicted each student's six-month training progress. An IP flew with his students according to the schedule; when he wasn't flying with or briefing a particular student about a flight, the IP discussed and taught procedures with all his students. When the IP wasn't there, the students were expected to study unless scheduled for other training activities, such as flying in the simulator.

The first phase of T-37 Primary Training was pre-solo contact flying—learning fundamental visual aircraft maneuvers and landings—stick, rudder, and throttles stuff. That took a student up to his first solo. After that the student was scheduled for a mix of dual or solo contact flights. Throughout the six months of Primary Training, students went through phases of instrument, navigation, and formation flying while sometimes night flying and flying cross-country or out-and-back navigation flights.

That first solo is a big deal. The first half of the flight is flown dual. The IP and student fly to a designated training area and the student performs stall, unusual attitude, and spin recoveries. If the student performs those satisfactorily, they return to the airfield and practice patterns and landings. If the student performs those satisfactorily, they pull the aircraft onto a taxiway and shut down the right engine. The IP climbs out the right side with his parachute and helmet and the student restarts that engine. As the student taxies for takeoff, the IP walks to the mobile control shack—a small, glassed cubicle on the side of the runway staffed by two other IPs who supervise and control aircraft in the landing traffic pattern. The solo pilot takes off, makes a couple of touch-and-go landings, then brings the bird in for a full-stop landing and taxi back to parking. Throughout all this his IP sits inside the mobile shack, sweating bullets and chewing his nails to the quick.

I really don't remember my own first solo. I just don't. I received a certificate for it, so I'm pretty sure I did it, but I'll be damned if I can remember it. Scared brainless, I guess. But I sure as hell remember the first time I soloed a student. I remember every exquisite detail about it. He did fine . . . but I was a nervous wreck until it was over.

At the end of the day any students who flew their first solo were marched by their flight mates to the dunk tank behind the squadron building and unceremoniously thrown in with all clothes on. That night they bought everyone drinks in the bar. Every so often someone actually drained and cleaned the solo tank, an old cattle watering tank. But it would be weeks from one class's solo phase until the next class, and during those weeks no one cleaned the dunk tank. When the next solo came along, someone usually scraped the green scum off the top before the solo guy hit the pond. In winter they occasionally broke the ice first.

One of the most difficult feats for student pilots is learning how to talk on the radio. Walking and chewing gum is child's play compared to flying and talking over the radio. Airplanes fly fast and run out of fuel quickly, so there's no time for extraneous chit-chat or long explanations. Over time a particular language has developed for the aviation world. Its lexicon is loaded with acronyms and short phrases that convey a lot of meaning without superfluous explanation. It becomes ingrained in pilots' speech over the years, e.g., "Roger" replaces "Yes;" "Negative" means "No." But there's truly nothing more hilarious than first-time student pilots trying to transmit on a radio while also flying an airplane. One skill or the other is bound to be mangled.

A typical contact training flight begins with student and IP going to the parachute shack to gather and inspect their parachutes, helmets, and oxygen masks, then catching the flight line trolley to drive them to their assigned aircraft. At the aircraft student and IP check the aircraft maintenance log and then perform exterior and interior preflight inspections. Once strapped into their seats, they start engines, taxi, takeoff, and depart the airfield.

Each flight is assigned a reserved training area to practice "area work"—basic flying maneuvers such as stalls, unusual attitudes and acrobatic maneuvers like rolls, barrel rolls, loops, and spins. After doing their area work and burning off some fuel weight, the pilots descend and follow prescribed procedures to return to the airfield. They enter the traffic pattern under the tower's control to practice normal and emergency approaches and landings.

Spins are the biggest area work challenge for most students. Most aircraft types are restricted from intentionally spinning because either the aircraft may be overstressed or the recovery is uncertain, but the T-37 was purposely designed for spin and spin recovery training. Because a spin is a free-fall maneuver, it must be initiated above 20,000 feet and must recover by 10,000 feet. Twenty-thousand feet is pretty high for an unpressurized airplane, and if you suspect you might be developing nasal or sinus problems, a rapid descent from twenty grand will tell you for sure. A sinus block feels like a bee is stinging you smack in the face.

A spin wraps you up pretty good and can be quite dizzying. The first recovery step is to "Determine the direction of spin." That's not always as easy as it sounds. The recovery method is a fairly violent

30

maneuver, calling for you to rapidly move stick and rudders full and hard to their stops. If you just milquetoast your way through it, the aircraft won't snap out of it—it'll spin faster. Might even flip upside-down. You only get a couple of chances before you run out of altitude. If you blow it, that's when the IP takes over, recovers, and begins the long climb back above 20,000 feet for another chance—time and fuel permitting.

The T-37 had a primitive air conditioning system that was woefully inadequate in Arizona's summertime heat. The infernal air conditioner was just a small ram air expansion cooler. It worked worst at slower speeds and lower altitudes where our landing training was done. Summer cockpit temperatures in the landing pattern reached 140 degrees.

No one handled the cockpit heat worse than classmate Bob Yant. Bob had been an accomplished college wrestler—a stocky, muscular guy who could bend iron. He was nice as all get-out, always friendly and jovial. But Bob was a sight when he returned from one of those very hot, summertime training flights. When Bob and his IP walked into the flight room, the IP's flight suit might have a sweat stain or two, but every inch of Bob's flight suit was drooling wet. Bob actually dripped a trail of sweat on the floor wherever he walked. I think his boots squished, too. Flight training wasn't going well for Bob, and we all felt bad for him. Eventually Bob was eliminated, but throughout his endurance contest Bob gave it his all, smiling all the way.

## Arizona

I chose Williams as my pilot training base partly because I wanted to see the desert southwest. I wasn't disappointed. I really enjoyed Arizona during pilot training and many years afterward. I had a preconceived image of endless sand dunes, but the Sonoran Desert was far different. It abounds with desert plants and wildlife. Unlike the eastern seaboard, its heat is dry and very tolerable.

As intense as pilot training was, it wasn't all work and no play. For the first half of the year we were required to live on base. I lived in

31

Bachelor Officers Quarters sharing a duplex apartment with another officer who worked elsewhere on base. On-base living brought classmates together and we often met after work in the Officers Club or enjoyed parties, picnics, and sports outings.

Arizona's vast desert beckoned and I enjoyed venturing into the wilds. One day I looked at a mountain and simply climbed it. I sat up there alone for quite some time, looking over the big valley below.

I remember my introduction to "tubing." All of us from our flight along with wives and girlfriends set out one weekend to the waters of the Salt River northeast of Phoenix. Supplied with tire inner tubes of various sizes plus some cooler chests of beer, we leisurely floated down the lazy river through desert wild lands to where we had pre-parked our cars. It was beautiful, and we were all tipsy with sun and beer after a day of that. I, of course, burned to a crisp.

Phoenix wasn't too far away to drive there for night life. Several night clubs attracted singles, and there was a nice live jazz scene around town.

Some of our activities were organized by the Flying Training Wing, and I attended my first Dining In—a very formal dinner affair that exuded protocol. As officers we were required to buy our formal dinner uniform, called a mess dress. It cost a lot, but formal wear was part of an officer's life. Plus, it provided added encouragement for me to stay slim—I didn't relish having to buy another costly mess dress for a while.

An intense year with my fellow student pilots produced strong bonds and friendships. We came from all over the country and brought together different backgrounds and personalities. Despite differences, it was surprising how compatible we were. I really can't recall any significant disagreements.

There were also seven Germans in my flight: five Luftwaffe officers, one sergeant, plus a German Navy lieutenant. After pilot training the Germans all moved to Luke Air Force Base northwest of Phoenix to complete their US training in the F-104 Starfighter.

32

I longed to move off base when my six months were up. I started putting out feelers for an apartment roommate. A friend told me of a guy in our sister squadron looking to do the same thing, and we established contact. His name was Bob Kimball. Kimball and I were on opposite schedules, and we just couldn't hook up, so we arranged everything separately by phone. I found an apartment in nearby Mesa, and we each signed the lease separately.

In fact Bob and I never even met until we had been living together for two weeks. Working on opposite schedules, we came and left at different times.

It was a Sunday morning, and I had enjoyed the previous night's party all too well. I rolled out of bed and stumbled out of my bedroom just as some other apparition came out of the other bedroom in no better shape than I. We looked at each other in confusion for a moment and then he said, "You must be Saboski." I said, "You must be Kimball." And so we were mostly Kimball and Saboski to each other from then until the end of pilot training. Funny guy, and a good pal. Bob ended up flying B-52 bombers someplace.


## The Germans

Spending a year with my German classmates was quite entertaining. They really ate up Arizona's Wild West atmosphere. They bought garish western gear with tall boots and even taller hats. They even bought six-shooters—real ones, although the rules said they weren't allowed to have guns. The German class leader, a barrel-chested gymnast named Peter, was practicing his quick draw out in the desert one day and didn't quite get his gun out of the holster when it went off, putting a hole through both his foot and his brand-new boot. That episode knocked him back a couple of classes while he recovered. They almost sent him home.

The Germans were required to live the year in Bachelor Officer Quarters on base under the watchful eye of their liaison officer, a lieutenant colonel. One evening Peter walked out of the BOQ to tend his dinner on the outdoor grill in time to see a cat perched on the picnic table, eating his steak. Furious, he went inside, got his gun and shot the cat. His liaison officer heard the shot and came outside. Peter was caught red-handed with smoking six-shooter in hand— prophetically like the western movies he enjoyed. If he hadn't been so close to graduation he surely would have been sent packing.

One of the Germans, Frank, became a good friend. He had been an accomplished Olympic fencer. But Frank was prone to take chances that often made me uncomfortable. After Peter shot himself in the foot, the German liaison officer started inspecting his students for any other weapons. Frank asked me to stow his gun and holster in my apartment, which I did, reluctantly.

On our first T-37 solo flight to an assigned training area, Frank and I were scheduled to take off about the same time. Frank said, "Art, let's meet over Coolidge Dam." Coolidge Dam was just outside the boundary between our two training areas and to rendezvous there would violate airspace restrictions. I didn't want to do that, and I sure as hell didn't want to be caught if I did.

Frank fixed a time and said he'd be there. I pretended to be non-committal, but in my mind I wasn't about to do it. When the time came I flew over toward my area boundary and looked around, but carefully stayed inside the boundary and didn't overfly the dam. I scanned the skies but didn't see Frank's airplane.

Back on the ground Frank asked whether I had showed up. I told him I had flown nearby but didn't see him. Frank said that was because he was flying down on the deck. He had actually descended to reservoir level, skimming just above the water, looking at boats to either side of him. But as he told me this his voice got quieter and his eyes bigger as he described what happened next. When he looked back to the front he suddenly saw the huge dam looming up before him. He quickly pulled up, just missing it. He said to me in his thick accent, "But Art, I really scared myself." Frank was like that— frequently sticking his neck out too far just for thrills.

Decades later our German classmates arranged a reunion for us all back at Williams AFB. It was our one and only class reunion. The Germans flew in from Europe and almost everyone showed up. Frank didn't show. I asked the other Germans where he was and they told me Frank had crashed his personal airplane, killing himself. Neither they nor I were surprised.

## The Good Captain Wallace

Sometimes nothing goes right.

One day as I entered the squadron building a most pretty lady was also entering before me. I couldn't help but take notice and quickly moved to open the door for her. Smiles were exchanged, and I unknowingly let the spring-loaded door slam shut behind me—right into the face of her husband who was trailing behind.

Captain Wallace was a check pilot—one of those who evaluated and graded lowly students like me. For some reason I kept bumping into the guy after that, and always under the worst possible circumstances. He caught me eyeballing his wife on yet another day, as impossible as that seems. One day I got the last stall in the men's room just before him when he was obviously in a big hurry. Another day he was waiting impatiently at the snack bar when I nonchalantly walked in and got served first. Stuff like that. We didn't know each other, but there was a shadow of gloom hanging over him when I was around. He gave me nasty looks in the hallways.

I tried to avoid Wallace when I could, but when I came due for my contact check ride, to my dismay I saw that he was scheduled as my check pilot. I knew what the results would be before we even left the building. I flew well, but he gave me a marginal "fair" grade on the ride. Yes, his judgment was superior to mine, but I wasn't completely without smarts, and I knew I had flown far better than the grade I got.

When my IP saw the grade sheet he went ballistic. Harlen marched down to the check section and had it out with the good captain, but to no avail (Harlen didn't like Wallace, either). Harlen came back, red faced. It was my only bad grade. Even with that, I finished seventh in my class of about 80.

I should never have eyeballed Wallace's wife the way I did, but I suspect I wasn't the only one.

## From Tweet to Talon

After a half-year in the Primary Phase, all of us from John Black Flight who were still in the program migrated to Gombey Flight to begin our Basic Phase. My new IP was First Lieutenant Sam Porter—a solid instructor and an all-around good man. Sam had that fighter pilot swagger.

We were introduced to our next aircraft, the T-38 "Talon," the twin-engine, afterburning, tandem-cockpit, high-performance supersonic trainer that once held the world's time-to-climb record. The T-38 was also manufactured and sold to other nations as a front-line fighter aircraft, the F-5.

The T-38 was a real sports car. Its speed and acceleration were phenomenal, and it was quite a challenge after flying the subsonic "Tweet." Aircraft speed compresses a pilot's reaction and decision times—shortens the flying time available before something goes horribly wrong.

My first T-38 flight was, let's say, eventful. I could hardly wait for it: the so-called "Dollar Ride," named such because tradition requires that you pony up a dollar to the instructor for introducing you to a new airplane.

I was in the flight room with my nose in a book when the phone rang. I was told to get my flying gear and hustle out to the T-38 parking ramp to meet an IP and fly my first flight. I was pumped. I hurried to the line shack, grabbed my helmet and parachute, tested my gear and jumped on the flight line trolley. As I got off the trolley and hustled to my airplane, the waiting IP said, "Where's your G-suit?" I was dumbfounded—after flying the T-37 for six months, I forgot I needed to wear a G-suit in the high-performance T-38. He said, "Never mind, let's go," and off we went.

36

The first T-38 flight is intended for the IP to demonstrate the aircraft's capabilities. I sat in the front cockpit. We did everything, including going supersonic—my first and only time while in UPT. Others told me before hand, "Don't blink or you'll miss the takeoff," and that pretty much describes the way it was. Everything happened ridiculously fast.

The T-38 was light weight and very fast. The controls were very sensitive and the aircraft response rate was quick. A slight touch to the control stick was all that was needed to perform almost any maneuver. The rudders were used mostly to provide a place to rest your feet.

The takeoff acceleration in full afterburner pinned me to the seat and we were suddenly airborne. We climbed steeply and quickly through ten thousand feet and proceeded to our designated training area. My IP demonstrated a max performance roll by first telling me to brace by putting my hands against my helmet with my elbows pressed against the canopy. Then he slapped the stick sideways. My head banged against the canopy, and in an instant we had rolled more than 360 degrees, ending up inverted.

Then he put the bird through a series of steep, high-"G" maneuvers. The T-38 can pull seven positive Gs (one G = the force of gravity) and two negative Gs. This was flying like I had never experienced before. I was just beginning to catch my breath and relax a little when he eased the aircraft nose down into a steep dive, accelerating rapidly. As he pulled out of the dive I felt strong G forces pushing me into my seat. I realized he was beginning a loop. As we pulled through the bottom we were probably pulling 4-5 Gs.

During high positive-G maneuvers pilots are taught to perform an "M-1" maneuver in which you tighten all your lower body muscles and grunt. Its purpose is to prevent all your blood from flowing from your brain and heart and pooling into your lower body; that's what the lower torso G-suit does automatically—if you remember to wear it. I performed the M-1 maneuver, but too late. By the time we had pulled into the vertical climb, I had blacked out. I never saw the rest of the loop.

As I regained consciousness I realized we were flying straight and level. My head was lying helplessly on my right shoulder. It stayed there as my vision slowly came back as if I were emerging from a tunnel. At first I couldn't move. Then I slowly raised my head. I heard my IP chuckling. He asked if I was okay and I said I was. Then he said, "I'll bet you never forget your G-suit again."

I paid him a buck for my Dollar Ride and fought a nagging headache for the rest of that day.

## Flying the Talon

The Primary Phase of undergraduate pilot training essentially followed the same pattern as the Basic Phase in the T-37. There was more emphasis on formation flying in the T-38, and we flew in four-ship formation for the first time. The T-38 wasn't designed to spin, so we didn't do spin training. In fact, among all pilots—military and civilian—there are very few who have actually trained in spin recoveries. Air Force pilots spin in the T-37 during UPT and likely never spin again unless they return to the T-37 as an IP. Later on in flying the F-4 Phantom, the spin recovery was quite simple: deploy the drag chute.

One difference with the T-38 was its greater range. The Tweet could only fly about 400 nautical miles before having to refuel; the T-38 flew twice that distance. T-38 cross-country navigation was much more interesting because we flew to more distant—and more interesting—destinations. And we got there much faster.

I was doing well in pilot training, gaining experience and confidence daily. There was simply nothing else I would rather be doing, and I was amazed I was actually being paid to do this.

The intensity and level of learning were very high, and it all came at us very fast. Those who didn't, or couldn't, manage were eliminated, usually migrating to navigator jobs. By the end of the year, 28 percent of my classmates had been eliminated.

Formation flying was the last phase of training prior to graduation. I looked forward to the challenges of flying formation. It was pure fun, particularly because we flew 4-ship formation for the first time. "Fingertip formation" describes when airplanes fly with their wings close together, such as your hand looks when your palm is extended. The lateral wingtip separation is a mere three feet, slightly staggered fore and aft. Formation flying demands precision, skill, and anticipation.

Trail formation is when one bird flies closely behind and slightly lower than the other. Flying in trail has military combat applications. Close trail is exactly that—you fly closer, without colliding.

I was in the Number Two position, flying solo in close trail behind Sam and another student in the lead bird. All was normal until the other student inexplicably pitched his aircraft down without warning. I had no time to react as he flew directly in front of me. I found myself staring at his tailpipes up close.

My bird bounced violently, and the exhaust from his engines caused both my engines to stall. I rapidly lost power as my engines wound down. They reached a very low rpm. I pulled back the throttles and then eased them forward slowly. The engines responded, and I got the power back. If I hadn't, it was ejection time.

Sam knew right away that I was probably in trouble, and he radioed to ask if I was okay. I wasn't—until the engines came back to life. We called it quits for that day, and I limped back to base on two damaged engines.

\* \* \* \* \* \* \* \* \*

I was feeling very comfortable at this point in my training. Pilots put it this way: confidence is when you're flying the airplane, not the other way around. As graduation approached I was feeling confident—and maybe cocky, too.

Before leaving the flight line one day I looked at the scheduling board. I had already passed my formation check ride—the last one— so until graduation I flew some flights just to maintain proficiency while other students were finishing up. The board told me I wasn't scheduled to fly the next day.

That night some of us gathered together, and one drink turned into one too many. When I showed up the next morning I wasn't feeling very well. I sat down at our table, and Lt. Porter eyed me a little. He asked, "Are you ready to fly?" I turned around in my chair to look at the scheduling board. It was blurry—my eyes wouldn't focus. I thought, "This is really bad. I can't even see the board." I got up and went closer—and saw I had been scheduled to fly. I looked back at Sam and said, "Yes." He looked at me skeptically.

It was a two-ship formation ride. I was flying solo with Lieutenant Porter and another student flying dual. The student was preparing for his formation check. I was to fly solo lead for the first half of the flight and then we would swap positions.

At this point of my training I felt I could do it all blindfolded, and that's almost the way it was that morning. It felt like I was a zombie flying on autopilot. We pulled our aircraft out of parking, taxied to the runway, lined up in formation, and I took off first with them trailing eight seconds behind. We joined up during the turn out of traffic and proceeded to our training area over the Superstition Mountains.

I led us through several maneuvers and then it was time for us to swap positions. They pitched out, and I took spacing before making my pitchout so that after the 180-degree turn, they'd be in front with me behind, both on the same heading.

The pitchout is a 60-degree, two-G turn—G-forces sort of like going up in a really fast elevator. But when I rolled out and looked ahead for them, I saw stars. That mere two Gs put my eyes out of focus thanks to my unrestrained night of partying.

I thought, "This can't be happening." It took several seconds for my head and vision to clear. The other bird was nowhere in sight. I pushed the throttles forward to catch up to them, wherever they were. Then I saw them immediately above me. I pulled the throttles to idle, popped the speed brakes, and abruptly pulled up onto their left wing in perfect wingtip position. Very unorthodox, but it worked. Their heads were both turned to the right, looking in vain for me to rejoin on their right wing. When Porter turned his head to look left, there I was right next to them. Both he and the student did perfect double-takes.

We finished the flight with me on their wing and came home, uneventfully.

When we walked into the flight room, Sam walked to the podium and got everyone's attention for an announcement. Without naming names, he simply gave everyone there some advice. "After getting your wings," he said, "there will be days you shouldn't fly. Respect those days—and don't."

He came back to our table and gave me a wink. Nothing more said. We graduated later that week.

## Hazardous Duty

The real cost of pilot training became apparent in other ways. A fellow student pilot named Ken and his IP had to make a high-speed takeoff abort one day. Stopping an aircraft on the runway after accelerating to near-takeoff speed is dangerous. Their T-38 was still going fast when it reached the departure end of the runway. As it rolled into the overrun it somehow skipped over the arresting gear that's supposed to catch and stop aborting aircraft. It sped off the runway into the dirt, sheared off the landing gear, and skidded to a stop without catching fire. Neither pilot was badly hurt.

Not long after that Ken was taking off on an instrument flight. When practicing instrument flying the student sits in the rear cockpit with a cloth hood pulled across the rear cockpit canopy to prevent him from seeing out.

As Ken and his IP took off and made a slow climbing turn, another T-38 took off behind them and made a steeper turn, putting the two aircraft on a collision course. The two airplanes hit, shearing off the nose of Ken's aircraft. With the hood over his cockpit, Ken couldn't see anything. When he felt the impact he asked his IP what happened and the IP didn't respond. Ken pulled the hood back and saw his IP unconscious or dead in front with a big crack down his helmet. The entire nose of the aircraft was missing. The aircraft began to roll inverted, uncontrollably. Ken ejected while upside-down and parachuted safely to ground. The other aircraft and pilots were lost. Ken was quite bruised from his inverted ejection, but otherwise okay.

The hazards of what I was doing became very apparent. It was another important flying lesson—one that wasn't written into our syllabus. I also learned why we got flight pay.

## The Real Meaning of It All

As my year of pilot training progressed I assimilated a lot of practical knowledge that didn't come from instructors or textbooks. I learned that this new life I had chosen contained lurking risks and pitfalls. It sure wasn't the benign life of a department store business manager, and it was far different from the careers of my college classmates. It demanded energy, concentration, alertness, and continual study. Flying at this performance level was extremely unforgiving, and mortal danger was the consequence of lapses in judgment or poor decisions. It also demanded extreme self-confidence, and that only came with high levels of practice and proficiency.

If there was any single consequence of that year in pilot training I would cite the huge change in my personal confidence level. I became demonstrably stronger in everything I did. Pilots of complex aircraft are said to exhibit a certain swagger, a certain boldness. That's probably true, and it comes from knowing that you've accomplished something that few have tried and even fewer have mastered. It comes from realizing that you've completed over a year of intense, demanding, all-consuming training that is easily the equivalent of years of higher education. It comes from the feeling and knowledge that from this achievement you have the ability and toughness to take on all else—including combat, which is ultimately the difference

42

between military pilots and all others. Like the popular TV show of that day, you've truly become a Million Dollar Man.

I discovered other, more subtle changes in me and those pilots around me. Our jobs necessarily demanded supremacy in our working lives and character, but we weren't necessarily so good in other aspects of life. I remained a bachelor for 38 years, meeting Eileen only when I had pretty much accepted that I would likely remain a single man. I watched my married pilot friends try to balance their very full lives as military officers and pilots with their family lives, and not always very well. Flyboys don't necessarily make good family men.

I found it difficult to reconcile how I could be a pilot while marrying and having kids. For sure, the romantic temptations were there. Some romances became serious but not committal, and as time went on I became better at just remaining single. I was becoming a perpetual bachelor.

I imagine my parents at times regretted my career path. It took me further away from them in time and distance. It also separated us in other ways. Over the years the primacy of my Air Force duties was hard to explain to them. Dad was always supportive, and I believe proud, of my career; Mom was less enamored by it. I believe she missed the family I might have had with an early marriage, although she never brought it up directly.

My forays to distant places weren't conducive to regular visits back home. It was difficult for me to explain the nature of my work and its demands. It was obvious to them that I cared a lot about what I did, but it was impossible for me to convey how flying and aviation consumed me. Later on, through the U-2 and my advancing positions, I dealt with matters in my job that I simply couldn't divulge to them because of their high classification. It was hard for me to keep such secrets from my Mom and Dad.

Years later Mom and Dad visited me in the Pentagon for my promotion ceremony. I worked in a special intelligence vault, inside another vault, behind a guarded entrance. As we walked in I realized I had left a classified document face-up on my desk. Instinctively, I flipped it over to hide it. Mom was quick to notice and asked why I had done that. I simply said because it was classified. She was miffed and admonished me, "But I'm your mother!" There was nothing I could say that would remediate that moment, and I didn't even try.

Getting my wings was the culmination of the most arduous year of my life to that point—and by far the most gratifying. I had found myself in the perfect job and perfect career. I had gotten there by personal choice, choosing to enter military service on my terms rather than through the draft. I never imagined I would like it so much.

Naysayers contend that military service is too regimented and that everyone's life is cast into the same mold. I say the opposite: most people would benefit from rising to a higher plateau of challenge and taking on more self-discipline.

I look at military service with a more positive spin: everyone with me in the Air Force was a volunteer—no one was drafted into a blue uniform. What appears to outliers as regimentation and coercion is in reality an eminently practical system of organization that serves to preserve and protect everyone on the team, especially in combat. I truly believe that of those who criticize the military, most could never hack it even if they tried and were having their best day of their lives, every day.

Air Force people—service members and their families—are typically imbued with a sense of patriotism, pride, and fulfillment that isn't ordinarily found in the general population. I look at civilian life as mostly a chaotic society—tamed somewhat by the laws of government, but a society in which many people make horrible choices and then rely on others to pull them out of the muck.

We are a democracy in which individuals make or do with it what they will—sometimes successfully, sometimes not. So many people spend much of their lives forever finding themselves, searching for a livelihood, happiness, structure, and organization. I discovered that the Air Force was already organized for success. It gave young entrants a jump start on all of that, and it was filled with surprisingly talented, educated, focused people. It allowed newcomers like me to hit the ground running.

44

The Air Force was then, and is now, a youthful organization where people are charged with immense responsibility and challenges at an early age—an organization in which the principal rewards aren't monetary. The rewards you earn come from knowing that your service truly matters to our nation and its people. These feelings muster when our flag is flown and when a mission is accomplished.

It's no ruse—the emotions play a big part. I've seen such pride well up and produce tears of happiness or grief in the most stalwart of men and families. It's the answer to a calling, and to those on the "outside" it's often very difficult to explain why you love what you do.

## The Next Assignment

Graduation neared, and it was time to learn what my next assignment would be. The day of reckoning approached. The needs of the Air Force always came first, so all of us in Class 66H received a block of available assignment categories as determined by higher headquarters. Each available category listed a type of aircraft, the organizational command in which it operated, and the number of assignments to be awarded to that category. We listed our preferences in rank order, and the assignments were awarded according to each student's class standing. I wasn't the top student in my class, but close enough to know I'd likely get my first choice.

The block of assignments finally came down from headquarters and was posted on the board for all to see. To the surprise and shock of us all, they were almost all either fighter or UPT instructor assignments. That suited me, but in our class a large number had hoped to fly multi-engine transport or bomber aircraft, and they were quite disappointed.

Our top classmate, Lou Distelzweig, was rewarded by getting a choice assignment as an exchange pilot with the British Royal Air Force. The RAF was just getting "Harrier" vertical thrust jet fighters—the "jump jet." It was just months after graduation when I learned Lou had died. He was lifting off in his Harrier when some

45

catastrophic malfunction occurred. The bird crashed right where it had lifted off. When they examined the wreckage they discovered that Lou had never pulled his ejection seat safety pins. He likely tried to eject, but couldn't.

I wanted to fly fighters, and for most of that year had aspired to fly the F-105 Thunderchief—the "Thud"—single cockpit, single engine. I immediately focused on the two F-105 slots that were listed, but I was also intrigued by the very large number of new F-4 Phantom II assignments to Pacific Air Command, to European Command, and to Southeast Asia. However, the F-4 was a two-seat fighter, and junior pilots were being placed in the rear cockpit. I swallowed hard at that.

I wondered what one of the listed assignments was about: "F-4s to Southeast Asia." There was no accompanying information, so we were left to guess what we didn't already know. When some of us asked, we were told it offered a chance to go directly to Vietnam, and the lollipop for doing so would be a fast upgrade to the front seat.

That posed a new twist to my plans. One of my goals was to fly my own fighter either solo or at least in the front cockpit. I now had a choice that might land me in the hottest fighter in the world and get me into that front seat in short order.

I really didn't know what to do: F-105 or F-4? We were given just three hours to decide. I walked next door to the F-5 training squadron. That's where American IPs were training mostly foreign nationals to fly the F-5 Freedom Fighter, the fighter version of the T-38. In that squadron was a number of real combat fighter pilots newly returned from Vietnam.

I walked in, introduced myself to the first guy I met, and explained that I needed some advice—quick. Several of the IPs gathered around, and I got lots of advice. To a man they said the F-4 was the up-and-coming fighter and I should go for it. They said that the "Thud" was too old and dated, and besides the F-105 was a plumber's nightmare—it had hydraulic lines that were especially vulnerable to enemy fire. They affirmed that back-seat F-4 pilots were upgrading to the front seat rapidly and convinced me I should bypass the F-105 and go for F-4s to Southeast Asia.

Armed with this info, I returned to my squadron and listed F-4s to Southeast Asia as my first choice, with the implied promise for an early upgrade to the front seat by choosing to go straight to Vietnam.

That turned out to be a promise not actually made and certainly not kept. Yes, back-seaters (the GIB, or Guy-in-Back) were upgrading to the front rapidly at that time, but it was eight months before I got there, and by then a tidal wave of brand-new GIBs like me had put the front seat entirely out of reach for years. We had all been led innocently down the garden path.

But my decision was made. I got my first choice, and soon I was on my way to the back seat of an F-4.

## Graduation

Graduation was something special—the occasion, the ceremonies, the sense of accomplishment. Mom and Dad traveled to Arizona to be there, and that was very special, too. It was the culmination of a very full and auspicious year. I could see that Mom and Dad were proud, and I felt pretty good about myself—a lot better than after my tepid college performance.

Our class speaker was Colonel "Chappie" James, who gave an inspiring speech. I would see him once again during my F-4 training in California and again in Thailand. General James went on to become Chairman of the Joint Chiefs of Staff, the first black man to do so.

Receiving my wings marked the beginning of more travels ever-farther from home and from my parents, and then overseas to Vietnam.

Many years later Williams AFB closed and was turned over to the state of Arizona for civilian use. In years that followed while living elsewhere in Arizona, I watched as the old buildings came down and were replaced by new development. At one point only the old control tower remained. Eventually even that was removed. "Willy" is now the Phoenix Gateway Airport. Whenever I fly out of Phoenix commercially, I look down at the "Willy" runways and remember it all.

# *The Phantom*

I graduated from UPT in June of 1966 and arrived in Vietnam in January, 1967. Before arriving in Vietnam I had eight months' more training before me.

The first step was Air Force Survival School in Spokane, Washington. I drove there in my car with two of my pilot training classmates, Johnny Hobbs and Bob Whelton. We travelled from Willy to the California coast, then north up Route 1 to stop in San Francisco. It was a fun ride and very beautiful along the coast. In pilot training I had taken my first cross country navigation flight that way, skimming the water and looking up at the cars along Route 1.

Our first stop was in Bakersfield. We ate at an upscale hotel restaurant with live entertainment. I remember ordering sweetbreads before I knew what they were. A Mexican mariachi band was playing, and one of the guitar musicians caught my eye. He was the spitting image of my old college roommate. When I tried to tell him that, I realized he spoke no English.

We played tourist briefly along the Embarcadero in San Fran, then made our way to Spokane and Fairchild AFB, home of Air Force Survival School. They don't call it survival school for nothing—you had to survive the school before living through anything else. Survival School was purposely tough. It was intended to impart strength, endurance, and knowledge by placing us in survival situations both in surrounding forests and also in a very realistic, mock prisoner of war camp. There was nothing to like about any of it, but it was necessary.

For the first week we studied survival techniques, self defense, hand-to-hand combat, and escape and evasion. Our classroom studies

49

were followed by internment in the prison. After that we proceeded to the forests north of Spokane to practice wilderness survival, escape and evasion. While in the field we ate only what we caught or killed. Ours was just the second survival school class since the school had relocated from Nevada, and the wildlife hadn't been depleted yet. We were able to catch a few small fish and find some berries. Each of us was allowed to take with us into the forest an onion, two potatoes, and either a pack of candy or gum. Each group camp of twelve was provided a live rabbit. I learned that rabbit eyeballs are a good source of salt.

After spending a few days in group camp, we split up and trekked day and night through the forests and mountains in two-man escape and invasion (E&E) pairs. We went days without meaningful food. I learned that the most wonderful food God ever created was a raw onion. After I became really, really, really hungry that onion tasted really, really, really good.

At age 23 I was still quite slim but had a voracious appetite that belied my youthful figure. Unfortunately I brought that appetite with me to survival school where food was scarce. The school taught me that when you're starved you can't concentrate on anything except your longing for food. When I wasn't swatting mosquitoes I daydreamed of hamburgers.

The E&E pairs were instructed to make our way for miles across rugged terrain to a supposed "friendly" partisan enclave where we would find assistance and food. Meanwhile the staff was attempting to find us and send any who were caught back to the starting line. To escape and evade we had to navigate at night using a terrain map and our survival compass. We had flashlights but were told not to use them. It took a couple of days, but all pairs eventually came wandering into camp and were served some soup by the "partisans."

John, Bob, and I all had different E&E partners. John's trek turned out to be a little different from ours.

Johnny Hobbs was an all-around good guy. He and I roomed together in Tucson following survival school. Johnny had an easy-going, self-effacing way. He was also very funny. John was somewhat blacker than the rest of us—a graduate of Rutgers University and a self-described "ghetto kid." John would look you in the eye and swear that until survival school he had never seen a tree. He attracted women like a magnet. In later years Johnny J. Hobbs, ghetto kid, rose to the rank of major general in the Air National Guard.

After we returned from the field Johnny told Bob and me the story of his E&E jaunt. John's E&E partner was a navigator. This guy took outdoor survival somewhat more seriously than John and had obvious wilderness survival experience. The Nav always walked in the lead with John following. He'd nimbly step over logs and dodge limbs whereas John took every limb full in the face and barked his shins on every log. He'd easily dodge or jump over puddles while Johnny would step in mud knee-deep. John would pour over the map to figure out where the hell he was, while the Nav would simply look up at the stars and say, "This way."

John had had just about enough of the Nav and his survivalist ways. The guy was really irritating. John was tired, hungry, and the mosquitoes were eating him alive, so they stopped to rest. When they did a mosquito landed to feast on the Nav's arm. Instead of swatting it, the Nav looked at it a moment and then slurped it into his mouth. After all, it was food, sorta. Protein, too.

That did it. John said farewell, and he and the Nav parted ways. They weren't far from the partisan camp, and John eventually straggled in alone.


## Imprisonment

Survival School's prisoner camp taught me that humans can be very brutal without causing lasting damage or drawing blood. We got there by first going through a nighttime obstacle course on our bellies, dodging trip wires and flares. It was late at night, and at the end of the course the "enemy" waited. As we each came in we were "captured," stripped naked in the cold, bound, and had a gunny sack placed over us. We stood there, trussed and shivering, for a long time while guards yelled at us. Then we were marched to a building with

51

cells so small you couldn't stand up. No bathroom facilities—so we did what we had to do. We spent hours locked up and were then marched to a room and squeezed into plywood boxes in stress positions. That's enough of this telling—I won't go on with the description.

The interrogation and treatment methods applied to us were starkly realistic without causing physical injury. We were briefed that our "guards" weren't allowed to physically hit us, but they didn't have to in order to create a realistic effect.

Fear is a very real emotion. After Survival School I decided I'd rather go down with my aircraft than be captured. I reached that decision while pondering Survival School's lessons on my long journey to Southeast Asia and the war.

After two and a half weeks of luxury living in the wilds of the Pacific northwest we weren't interested in sightseeing, so we drove nonstop back to Arizona. On the long drive back John and I played "Name That Tune" as we listened to all-night music. Despite our fatigue we laughed and joked all the way as Bob slept in back.

## Tucson, Then to the High Desert of California

My first F-4 training was a two-month school at Davis-Monthan AFB in Tucson to learn how to operate the rear-cockpit radar, navigation, and weapons systems. It was mostly classroom work accompanied by equipment simulation and operation. We lived in apartments outside the front gate. Another UPT classmate, Bill LaFever, roomed with Johnny and me. The school was routine course work on a regular daytime schedule, leaving some time for basketball and sightseeing. I liked Tucson and was glad to return there several years later.

After Tucson it was off to George AFB in the Mojave Desert of southern California to learn to fly the F-4D. That's where I met the front seat pilot I would be paired with throughout my Vietnam duty— Homer "Pinky" Lee.

Captain Homer Lee was a tall, good ol' boy from Georgia with a deep, booming voice, a sharp mind and good sense of humor. I first knew him—or knew of him—from pilot training. He had been one of the check pilots who gave flying evaluations to us students. The students called him "Pinky" Lee—not because he was funny like his namesake comedian, but because of all the red ink he used when scoring student evaluation sheets.

Back in UPT I quaked in my boots with thoughts he might be the next one to give me a check ride, so when I arrived at George my jaw dropped when I learned the famed "Pinky" Lee would be my aircraft commander.

But Homer's reputation was pure fabrication. He was anything but the ogre students portrayed. He was a fair and very capable pilot, truly the best of the best, and I'm forever thankful that he was my wartime aircraft commander. In his deep, booming voice he loved introducing me to others as his "big-nosed Polack" (as if his nose was any smaller). But that was okay—as I got to know Homer and his abilities, I was to glad fill that role. But just for the record, Homer sported a proboscis twice as big as mine. I should have had it measured.

Homer liked to introduce himself at social events by extending his hand and drawling, "M'name's Earl Scrotum . . . from Mineral Wells." Invariably the person at the other end of Homer's handshake would screw up their face and timidly ask, "Earl Scrotum??" And Homer would grin and say, "That's right—from Mineral Wells."

At George all of us trainees were in a Replacement Training Unit (RTU) squadron under the command of Lieutenant Colonel Ernie Craigwell. Several of my UPT buddies were there, and I rented an apartment in nearby Victorville with two classmates. One of my roommates was later shot down in the war and captured.

Our class was divided into front- and rear-seat pilot crew pairings, the guy in front being the Aircraft Commander (the AC) and the guy in back being simply the Guy-in-Back (the GIB). No GIB wanted to be called co-pilot. It was a bone of contention, because none of us

53

wanted to be officially titled "co-pilot" in a cockpit that didn't even provide us a gear handle. The Air Force respected that distinction and nominally called us "rear-seat pilot."

Pilots, instead of navigators, were placed in the back seat during the war because someone had decided that a backup pilot was needed in case the guy in front became incapacitated. Fat chance—if the front-seater took a hit, the GIB was likely to get hit, too. Besides, the ejection seats were wired so that if the AC ejected the GIB's seat would fire first. That's so the GIB wouldn't be burned by the AC's ejection seat rocket. The chances of a GIB flying the aircraft home alone were pretty slim.

It was the objective of every GIB to get out of that back seat job as soon as possible—hopefully by upgrading to the front seat.

The F-4 was the hottest, fastest fighter in the Air Force inventory at the time. In RTU training we flew D Models; in Vietnam we flew older C Models. Go figure that one. The F-4 was designed as an air interceptor to guard against long-range aircraft attack. For that reason it was built to carry air-to-air missiles instead of short-range guns. It wasn't designed for the air-ground attack mission or close-in dog fighting of the Vietnam War, but that's the way it goes. When someone designs a fighter they never know what kind of war we'll be fighting next.

We studied all aspects of flying the F-4 just like I had done throughout pilot training. The F-4 had some good features, such as a better engine fuel control system that allowed pilots to be more aggressive with throttle movements. And it had lots of power. It had so much thrust that if you advanced both throttles to full power with the brakes on it would cause the tires to rotate on the wheels.

The F-4 carried two air-to-air missile types: the radar-guided Sparrow and the infrared, heat-seeking Sidewinder. For actual live fire, we flew out to Catalina Island off the California coast and shot the Sparrow at a target towed by another aircraft.

Our training included practicing air-to-air intercepts: two F-4s running head-on at supersonic speeds. First the GIB used his

54

acquisition radar to find and track the target aircraft. As the target aircraft came within range of the Sparrow, the GIB put the radar into a lock-on mode so the Sparrow could be guided to its target, and if it were an actual enemy, the AC would then fire the missile.

I recall the first head-on intercept we performed. I acquired our "enemy" on my radar and tracked him as we flew at supersonic speeds toward each other. I remember seeing the picture on my radar scope, indicating we were closing at 1600 nautical miles per hour. He was at a lower altitude from us, and as we passed I looked down and was surprised at what I saw. I had never seen a supersonic shock wave before, but there it was. Coming off the other aircraft I saw a thin, "V"-shaped line. It looked like someone had etched a wedge shape in the air using a very sharp pencil. The line I saw was the effect of molecules of air compressed into each other so hard that it produced a visual disturbance.

On another day of training I saw an object on my radar to the north of us near the test range at Edwards Air Force Base. As I watched the object accelerated at a fantastic speed away from us while climbing until it disappeared off my scope. Later that day the national news reported that test pilot Scott Crossfield had test-flown the X-15 rocket plane at Edwards that very day. No doubt that's what I had seen on my scope.

We also practiced air-to-air refueling, stopping to gas up behind a KC-135 tanker. The F-4's refueling receptacle is directly behind the GIB's canopy, so when the tanker's boomer tries to plug the probe into that receptacle the boom comes within just a few feet of the GIB's head. And yes, there's at least one case where the boom busted a GIB's canopy.

Air refueling was mostly Homer's show, but I got a little practice, too. Over Thailand I got to do it often.

As aircraft complete a major maintenance overhaul they must pass a functional check flight (FCF) before being returned to service. An FCF pilot flies the aircraft and performs detailed checks of the airplane's systems before certifying it's ready for operational service. Since the F-4 was a two-cockpit aircraft, the FCF pilot is accompanied by a GIB to check rear cockpit systems. I had volunteered to be on weekend call should a GIB be needed for an FCF, and one day I got that call.

Most of the flight consisted of the FCF pilot and the GIB each running through their separate checklists. Then the time comes to speed-check the aircraft. The F-4's max speed is 2.5 times the speed of sound, or Mach 2.5. Max speed in the T-38 was Mach 1.2.

My AC put the bird in a steep dive at full afterburner. I watched the speed on a groundspeed readout with a display showing four digits. As we bottomed out of the dive the first two digits were reading 1 and 5; the third and fourth digits were spinning too fast to be readable. Still in max afterburner we climbed almost vertically until we ran out of thrust to go higher. That took us to over 62,000 feet. It would be years before I flew higher than that, piloting a U-2. Were my FCF pilot and I the fastest humans on earth that day? Probably, but who knows? Who cares?

The ACs initially flew several missions with instructors to the gunnery range to learn how to drop and fire weapons. Then I got to go along with Homer.

The gunsight and arming switches are in the front cockpit, so the GIB is relegated to determining various sight settings for whatever weapons are aboard. He gives the settings to the AC who dials them in. Rear seat forward visibility is poor, so the real fun of making bomb drops on the range is lost on the GIB—he just can't see much from back there. The practice bombs had little weight and charge—they go poof when they explode, just enough detonation to mark where they hit. When we bombed for real during the war, it was unmistakable to feel when multiple 500- and 750-lb. bombs dropped off the wings. We also carried the 20 mm Gatling gun (the "pistol") mounted in a pod strapped to the bottom of the bird. When it fired it felt and sounded like a jackhammer pounding on the aircraft.

We also simulated realistic ground attack. At the China Lake range there were old vehicles laid out like a convoy, and we practiced approaching and attacking as we would a defended target.

We trained in air combat tactics, or ACT: intercepts of enemy aircraft and dog fighting. For long range targets many miles away the F-4 carried AIM-7 Sparrow radar-guided missiles. The radar controls were in the rear cockpit, and it was the GIB's job to acquire the target and then illuminate the enemy aircraft with an intense radar beam before the AC fired the missile.

For closer-in dog fighting, the GIB's role was to act as a rear-seat observer who can look backwards at enemy aircraft. But it was primarily the AC's job to engage in dog fighting. The F-4 isn't particularly suited for close-in dog fighting since in those years it didn't carry an internal gun. Its only short-range weapon was the AIM-9 Sidewinder heat-seeking missile, but it required a tail shot up the enemy's tailpipe.

ACT was high-performance stuff, flying F-4s against each other at full power in high-G turns. Although close-in ACT was mostly the AC's job, I got to play the game a little, too. In my first engagement Homer gave me the controls with another F-4 behind us. I began a sharp turn right, then tightened it up as our opponent pursued. At some point as I applied stronger controls to the right, our bird instead reversed to the left. I had inadvertently stalled, causing adverse roll in the other direction. I had a lot to learn in my second year of flying high performance aircraft.

Prior to course completion we were visited by Colonel "Chappie" James. Craigwell prepared to entertain him with gusto. He laid on a party at the Officers Club for a Sunday night. Monday was a fly day, but Craigwell wasn't bothered by that. He said that as fighter pilots, we had to learn how to drink and fly. Hmmm. So he and James—two pretty big-sized black men—spent time toasting and slapping each other on the back that night. All of us joined in, too. It was a pretty good bash, and some of the guys didn't know when to quit.

The next morning was a sorry sight. Craigwell surveyed his pilots as they came in, and he realized he had encouraged drinking just a tad too much. A number of them were completely sloshed that morning while others were just tinged a little. I wasn't flying that day and was pulling duty in the ops room—the center of activity where our radios were.

Craigwell started sweating as he surveyed the condition of his pilots. Our senior crew, with Lt. Col. DeRaud in front and Bob Whelton as GIB, were particularly bent. DeRaud barfed on the tarmac on the way out to their bird. When they returned (safely, fortunately) Bob barfed on the ramp walking in. There were no accidents or incidents, but I watched Lt. Col. Craigwell nervously pace back and forth across the ops room all morning, listening intently to the radio chatter from the pilots.

We finished RTU training and it came time to deploy to Southeast Asia. Half our class was assigned to Da Nang Air Base in South Vietnam and the other half to Ubon AB in Thailand. The guys at Ubon lived in the lap of luxury compared to us at Da Nang. They ate real food there; we ate a lot of reconstituted stuff they called food.

After RTU training the west coast guys went home to say goodbyes before heading overseas. I headed for San Francisco to catch my flight to the Philippines. I arrived late and spent the night in the Marines Memorial Hotel rooming with two Marine gunnery sergeants. One was returning to Vietnam for his third tour of duty, the other for his fourth.

We rendezvoused at Clark AB in the Philippines to attend Jungle Survival School. Homer and I roomed in an open bay, screened hut with one of the other GIBs. Prior to arriving at Clark we heard rumors that our class was too big to be accommodated in jungle field training, so some of us would receive only the academic portion. Furthermore, we learned that the class before ours was hit by tragedy when a mudslide buried and killed several guys.

When we entered the school's assembly room, there was a mad scramble to get seats at the back. I got one, and sure enough an instructor started counting numbers beginning at the front row. He ran out of numbers when he counted the seat just before mine. Those he counted went to the jungle. The rest of us didn't. That was okay with me—after two full years of training I wasn't eager for a survival school field trip where guys could be killed. Instead I spent those days at a hotel pool sipping gin and tonics and eating spring rolls in the company of American stewardesses.

# Young Pilot in War

We flew into Da Nang on a dreary, rainy day. It was a dismal place, but at least the Air Force had replaced their tents with hard buildings by 1967. On one side of the airfield were the Marines; the Air Force had the other. Being Marines, they still lived in tents mounted on dirt. I think they preferred it that way. I only went over to their side a couple of times, but it was pretty bad living, especially during monsoon season. That's why the Marine officers always came across the airfield to our Officers Club.

Homer and I shared a room on the second level of the barracks. There was just room enough for our bunk bed, a steel desk and chair, and a steel locker. I had the upper bunk, of course.

I was still very young, and all that I encountered—living overseas, the war, the threats, the flying, squadron life—was new. Da Nang exemplified the war zone. Aircraft were parked in revetments and sand bags were everywhere. From time to time sirens wailed in warning of a possible rocket attack, which had happened just before our arrival.

One night soon after our arrival we were flying back to Da Nang after a strike mission and were told to divert to Ubon Air Base in Thailand. Da Nang was under rocket attack again.

We landed at Ubon and spent the night. I had a drink with some RTU friends in the Officers Club. The next morning I had pancakes for breakfast. Yes, they actually had pancakes with real syrup and fresh fruit. I was ready to jump ship and remain at Ubon just for the pancakes, but I just couldn't let Homer return to purgatory alone.

After breakfast we flew back to Da Nang-By-the-Sea with its powdered milk and eggs and its reconstituted ice cream that tasted like . . . .

A lot of the base population carried weapons. Vietnamese workers performed various jobs on the base, but there was no real distinction in who was friendly and who wasn't. Sanitation wasn't good, and the place stunk. When guys started getting sick after eating at the O Club they discovered that Vietnamese helpers were washing the silverware in drain water.

I was still learning about everything—flying, the Air Force, the war, and about the Marines who populated the other side of the airfield. I know the Marines are a lot about "hoo-rah" and achievement against all odds, but my biggest lesson came from watching how they attacked the Air Force Officer's Club.

To entertain themselves they had invented a little contest. In the tropics every building had overhead fans, and so did the bar at the Da Nang O' Club. Their game was for one Marine to climb on another's shoulders. That two-man team competed against other teams, and the objective was for the guy on top to raise his head sloooowly into a fast-spinning overhead fan, causing it to eventually stop. The team that stopped the fan first, won—free drinks plus side bets.

This one night we Air Force folk were watching the Marines entertain themselves (and us) this way. One team—quite snockered—kept losing consistently and wasn't taking their losses well. Fed up with it all, they challenged the winners again, but this time tripled the bet. Both teams mounted, ready for the contest. But this time the losing team decided they would lose no more. The top Marine simply thrust his head straight up into the spinning fan. The fan blade caught him pretty good, knocking him out cold. Cheers went up all around the bar. His three mates hoisted him up, laid him flat on the bar, and enjoyed celebratory drinks over his prostrate form until he came to. When he revived, lying there on the bar, he asked, "Did we win?"

I was one of many GIBs at Da Nang. We were oversupplied with back-seaters. Besides killing any chance for a front-seat upgrade, it also meant we would fly less. Fewer flights meant fewer "counters"— missions north of the DMZ that everyone wanted because every 20

61

counters lopped one month off your 12-month tour of duty. But even though we were overloaded with GIBs, Air Force personnel kept sending in more.

## Flying the Phantom in Combat

Our missions at Da Nang included a mixture of ground attack and combat air patrol, which we flew to guard our fighter-bombers flying out of Thailand against enemy fighters over North Vietnam. We flew missions into North Vietnam, South Vietnam, the Demilitarized Zone (DMZ), and Laos, day and night.

Some combat missions were routine and uneventful, attacking ground targets based on intelligence reports and denoted by map coordinates. Sometimes enemy ground defenses gave us some "feedback" to tell us we weren't wanted. My aircraft was hit by enemy fire only once, and that was with minor tail damage. Others weren't so lucky, and some pilots didn't come back.

My first two flights were familiarization missions flown with Major Windy Schuler as my AC. Windy was a seasoned veteran of the war. After that I regularly—but not always—flew with Homer in front. Flying in the rear cockpit I had responsibilities for our safety and effectiveness, and I knew I had better learn them well.

The consequences of a botched mission greeted us when we first arrived. A strike mission flown just before our arrival hadn't gone well. Two F-4s from our sister squadron next door had bombed the wrong village in Laos. They went before a judicial, "Article 15" board. The AC and GIB of the lead aircraft, plus the GIB of the wingman, were found negligent and were fined, the fines going to the village as reparations.

On our first mission together Homer and I flew on the wing of Windy and his GIB, Doug. It was a night ground attack mission over Laos. Laos at night is pitch black—no lights of any kind. We were directed to rendezvous with a forward air controller (FAC) who designated the targets we were to strike. The FAC marked the targets with flares. Windy and Doug went in first, making several passes until they had expended their ordinance.

It was our turn—our first taste of combat together. We dived in, Homer fired rockets, and we pulled off. As we did I saw tracers coming close off our left side and told Homer, who jinked to the right. I felt a lump in my throat—our first time under fire. We made a second pass and the same thing happened. The tracers appeared in the same spot. They were red tracers that seemed to float up to us from the darkness below, and they really lit up the night sky. My voice was about an octave higher when I told Homer the proximity of those tracers.

We made a third drop. As we pulled off the tracers appeared as before. I was getting used to this and probably sounded just a little cocky when I nonchalantly said to Homer, "They're shooting at us again, same place." Then I casually looked over my right shoulder and saw a shower of tracers just off our right wing, big as life. I let out some kind of expletive and shouted at Homer, "Turn left, turn left! It was just one more lesson I learned the hard way: there was no room for complacency in this work.

Homer and I flew a mission another night to the infamous Mu Gia Pass area of Laos. It was heavily defended. After expending our hard bombs we were left with rockets. We had come under fire from an anti-aircraft artillery site, so Homer rolled in on it. Tracers began coming at us from the AAA site. The tracers were passing off to our left, and we were firing rockets down their throat in a classic "pissing contest." After Homer squeezed off the rockets, he announced "Off left." It was an instinctive thing he did, molded from repeated passes on the firing range and combat anxiety, but if he had turned left we would have turned directly into the Triple A fire. I quickly yelled, "No! No! Pull right! Pull right!" and put my left hand against the stick to prevent him from rolling left. Homer let out an "Oh shit!" and quickly reversed his attempted turn.

There are those who argue vehemently that there was no need to put pilots in the back seat of the F-4s in Vietnam; navigators would do just fine. But no navigator would have interceded like that, at least not to the point of putting his hand on the stick. That was pilot-to-pilot teamwork.

We were returning from a strike mission over Laos, headed into Da Nang one day in a two-ship formation. We were flying as the Number Two. As we came across Monkey Mountain which lies just north of the airfield, we descended into our landing pattern. Our lead aircraft just ahead of us hadn't pitched out to begin his landing, and Homer and I wondered why not. Just then lead radioed that they had lost hydraulic pressure and couldn't control their aircraft.

Both pilots quickly ejected just a few miles off the end of the runway. We were almost touching down when they had called. Homer pulled up and we flew over their crash site. We could see both of them below standing next to their parachutes, apparently safe. As we orbited overhead a rescue helicopter quickly came from the base to pick them up, and then we landed.

When we walked into the squadron building our Lieutenant Colonel DeRaud was standing there wearing a hard hat and flak vest and carrying an M-16. He looked more like a grunt than an airman, and we had a laugh over that. He was heading up a team to go to the crash site and investigate.

All of this happened within only an hour after the crash, but by the time DeRaud and his team arrived, the Cong had already planted booby traps at the wreckage, and the team came under enemy fire. They were pinned down for half an hour until Marines went in and pulled them out. Later the maintenance guys told us that our aircraft had also been hit, and we surmised that both birds had been hit when flying over Monkey Mountain.

Another day, another strike mission. We were headed home and touching down at Da Nang when the tower instructed us to pull over to the left side of the runway as we rolled out. Just then an F-105 rolled past us at high speed on our right and engaged the arresting gear at the runway end in front of us. After we parked we went over to look at the F-105. It was a bird based in Thailand, and it had been shot up pretty bad before making its emergency landing at Da Nang. The entire right side stabilizer had been shot off, and it's a wonder the pilot was able to land it. We talked with the pilot at the Officers Club later. A couple of days after that we learned that he had been called to headquarters in Saigon to receive an award. As he flew in on a transport, the aircraft crashed in foul weather and he was killed.

I was still relatively new at Da Nang and the war when I was tapped for a special mission. We were preparing to fly a CAP mission (combat air patrol) to guard the strike force coming from Thailand to bomb targets in North Vietnam. Flying high above the strike force, our fighters provided aerial protection from North Vietnam's MiG fighters. On CAP missions we carried both Sparrow and Sidewinder missiles, but we had no gun. A Gatling gun could be mounted under the aircraft centerline, but that's where we put our big 600-gallon fuel tank. Without a gun for close-in combat with enemy fighters, the F-4 would only be effective at greater distances; once the MiGs closed in, the F-4 couldn't shoot effectively, and the MiGs were superior.

The MiG pilots soon figured out that we couldn't shoot at close range, and so they maneuvered to take advantage of it by closing in.

Having had enough of that, Colonel "Boots" Blesse, our Wing Commander, decided to change the tactic. He decided to carry the Gatling gun in place of the centerline fuel tank on the next mission, hoping the element of surprise would overcome the MiGs.

Da Nang normally flew two CAP missions per day consisting of a morning and afternoon "gaggle" of eight aircraft in two 4-ship formations. The day we were to carry the gun for the first time, I was chosen as lead GIB to plan the morning mission. Why me? I don't know.

I planned it and crossed my fingers, but our mission was canceled for bad weather up north. However, the afternoon mission flew, and to everyone's delight they bagged three MiGs: two with Gatling guns and the third with a Sidewinder. The mission results were radioed back to the squadron, and we met the returning crews on the flight line with Champagne.

I could repeat this over and over but I'll say it here just once: During the war I really learned to appreciate Homer's abilities and insights. He was sharp, calm and collected in combat—he knew his stuff, which is no doubt why he had been a UPT check pilot. We were both learning about flying in combat, but his flying experience and savvy were already considerable. I could tell that others in our flight respected him that way, too. He saved our butts many times.

I learned only recently that Homer passed away. He and I had spent a year flying together. We crewed and lived together. He was a remarkable man.

I still think his nose was bigger than mine. We should have measured.

## Stuff Happens

One welcome feature of the F-4 was its rocket ejection seat. Instead of older seats with essentially a cannon charge underneath, the Martin-Baker seat lifted pilot and seat with a rocket that continued to elevate them to considerable distance from the airplane before a "butt-snapper" kicked the pilot away from the seat and chutes deployed. The Martin-Baker seat meant that a pilot could safely eject under zero-zero conditions: zero airspeed and zero altitude. And the rocket wasn't so likely to break the crewman's back in the process.

But the seat's design anticipated the pilot would be strapped in before ejecting. On one unfortunate day one of our GIBs did it differently. The GIB went to his aircraft and began his preflight checks. To inspect the upper part of the seat you had to stand on it. Somehow his seat wasn't pinned, and as he stood on it his movements caused it to fire. He was sent up, then came down, landing head-first on the wing without a helmet. He was killed instantly.

Da Nang was one of those places in the South that was only marginally secure. Normally we left our sidearms at the squadron building and checked them out when we flew, but occasionally we were told to check them out and take them to our quarters because of possible base attack. We kept our flak vests and hard helmets in quarters under threat of possible rocket attack and base invasion. I had worked out in my mind what I would do if the base came under attack. I kept my helmet on my bedpost with my flak vest in the locker. I played mental games, going through the steps in how I'd respond to an attack if I were in barracks.

I had been at Da Nang for a few weeks when one night I was suddenly awakened by a loud explosion that shook the building. I had been in deep sleep. I didn't know what had happened and my mind was foggy. I heard nothing else except Homer snoring beneath me. I thought, "This is it. We're under attack." So I said to Homer, "I think we're under attack." His response was more snoring.

It was time for me to put my attack plan to work. We had no windows and the room was pitch black. I sat up in bed and pivoted to swing off my top bunk—except I turned the wrong way, rammed my head into the concrete wall, tumbled backwards and did a half-flip onto the floor. Somehow I landed on my feet. I just stayed there, squatting in the dark. Homer stirred and said, "Saboski, what the hell are you doing?" I replied, "I think we're under attack." Homer began snoring again. I just squatted there a while, listening. Finally I stood up, found my hard hat on the bedpost, and put it on, still squatting. Homer never stirred.

Just then I heard voices outside our door—laughing. I stepped out into the lighted hall to see several of the guys there. They turned to look at me and laughed harder—I was standing there in my skivvies with a hard hat on.

From our balcony we saw the airport was lit up by fire, and then there were secondary explosions. It wasn't an attack. We later learned a Marine A-6 Intruder had been taking off when a C-141 transport was cleared onto the same runway by a different controller, and they collided. The Intruder was carrying a load of bombs. Both aircraft were fully loaded with fuel, a fire ensued, and the Intruder's bombs cooked off. Lives were lost.

That was in 1967. Fast-forward to 2001 when I was an assistant professor teaching aviation subjects at Embry-Riddle Aeronautical University in Prescott, Arizona. Our faculty were almost all former military pilots at some point in their lives. Retired Marine Colonel Fred Cone was one. Fred had been inducted into the Arizona Aviation Hall of Fame and had many interesting aviation stories to tell. One day while in some meeting or other, someone asked Fred to tell about the aircraft accident he had in Vietnam, and Fred told his tale. In one of the most remarkable coincidences, I learned Fred had been the pilot of the Intruder that night at Da Nang. Fred had crawled out of the wreckage severely injured, but he eventually recovered from those wounds.

But there's one more twist to the story. After hearing Fred tell his story, I remarked that I had also been there on that night and remembered the crash quite well, having gotten a lump on my head because of it. Then Nick Manderfield spoke up. Nick, another faculty guy, had also been there, working as an Air Force hospital administrator. How bizarre that all three of us would be reunited on the same faculty team in Arizona after all those years.


## Flyin' With Chuck

I seldom flew missions with anyone besides Homer, but one day I was paired to fly with a front-seater named Chuck. I can't remember why that happened, but off we went on a route reconnaissance ("recce") mission, scouting roads in the Demilitarized Zone. The DMZ was a no-man's land where VC trucks conveyed weapons and materiel into the South. Our route recce mission that day was to find and strike targets of opportunity along those roads.

Chuck was a somewhat flamboyant character, never reticent about expressing himself around the squadron. He was also a bit of a braggart.

We performed our pre-flight duties and took off in two-ship wingtip formation. As we approached our target area, we repositioned to a fighting wing formation with our airplane trailing loosely behind lead.

All was normal until we dropped down into defended territory and began surveying the roads at low level. That's when Chuck's voice went up in tone and volume, and everything he said resembled a panicked yell. Our entire route recce mission went that way—he was one excitable guy. I got tired of it and went into silent mode. He was really wired. We never really saw any targets, and the mission was a bust. But Chuck remained in a highly agitated state the entire time. He certainly wasn't the cool guy he professed to be around the squadron.

As we joined up with lead and climbed up to head home, Chuck regained his composure. It got real quiet in our airplane as we flew south. After a while he said something to which I responded, then more silence. Then he simply apologized to me in a lame sort of way, confessing that maybe he got a little over-excited back there. I acknowledged him, and that was it.

After we landed I made a beeline to Chuck's regular GIB, Mel. I described what had happened and asked Mel if Chuck was always like that. He stammered a bit and then acknowledged, yes, he was.

Sometime after that Chuck's bird got shot up. Flying his F-4 back home it lost hydraulic pressure and went out of control. Chuck and his GIB ejected, but the aircraft had already gone supersonic before they got out. The GIB ejected safely and was only bruised from the shock. But Chuck had a bad habit of flying with his visor up, and when he ejected the supersonic wind blast caught him full in the face.

It was several days before Chuck got out of medical and appeared in the squadron. The supersonic airflow had stretched back the skin

69

around his eye sockets, and his loose lower eyelids drooped down low onto his cheeks. Pretty ugly. He looked like a sad Bassett hound.

After I had left Da Nang for parts south, I heard that Mel had ejected, was captured, and became a prisoner of war. I knew two others who served out the war as prisoners. One was my roommate during F-4 RTU training, Mike Silva.

## Denny Chambers, POW

The other was Denny Chambers. Denny was over six feet tall, a handsome, muscular guy I had known from pilot training days. Denny had been in our sister flight during UPT, so he and I were classmates on opposite morning-afternoon schedules. We also went through F-4 RTU training together at George.

Denny got shot down over the DMZ. He ejected and parachuted into dense jungle in the midst of enemy ground forces. His wingman flew overhead and talked with Denny on his survival radio until the fuel ran low. Rescue aircraft had been alerted and immediately headed for Denny's position.

First to arrive were the "Sandies." The Sandies were A-1E Skyraiders—propeller-driven fighter-bombers that carried a massive amount of weapons and flew slow enough to provide defensive cover for a downed pilot. Denny kept talking to the Sandies so they could pinpoint his position. Meanwhile the rescue helicopter, the "Jolly Green," was moving in to pluck him out. Denny kept talking, but he began talking quieter because he could hear the VC moving around him. Then there was a pause in his transmissions. Just before the Jolly Green arrived, Denny said, simply, "I've got to go now—this little guy wants my radio."

After Jane Fonda enjoyed a nice vacation in Hanoi and revealed whose side she was really on, and after the war had ended, Eileen and I were at Maxwell AFB in Alabama as I attended the Air War College. It was 1983, and the POWs had just been repatriated from North

Vietnam's prisons. For their recovery and re-introduction they were brought to Maxwell.

Eileen and I were driving onto the base one day, approaching the front gate entrance, when a line of staff cars was exiting the other way. As we briefly passed I glanced into one of the cars. In the back seat I saw Denny Chambers—or what was left of him. Denny had been a big, strapping guy when I last saw him. What I saw now was a blank face with sunken eyeballs and prominent cheekbones showing. I stared, probably showing the shock I felt. He stared straight at me with an expression that showed faint recognition, but also confusion. That's the last I saw of Denny. I still remember that apparition.

## Strange Circumstances

On two occasions flying F-4s at Da Nang I was tapped for unusual duty under strange circumstances. On the first, my flight commander asked me to fly with another front-seater, an older lieutenant colonel. He wanted me to secretly evaluate the guy, providing feedback of his flying abilities.

I knew the lieutenant colonel from our F-4 training back in California and I liked him. But on our mission that night he showed definite flying problems, culminating in a "hard" landing with bombs on board. That's dangerous. I reported what I observed to my flight commander, but I was most uncomfortable. I was a mere first lieutenant tasked with evaluating a lieutenant colonel, a fellow classmate I liked and respected. Why me? I never found out, but the colonel was removed from our squadron soon afterward.

The other occasion was more unusual and had far more serious consequences.

I found myself scheduled to spend a day on alert duty paired with a Major Malm whom I had never flown with or even knew. That was very odd. Homer smelled something skunky and started asking questions. He was really concerned. Later in the day he told me that

71

"something was going on" but he couldn't find out the particulars. But he cautioned me to be very careful.

Whenever we pulled "Coyote" alert duty, two crews waited in full flying gear in an alert shack at the end of the runway. Their two F-4s were parked just outside, loaded with mixed weapons, cocked with electrical power turned on, and affixed with starting cartridges to expedite the engine starts. If called to respond to a request for rapid close air support, the alert crews could be airborne in mere minutes. Our Coyote flight was scrambled twice that day.

Windy and Doug were crewing the lead aircraft with Windy in charge. We all met Malm for the first time in the alert shack. Windy briefed Malm on coordinated procedures. Malm acted coolly, didn't join in any conversation and avoided any casual conversation with us.

Malm had only a few words with me about my flight duties. That was highly unusual, and I was very ill at ease about it. We three played some cards as he sat in a corner by himself and read. Windy was a pretty gregarious guy, but I detected there was a certain unease when he gave instructions to Malm.

I had never flown with any AC who just wouldn't talk. These airplanes are meant to be flown by a crew of two, and they had better discuss and know what each is doing. This guy wouldn't open up, and it was very apparent he expected me to just be along for the ride.

On our first scramble we flew to the DMZ to hit ground targets under direction of an airborne FAC. Malm still wouldn't communicate with me. We perfunctorily accomplished our checklists, and that was all.

Windy and Doug worked over the target first until their weapons were expended. When it was our turn to roll in on the target, Malm released all our hard bombs in a single pass instead of in pairs the way we were supposed to. I was caught by surprise, not knowing why all that tonnage had suddenly dropped off the bird. With only the gun left, he rolled in again, briefly fired a burst, and then pulled off "dry." Windy asked why he wasn't making any more passes, and Malm answered that our Gatling gun was jammed and all bombs had been dropped. So I'm the other pilot in this airplane sitting just a few feet behind him, and he never said a word to me about a "jammed gun" or why he unloaded all bombs in a single pass. If Windy hadn't asked, Malm likely wouldn't have said anything.

This was all wrong. When we got down Windy and Doug asked me about it, and all I could do is tell them that Malm wasn't talking.

Our second scramble was disastrous and lethal. We were alerted to the Vietnamese village of My Lai, the place that was later catapulted into national news and infamy by Army Lieutenant Calley's massacre. During the entire flight south, Major Malm was as mum as before.

Windy and Doug made several attack passes under the FAC's directions. When the FAC cleared us in to hit the target, Malm instead flew us overhead in a shallow turn at about 10,000 feet over the city. I didn't know what the hell was going on; I thought maybe he was just reconnoitering the target.

Unknown to me, Malm had released our cluster bomblets on that pass. Cluster bombs are tiny bombs contained in a pod under the wing. They trickle out when released—you can't feel them come off as you can with heavier weapons, and I could see nothing—the GIB can't see downward because of the big engine intakes on either side of his cockpit. Until Windy radioed us, I didn't realize Malm had already released the weapons. It was extraordinary.

CBU bomblets are designed to scatter, and so they were supposed to be released at low altitudes. When Malm released them at high altitude they scattered widely all over the area. We learned later that one bomb hit a boatload of Vietnamese refugees transiting the river south of the city. Seventeen in the boat were killed, including a US Navy lieutenant who was there on a clandestine mission.

It was a bad, bad situation. Malm did other things that were highly irregular. When we landed, Windy and Doug came straight up to me and Windy said, "I hope that's the closest you ever come to a short round accident." I described what had happened, but Windy already knew something had gone horribly wrong. I had no idea of the consequences just then, but word about the accident soon reached

73

the base, and both Malm and I were immediately grounded. I was shocked.

To my surprise I was put back on normal flying duty the next day without any explanation. It was only then that I found out what had happened and why I had been scheduled to fly with Malm under such mysterious circumstances. It's a very sordid story. I had been set up.

Malm had been assigned to our sister squadron next door when he began acting erratically, aborting his assigned missions for no apparent reason. His actions were inexplicable, and his commander was concerned. It looked like dereliction of duty. Matters got worse when Malm left the base for Saigon on falsified orders provided by a friend. He was brought back to Da Nang and given another chance, but his squadron commander refused to have him back in that squadron, so he came to ours. I was put up to fly with him on his very first mission, and no one deemed it necessary to inform me. Homer sniffed it out and cautioned me. How and why I was chosen as Malm's back-seater always remained a mystery.

Time passed after that day on alert. Malm was brought before a flying evaluation board, but he beat that—there was nothing wrong with his ability to fly.

## Hawaii—on Business

It was months later. I had already left Da Nang for parts further south to be a Forward Air Controller when I received orders dispatching me to Hawaii to testify as a witness at Malm's military discharge board. Another witness who was to appear had since left Vietnam for Europe, and circumstances prevented him from traveling to Hawaii just then. The board was postponed for two weeks waiting for that witness, and I was told I'd just have to bide my time in Hawaii with absolutely no duties. My, how sorely disappointed I was.

It happened that Larry, another GIB from Da Nang, was also in Hawaii on R&R, so we paired up to enjoy our time there, splitting the cost of a rental car. Our problem was that Hawaii was expensive, we

74

were on lieutenant's pay, and we had big, young guy appetites—especially Larry, who was about three inches taller than me. Fortunately we found a Chinese restaurant just outside the base that served decent food in large quantities, and cheap. We ate there a lot. Occasionally I reminded Larry that, unlike him, I was there on official duty and was getting paid extra for it. I just thought he should know that.

Larry and I spent our days on the beach at Fort DeRussy, the Army's R&R resort hotel in Honolulu. It was nicer than the beaches in Vietnam that frequently smelled like the fishing villages nearby. Occasionally I'd roll over and remind Larry once again that I was getting paid for this.

That's where we happened upon two school teachers who were vacationing there. They were cute and friendly, we had a car, and so we linked up. We drove to the other side of Oahu where the surfing championships are held. We had visions of swimming there, but each time we approached the beach, the huge waves drove us back. Finally, we just perched on the rocks and watched. In the next day's news we read that a woman had been washed off that same beach that day and drowned.

We had a couple of days in company with the school teachers and saw all the sights. They were leaving the next day so Larry and I scraped our wallets and took them to dine at the Ilikai Hotel.

The Ilikai was a magical resort right on Waikiki Beach. After a really good dinner we went into the spacious lounge and got a table in one of their quaint, secluded booths. Each booth was private, one step up off the main floor, and featured a curtain of privacy beads hanging down in front. We ordered Mai Tais. I recognized right away that these Mai Tais were dangerous and should have come with a warning label. They were a blend of sumptuous fruit flavors and tasted wonderful. But they were really loaded, and soon we were, too.

Then the music started. The entertainment was a live, Mexican mariachi band. As I looked at the band, I saw someone I recognized. Of all the amazing coincidences, it was the same band that Johnny, Bob, and I saw back in Bakersfield when we were driving to Survival

School. Sure enough, there was my friend, the guitar player who was a twin for my old college roommate.

The band played for quite a while as the four of us eased into our Mai Tais. Larry was a big guy. His date was average size, and so was I. My date was a shrimp—cute, but tiny. The Ilikai should have offered pint-sized drinks for pint-sized people like her, but hers was as big as ours. That Mai Tai smacked her like a ton of bricks.

The band took a break and I motioned for my friend the guitar player to come over. Not understanding much English, he sat down and accepted a Mai Tai that I had provided to improve his language skills. I tried again to explain how he looked exactly like my college roommate, Fred, but that message didn't get through the translator. So I just called him Fred from then on.

The band's break was pretty long, and when they returned they were minus one musician. Fred was getting pretty happy sitting in our booth, and the curtain of beads kept him out of sight. The band members looked around but couldn't find him, so they struck up the music without him.

Fred was getting a little tipsy at that point. We suggested he'd better join his colleagues, and so he quaffed his entire Mai Tai in one gulp and got up. I could tell by the way he walked across the room that the Mai Tai had a grip on his legs. As Fred joined the band and played some notes, the others kept looking at him funny like he was a different person somehow.

That's when my date decided to make a trip to the little girl's room. She hadn't been on her feet for a while, and when she stood up she wasn't ready for the room to start spinning. She missed the step down from our booth and grabbed out in desperation, collecting an armful of hanging beads before I grabbed her and stopped her fall. The beads made a helluva clatter, turning every head in the place. She recovered, and Larry's date escorted her to the ladies room.

We cut her off right there. Heroically, Larry polished off the rest of her drink for her and chased it with another one. I had stopped drinking at one Mai Tai, and so had Larry's date, thank goodness. Two out of the four of us stayed somewhat sober. We managed to make it out of the place without further incident and went to an all-night coffee shop. It was after midnight. Larry was in near-pass-out condition with a strange smile affixed to his face. My date was in Neverland, and Larry's date was feeding coffee into his mouth with a spoon. We finally got Larry into the car. I drove us to the girls' hotel. We said our good-byes and got back on base as the sun was coming up. The next day Larry headed back to Da Nang and I was left there with one more day until the board convened.

Malm's board finally began and I was called in to testify. I related to the three senior officers about flying Coyote alert with Malm that day. They asked me very few questions, but when I described how Malm had ignored me they murmured and one of them shook his head in dismay.

There was a point in my flight with Malm that he wanted me to give him gunsight settings for the unfinned napalm we carried. Dropping unfinned napalm is like dropping water balloons—the cans tumble and there's no precision, so to deliver them properly you skim the treetops and use "Kentucky windage" to determine when to press the pickle button. A gunsight setting for unfinned nape is ridiculous. Malm asked me for sight settings. I was surprised—I had never done that with any other AC. When I gave him the settings for 5 and 10 degrees dive angle, he said, "Higher." I gave him 15 and 20 degrees. He said, "Higher," and I gave him the settings for 30 and 45 degrees dive. When he again said, "Higher," I was staring at the setting for 60 degrees. But I had had enough. I lied and said, "There isn't anything higher." We dropped unfinned nape at 45 degrees dive, and I had no idea where the cans went.

When I told the board that, I thought I was placing myself in real jeopardy for disobeying Malm's order, but the board members never said a thing.

My testimony was over quickly, and soon I was flying back to Vietnam. I don't know what happened to Malm. I never saw him since the day we flew, and I never learned anything further. I thought of Malm as a criminal who should have been prosecuted. He should never have been placed back in the cockpit, and I was angry that I had been duped.

I thought the whole episode was disgusting . . . except for the Mai Tais, of course.


## Back to Da Nang

Let's flash back to when I was still at Da Nang following the Malm incident.

The United States was now under a new president—Nixon. The Vietnam War was about to change drastically.

One day we were "fragged" to attack unspecified targets in South Vietnam. We realized something mysterious was going on. Homer and I were to be part of a four-ship formation. That in itself was unusual—four-ships don't normally attack targets in the South. Instead of receiving specific targets we were told to contact someone on a discrete radio frequency after takeoff.

After takeoff we pointed south and changed frequencies as directed. A controller changed our course. Instead of South Vietnam, we proceeded to Cambodia. Along the way we were joined by other formations of fighter-bombers.

The North Vietnamese Army had been using Cambodia—a neutral country—to transit its war supplies into South Vietnam, but although Cambodia was aiding the enemy President Johnson put it off limits to US air strikes. That day we hit targets in Cambodia for the first time. Everyone returned home and we were instructed to keep our mouths shut.

Among ourselves we celebrated. We were all glad to have the shackles taken off and to have struck the North Vietnamese where it hurt.

Since I first arrived at Da Nang, the Air Force continually over-supplied us with back-seat F-4 pilots, and my once-promised fast upgrade to the front-seat simply disappeared. It looked like I was doomed to be a GIB for a very long time.

I didn't like the prospects of being stuck in the back seat perpetually. I searched in vain for some front seat flying job elsewhere in the war zone, but nothing panned out. Homer understood my dilemma and helped me look. Our flight commander helped, too.

I had heard that T-28 (single-engine, propeller-driven aircraft) pilots were needed in Thailand to fly over Laos. My flight commander happened to be going to Thailand on business and he offered to inquire for me while he was there. When he returned he told me, "Yes, they want T-28 pilots, but they're looking for back seat T-28 pilots to fly with a Laotian pilot up front." No thanks. If I had to fly the back seat of anything it would be an F-4 with Homer in front.

We had been at Da Nang just over four months when Homer and I were sent to the Philippines for a few days of practice live-firing the Sparrow missile. While there I got to enjoy water buffalo steak, real eggs, and fresh fruit at the Officers Club.

When we returned to Da Nang the scuttlebutt on base was all about the announcement from headquarters in Saigon. There was a critical shortage of Class A forward air controllers (FACs) in the South, and volunteer replacements were needed immediately. Fighters couldn't attack targets in South Vietnam except under direction of a Class "A" FAC—someone with prior fighter experience. Someone like me.

Within a half hour of hearing that news I was knocking on my commander's trailer door, and in four days I was flying to the Mekong River delta region for FAC training. At last I was going to fly my own airplane—even if it was just a small one, and even if it meant extending my Vietnam tour by three months.

I was the first—and only—volunteer among all the Da Nang GIBs. That night I sat in the Officers Club and discovered I was the talk of the squadron. Not favorably, either. Many of the GIBs thought I was copping out.

I didn't mind. I had decided long ago that I wanted to fly either solo or in the front seat, and I made my UPT assignment choice accordingly. I blamed the Air Force for some deception in leading me to think I would quickly upgrade to the front seat of the F-4. But what really dogged me was how I had been set up to fly with Malm and the disastrous consequences of putting that sorry guy back in an F-4. Why hadn't someone given me notice about his prior behavior? Why hadn't they simply kicked him out? Peoples' lives would have been saved.

This critical need for FACs was a Godsend, and so I volunteered without hesitation.

Sitting pretty much alone in the O Club bar was strange, but soon I was joined by another GIB, then another, then others. They were all pumping me for information. They thought I knew something else about the call for volunteers. I didn't. I just knew what I wanted to do. They were enticed by the FAC assignment but afraid to make a decision.

Maybe those around me were afraid to face the wrath of those who stayed. Later in life I called that "union mentality." Maybe they were cowed because their tours would be longer.

In the next two days, three more GIBs volunteered. It was a way out of the back-seat pilot trap. Some of my fellow back-seaters languished in the rear cockpit for years afterward, watching their pilot careers go down the drain, and then quit the Air Force in frustration. After the war the Air Force began assigning navigators to the F-4's rear seat, but it was too late for many of the GIBs.

I left Da Nang three days after I volunteered. I said good-bye to Homer and never saw him after that. We wrote to each other and I learned of some more guys who were lost. Ken Huey, our flight commander, had been killed. Our correspondence trailed off as the war continued and we went separate ways.

After my four months at Da Nang in the F-4, I spent another seven months as a FAC and Air Liaison Officer. I got one month knocked off my 12-month tour for the "counters" I flew up north in the F-4.

# The Bird Dog

I reported for FAC training at Binh Thuy Air Base in the Mekong River delta region. Upon arriving I was greeted by the commander there, and his first words were, "Boy, am I glad to see you." That might not seem like much, but his greeting was the complete opposite of my reception at Da Nang, and it set a prevailing tone of welcome that lasted my entire time as a FAC.

When I had first arrived at Da Nang the place was already overloaded with GIBs. Every new arrival meant fewer "counters" and longer duty tours for the other back-seaters. That engendered an atmosphere of resentment among the GIBs of Da Nang. But at little Binh Tuy (Bin Tooey) I felt welcome and reassured that I had made the right choice.

Binh Thuy was decidedly smaller than Da Nang. I trained there in the little propeller-driven O-1E "Bird Dog" for several weeks, learning my forward air controller duties.

One day while I was on the flight ramp an airplane landed carrying noted comedian Jonathan Winters and his entourage. Winters mingled with a small crowd of us while his aircraft was refueled. I've never seen anyone so naturally and spontaneously funny as that man. For the short while he was there, he kept us in stitches. He was genuinely a nice person, too, and seemed to enjoy being with us. Much later I saw him on the Tonight Show, and he expressed those very feelings to Johnny Carson.

My other memories of Binh Thuy were of the raunchy smell of the nuoc mam (fish sauce) plant nearby. How something can smell that bad and taste so good is beyond me. I also remember the unusual bar

82

rule at the smallest Officer Club in the world. It was written on the ceiling so you could conveniently read it while reposing flat on your back. It said that if you buy yourself a drink, you must buy one for everyone else—a simple rule that instantly acquainted you with everyone else. It was the friendliest little bar I've ever known.

## Nha Trang and the Korean Army

With my FAC training completed, I moved from the delta region to Vietnam's east coast. I was assigned to the 21st. Tactical Air Support Squadron (TASS), attached to the 9th. Republic of Korea Army Division. The 21st. TASS provided the ROK army with air support for their assigned operations area along Vietnam's east coast from Tuy Hoa to Phan Rang. The 9th ROK Division consisted of three regiments—the 28th 29th, and 30th—lined up north to south along South Vietnam's central coast.

Along the coast was the north-south Highway 1, the main land route of South Vietnam. Alongside Highway 1 was a single railroad track. It, too, was a major transportation route. The Viet Cong loved to hit the two of them, sometimes simultaneously. Many mornings as I flew along I'd see smoke and damage from the previous night's attacks. There were some very vulnerable bridges that got hit frequently. The VC operated mostly at night. It looked peaceful from the air along the coast, but we knew they were there. I learned a lesson about that not long after I arrived.

## Complacency

Many of our airstrikes were "tree busters." The targets were determined by intelligence, and the FACs marked targets using the detailed terrain maps we carried. FACs flew to their targets before the assigned fighters arrived. The FAC reconnoitered the target to determine if there was physical activity, but not getting so close as to warn the enemy. Very often the target was nothing but a coordinate on a map, obscured because of the triple-canopy trees that made up Vietnam's jungle areas.

When fighters arrived, the FAC would describe the target and then mark it with smoke either from a white phosphorous rocket or simply dropping an exploding can. The fighters saw the smoke, and the FAC directed them where to strike relative to the smoke plume. After the attack, the FAC went back to the target—carefully—to perform a BDA (battle damage assessment).

The prevalence of tree busters was discouraging for both FAC and fighters—you struck something, but trees obscured any visual evidence of success.

I was still a new FAC when I flew north of Nha Trang one day to hit a target just west of Highway 1. I was meeting a couple of F-100s coming up from Phan Rang. Although still somewhat new to the FAC business, I had had enough "tree buster" missions to have grown tired of them.

I arrived at the target coordinates and saw nothing but jungle below. This would be another tree buster. The target was on a steep mountainside, and the terrain and prevailing winds dictated that the fighters and I make our run-ins from the south along a ridge. The fighters arrived, and I told the pilots their target looked like another tree buster. They were loaded with 250 lb. Snake Eye hard bombs, and the F-100 had an internal 20 mm. gun that is normally not effective firing into triple-canopy trees, so I had them drop only their bombs.

When they were done, I told them they could start heading home as I went in to survey the target. I expected to see nothing except jungle and there was no need for them to wait around. I dropped down and headed in from the south.

The VC had it all figured out. As I approached at low altitude along the mountainside, I was greeted by a shower of tracers coming directly at me. The tracers passed underneath my airplane, and I thought for sure I was hit. I racked the airplane up and rolled hard to the right. I was relieved that the enemy's fire didn't track after me. It appeared the VC had mounted a 30 caliber machine gun in the trees and lined it up to spot-fire through a hole in the canopy.

It scared the hell out of me, but I hadn't been hit. I told the departing fighters what had happened, and they turned around and came back. They strafed the target with their 20 mm guns and then went home with my sincere thanks. I didn't go back in for another battle damage assessment.

I was young and sometimes not cautious. The lesson learned that day was burned into my cortex for life. I had better be more careful and less complacent if I was going to live through the war.

## Working with Grunts

My airborne FAC duties were interspersed with ground duties, too. Our job was to support our Korean Army partners. Where Air Force and Army meet there is a dividing line—sometimes the line is like a chasm, and we have to learn how to bridge over it. Well, bridging over a chasm is the army way; we blue-suiters prefer to fly over such obstacles.

My first such encounter with the "grunts" was when I skirted around the draft by joining the Air Force. I was already prejudiced against the army when I arrived at the 9th. ROK Division.

The 9th ROK was an infantry division, and they were unaccustomed to using close air support. For my seven months there, we were continually attempting to convince them of the advantages of using air power to enhance their ground operations. I believe we were successful, particularly after the Viet Cong attack on the 28th Regiment's headquarters, which I'll describe in a moment. Through our efforts and theirs, we made significant progress over the months.

For my first four months I purely flew FAC missions. After that I flew two weeks and spent every third week performing ground duties as the Air Liaison Officer (ALO) for the 28th Regiment, and I mostly lived at their headquarters near Phu Hiep, just south of Tuy Hoa.

85

Occasionally I'd return to our TASS at Nha Trang. The food was better there.


## A Bunch of Cuties

As I mentioned, at first I lived mostly on base at Nha Trang, flying missions north and south from there. We were the Cutie FACs, and my call sign was "Cutie One Zero" or Cutie 10. "Number Ten" was the Vietnamese way to describe something unlikeable—something far worse than the exalted Number One—and my call sign quickly morphed into "Cutie Number Ten."

The Cutie FACs were a congenial bunch of guys, all of them older and of higher rank than I. I was quite content to be among them. A finer group of guys has never been assembled—at least not at Nha Trang, Vietnam. They quickly let me know that I was welcome and much-needed. That was a complete about-face from the circumstances at Da Nang where all the GIBs were focused on getting more "counters" to shorten their tours. I appreciated being among the Cutie FACs and doing my new job—and I was finally flying my own airplane.

At Nha Trang Air Base we actually ventured into the town— something almost unheard of at Da Nang. Our TASS had a jeep—a "slick" without FAC radios mounted on the back. Hardly anyone used it besides me. I'd simply ride around in my spare time to sight-see.

There was a nice French restaurant in downtown Nha Trang. Sometimes we'd drive the Jeep down there and indulge in decadent French food at ridiculously low prices. When I wasn't living in a tent or eating C rations, it was delicious to sup on good French cuisine sitting on the patio at La Fragats. I loved the fresh tiger prawns, big as lobster tails and better-tasting.

That didn't last, though. One night when we weren't there, someone hung a Claymore mine on the rear patio wall and blew away the customers sitting there.

Our area of responsibility (AOR) was coastal central Vietnam, the easternmost part of the country and a very beautiful place. On many days I forgot the war long enough to think just how nice it was to be flying my airplane solo, looking at the picturesque views. The waters of the South China Sea were deep blue and crystal clear, and I saw huge sharks meandering about the fishing boats.

We lived on the upper story of a two-story, open-bay barracks. The sea breezes blew through, sometimes supplemented by our overhead fans. At the center of our floor was our headquarters. That's where our scheduling board and beer refrigerator were and where we gathered at the end of the day. The rest of the floor was where we each had a cubicle, separated by room dividers. In each cubicle was a cot, desk with chair, and steel cabinet. It was home, except when we were away at one of the regiment headquarters.

Our barracks floor area was cleaned by a short, meager Vietnamese lady who weighed-in at just 47 pounds. We called her "Yardstick." She was very industrious and friendly, and we considered her one of us. When I finished my tour, I gave her my alarm clock that she always seemed to like.

I flew a lot. We were restricted by regulation from flying more than 100 hours a month, but that could be forgiven for up to 120 hours under combat circumstances. I flew right up to 120 hours in three successive months and was then advised to cut it back. Flying out of Nha Trang I sometimes flew north up to Tuy Hoa, sometimes south down by Phan Rang and Cam Ranh. Where we flew depended on where intelligence said our targets were and what fighters we were to meet. The FAC would fly to the target coordinates, reconnoiter the target area, and wait for fighters to arrive. Our lower altitude and speed gave the FAC better eyeballs for determining what the target and defenses were.

FACs normally flew higher than 1500 feet above the terrain to avoid small arms fire, but job requirements sometimes required us to fly lower. In those cases it was better to fly right on the deck than someplace in between. One time I put my wing under a tree limb to see where two VC were hunkered down.


## Dumb Mistake

One day I took off to provide escort for a convoy that was headed out of Tuy Hoa along the main road going west. It took a while to reach the area, and as I came across a mountain ridge and into radio range, I contacted the convoy commander. The convoy hadn't traveled far but had already come under fire. The convoy commander told me the VC were in the mountains north of the convoy, firing down upon them. My airplane would only go so fast, and it was several minutes before I arrived. I promptly flew over the mountain ridge where they were and down the other side, knowing that the sight of a forward air controller usually caused them to stop firing because they feared fighter aircraft were nearby.

My maneuver was a huge misjudgment. It was monsoon season, and the winds were coming strong from the east. On the back side of that mountain was wind shear—strong winds that pushed my aircraft down toward the trees below. I did all I could to pull up, but my airplane was still going down. Just before hitting the trees, I felt a cushioning effect where the winds pancaked out, and I pulled up just a few feet above the tree tops. Pure fear left the taste of bile in my mouth. That's the closest I ever came to killing myself. It was another lesson learned the hard way.

I recovered from my scare, but I was still a little shaken. My maneuver had stopped the enemy fire, though. The convoy continued on without incident. When it returned in a couple of days, I provided escort again but there was no trouble.


## My Encounter with the Press

On another day my FAC mission was to rendezvous with some fighters for targets in the mountains west of Tuy Hoa; but I was given a secondary mission, too. I had to first land at Tuy Hoa and pick up an Air Force photographer from Armed Forces Radio & TV so he could get some air strike photos. The sergeant was waiting for me on the Tuy Hoa ramp when I taxied in. I briefed him on what we would be doing, gave him a headset, and strapped him into the back seat. We took off, headed for the target area. I showed him where the targets were, and soon the approaching fighters—a 2-ship formation—called in.

Things got busy then. I got not just one set of fighters that day, but three of them in succession. Two sets had been diverted from targets further east for bad weather. I kept one set of fighters holding high and dry while I worked with another. As soon as they expended their weapons, I did the same for the next set and then the next. It was a real test to get it done before someone ran out of gas, but I was a pretty seasoned FAC by then and everyone got to play.

In typical FAC fashion I'd locate the target by using the intelligence information and my terrain map, mark it using one of my 2.75 inch white phosphorous rockets, then direct the fighter to aim for a spot in relation to where my rocket exploded. One by one I put the fighters in until all six had expended their weapons. To do so without everyone running into each other I had to really yank and bank my aircraft, looking high and low, firing rockets, dropping smoke canisters, and playing traffic cop. These targets were under a jungle tree canopy, so the enemy wasn't visible; it was up to the fighters to fire at where I put the smoke, so I would make a marking pass, followed by a fighter, then I'd make another marking pass, etc.

I completely ignored my passenger—the fighters had only so much gas, and I had no time to talk to him. When all was done I pulled off, low on fuel, and headed for base. I turned around to see how he was doing. He had his flight cap in his lap, and as I turned he threw up in it. He hadn't gotten a single picture. He was green around the gills and very quiet for the flight back to Tuy Hoa.

A couple of weeks afterward I was again directed to pick up a press photographer. Déjà vu. This time my passenger waited at Phan Rang AB to the south. I had no fighters scheduled, so my mission was to reconnoiter the area and wait in case fighters from another target were sent to me. When I pulled up to the Phan Rang parking ramp, it was the same guy. He looked apoplectic when he recognized me, but I assured him our flight wouldn't as violent as the last. I told him he likely wouldn't get any airstrike pictures, but I'd take him to some old WW II wrecks and ruins he might want to photograph.

It was a beautiful day, and ours was a leisurely flight. I dropped down and cruised the area like in one of those aerial scenic tours shown on the Smithsonian channel. We saw very nice mountains and flew through picturesque valleys. We flew along the coast, over the azure ocean. We viewed the wreckage of a submerged WW II ship under the crystal clear water and an old fortification on a hillside. I was absorbed in what we were seeing, and then I realized I hadn't heard from my photographer for a while. I looked around and he again had his hat in his lap, and once again, he barfed in it. I couldn't believe it—we couldn't have had a smoother, nicer flight.

I took him back. As he got out he said, "Captain, if you don't mind I won't do this again. I can't afford to buy any more hats."


## We Go Camping

The Koreans conducted two major ground operations in which they swept territory to the west of Tuy Hoa. I went along as air liaison officer along with the US Army Liaison Officer, Major Walker, and my enlisted radio operator. My job was to coordinate with the Koreans for US air support, working with our airborne FACs and our headquarters.

On the first deployment the Koreans pitched their headquarters on a hilltop. I slept in a tent shared by Walker, my sergeant, and the Korean liaison officer, Lieutenant Oh, a youngish officer who acted as interpreter. At base camp we ate C rations, shared a common privy, and observed blackout conditions at night. Just a few yards away was the camp perimeter with its guards and trip wires for flares and mines. On our first night Lt. Oh discovered a scorpion in his sleeping bag, and every night afterward he turned the place upside-down on a scorpion hunt before turning in.

Major Walker's Korean liaison officer was a very soft-spoken captain. Captain Koh was a nice guy who would quietly grin at a joke but never said much. I asked Walker about him, and Walker said he had been involuntarily pulled out of field duty and made a liaison officer after having been wounded ten times. His commander figured Koh had seen enough combat.

Our tent was pitched near the helipad, and I saw everyone who came in or departed by air. The Koreans would bring in Viet Cong prisoners. They were kept in a little barbed wire enclosure. They were walking when they arrived but often on stretchers when taken out.

The Korean offensive sweep was quite successful—so successful that it attracted the attention of the US Headquarters in Saigon. We were visited by a US Army 3-star general and his entourage. Major Walker escorted them and they remained with the Korean Regiment for about an hour before flying out again. I asked Walker how the visit went. He said the general was very complimentary to the Koreans. His only criticism was when he told them they should take more prisoners.

One day a Korean L-19 light plane flew over our encampment. I don't know what he was doing there, but he kept making low, slow passes with his flaps down, quite close to us. I could see there was a passenger flying with the pilot. I watched with concern because he seemed to be flying too close to stall speed. Sure enough, he stalled and crashed onto the hillside. A quick-thinking Korean pulled the passenger out, but the pilot burned in the fire.

The 9th ROK Regiment Commander was a lieutenant colonel. Walker came up to me one day and said the commander was interested in my revolver. It was my personal weapon; before going to Vietnam I was advised to take a sidearm, so I bought a .38 Special. I was too lowly in rank for the Korean commander to speak directly to me, so through Walker we arranged a deal. I had first qualified with a .45 automatic, so I said I would trade even for a .45. And that's what I got. Whether it was a captured weapon or not, I don't know—the serial number had been filed off. When I was ready to leave the war, I discovered I couldn't bring an unregistered weapon home with me, so it stayed behind. I traded it for a box of tools.

After two weeks the operation was over and we returned to the regiment's base on the coast. Some months later the division conducted another field operation. This one was closer to home—about ten kilometers west of Tuy Hoa. We softened up the area with US air strikes. However, one bomb missed target and cratered the main canal leading to the city. Canal water flooded the countryside, which was flat, consisting mainly of rice paddies. When we helicoptered in we set up our camp at the only high ground in the area—a US artillery battery. The high ground kept us out of flood waters except when we used the latrine, which was under about a foot of water.

High ground in a flood is also refuge for the beasties. Vietnam has rats—lots of them, big as cats. They moved in with us. We slept in hammocks in a half-underground bunker. On my first night we went into the bunker and my flashlight revealed that the rats were already there. They scattered but made noises all night long—along with the artillery. That first night two of them had a squealing fight next to my head. The next night, they were a little more stubborn, scattering only reluctantly. The third night, we had to kick at them. They were getting hungry. We used mosquito netting for the insects, but also to keep out the rats. On the second night my radio operator rolled over and a rat bit him on the forehead. He had to be evacuated to get rabies shots.

That operation was another Korean success. The Koreans proudly displayed a treasure trove of captured weapons. And this time they took prisoners.

The prisoners were kept at our encampment for a while until they learned better manners, the Korean way. Just outside our bunker the Koreans pitched a canopy and put cots underneath. The VC prisoners stayed there all day. They were taught to sing the Korean national anthem. As they sang, they were forced to sit in stress positions, such as on their tailbones without touching anything with arms or legs. Korean guards carried broomsticks, and any prisoner who moved to support himself received a whack.

I was back at regimental headquarters in a week, and life returned to "normal." The regiment was given the support of two US Army helicopter gunships. But the regiment commander didn't trust those guys, and neither did I. The helicopter pilots—warrant officers younger than I—would repeatedly come in and ask for some targets to hit. It wasn't my job to supply the US Army with targets, and those guys didn't work for me. I considered them reckless and irresponsible, and that came from personal experience.

My distrust began early one morning when I flew north out of Nha Trang toward Ninh Hoa, the location of the ROK Division Headquarters. The VC had attacked the division base just before dawn, and as I approached from the south there was a firefight going on. I contacted a US Army captain on the ground who said he thought they had pinpointed a VC mortar near the town square. I dropped down and flew at treetop level over the square. I couldn't see anything, and told the captain. I pulled off and took some small arms fire just to my left. I always flew my Bird Dog with the windows open, and I instinctively yanked my arm in when I heard the rounds shoot past my window.

Just then two Army helicopter gunships arrived. The captain gave them the same coordinates for the suspected mortar location, and the gunships opened fire—on the wrong coordinates! I radioed the captain immediately and exclaimed they were hitting the wrong target, but the captain had already seen that for himself, and he screamed at them to get the hell out of there—that they had fired on friendly positions.

When the Koreans had vacated the first field operation I described above, they had mistakenly left behind an ammunition dump. They didn't want it to fall in the hands of the VC, so they asked me to arrange for US airstrikes to hit it. It was a very small target, and they missed. The regimental commander tasked a gunship to fly up there and hit it, and two eager army warrant officer pilots came to me to ask for guidance. Those guys—as I already knew—couldn't read maps worth a damn. So at their request I climbed into the copter to show

93

them where it was. On the way there, the immature jerks just had show off to this Air Force captain by skimming low over the rice paddies, forcing Vietnamese farmers to dive off the dikes into the water.

When we got there, sure enough they couldn't see the ammunition dump until I pointed it out to them. Then they unloaded on it with rockets and machine guns—and couldn't hit it at point-blank range. The cocky pilots were pretty quiet on the ride back. After we returned, I said, "Don't ask me for any more favors, and don't hang around our camp anymore." Later that day a passing formation of Air Force fighters flying home with unexpended ammunition hit the dump successfully, causing a big secondary explosion.

## Kimchi in Self Defense

Then something happened that nearly changed the course of the entire war: the ROK Army in Vietnam received C-rations containing kimchi. For any uninformed epicureans, kimchi is a staple food of the Korean diet made from cabbage, garlic, and other spices that ferments in jars underground until it gets really, really ripe. With the arrival of C-ration kimchi the Korean army could eat kimchi anytime, anyplace.

My first kimchi encounter was when I arrived as a new FAC and visited the 9th ROK Army Division headquarters at Ninh Hoa. I had lunch with a handful of Americans there who pointed to the innocent bowl of salad and convinced me to try it. I began gulping it down until I realized it wasn't just salad. I grabbed my iced tea to quench the fire, not realizing that the Koreans used their sugar bowls to hold the salt I had put in my tea. After everyone had a big laugh at my expense, I think I said something like, "They should put that s___ back in the ground where it came from."

Later on, when I lived with the Koreans at the 28th Regiment headquarters I ate in their little mess hall. There was no place else to eat. Language was a mutual barrier, and all I could do was point and eat whatever I got. Although the food was always spicy hot, it wasn't

94

kimchi. I found a few foods from their kitchen that didn't taste like fire.

But along came C-ration kimchi, and soon it was everywhere. When someone popped open a can of kimchi in the headquarters building you could smell it instantly three doors down the hall.

Kimchi was especially popular at lunch time, and right after lunch was when I went to the headquarters planning room to lay out airstrikes for the upcoming days. Planning airstrikes required me to huddle with the Koreans over a map spread out before us. With the introduction of kimchi to lunchtime meals, huddling with the Koreans over a map became an endurance contest. I'd take a big gulp of air, dive into the huddle, then come up for fresh air when I couldn't take it anymore.

In the long run I finally gave in. The Koreans hosted a barbecue one night and I had some of the milder, summer kimchi—and actually liked it. I think my taste buds and smeller had been permanently altered by then because eventually I learned to even like winter kimchi—the stronger stuff that stayed underground all winter. By the end of the war I was a kimchi convert—it's pretty good stuff as long as everyone within a mile is eating it together. But for quite a while I really thought that I, and the war, weren't going to make it with C-ration kimchi floating around the war zone.

I no longer ate in the ROK Army mess. I had made friends with the American army officers at a US Army artillery battery nearby. They had noticed my plight and invited me to mess with them. I was eternally grateful.

Nearby was an army field hospital, and at the hospital were— nurses. An army captain buddy had been seeing one of the army nurses there. One night he told me that she had propositioned him, and he didn't know what to do. She asked him to get her pregnant so the army would send her home. He was married and so was she. He also told me it was a common practice among the nurses.

Years later when the political decision was made to integrate the sexes in American military combat units, I reflected on that. Our job was to win battles and wars. It made no sense to give wartime commanders a few contentious sexual problems just to see if they can handle it—as if fighting a war wasn't difficult and dangerous enough already.


## Living With the ROK Army

We in the TASS were now spending so much time at the 28th Regiment that the Koreans gave us wood and materials to build sleeping quarters. We also built a latrine—a building with a 3-hole privy and a shower. The shower was made from an old napalm can and fitted with an emersion heater for hot showers. The privy was a three-holer.

There was soon a problem with the privy. To do a Number Two, Americans sit, while Koreans squat. Our 3-holer was built for sitting, not squatting. To squat, the user had to balance his feet precariously on the front edge. Occasionally, one of our Korean visitors would miss his mark, leaving a present for the next sitting American.

We had a pet dog. Dogs are sometimes eaten in that part of the world, so we had to keep him in sight. He was a black short-hair of some indistinct breed, and we named him Dokebi, which we were told means Black Devil in Korean.

One regular visitor to our compound was a Korean doctor. Friendly, likeable guy, but, my, how he drank. He loved our little American parties where the booze was cheap.

We played volleyball with the Koreans. We'd have a mostly American team, supplemented with a few Koreans, going against an all-Korean team. But strict discipline prevailed over sports in the ROK Army. One day a Korean player was having a rough time, and our American team took advantage of his mistakes. Finally his sergeant had had enough. If he had been American, he would have been sidelined, but that wasn't the ROK Army way. The sergeant called him over, and as he stood two feet away, the sergeant smashed the volleyball into the guys face. That was it. The guy walked off the court with a bloody face. Our side still won.

One day I was planning airstrikes in the 28th Headquarters building when shouting interrupted us. From the planning room I could see into the regiment commander's office across the hall. Two majors were holding a captain by each arm. The commander was chewing him out, loudly. When he was done, the commander kicked him roundly in the crotch. The captain collapsed and was dragged down the hall by the majors. All of us quietly returned to the planning table.

The Koreans announced that an entertainment troupe was coming to visit the 28th. Festivities were planned. A large stage was erected and outdoor lights were placed all around. The regiment commander directed his US Army gunship to go out into the mountains and shoot a couple of deer. The venison was barbecued and served as Korean bulgogi—really delicious stuff to us Americans, and I think we ate most of it. The entertainment was quite good, and it was a pleasant diversion from the war.

For my last few months in Vietnam I was semi-permanently attached to the 28th and living there. Occasionally I still returned to the TASS at Nha Trang.

## The Aussies

American citizens are usually completely unaware that the ASEAN partner nations also participated in the Vietnam War. Most Americans think it was an all-US affair. Besides the Koreans, we also worked with the Australians.

The Aussies worked mostly from a tent encampment south of Nha Trang. They flew their Canberra bombers from Phan Rang Air Base. The Canberras (like our B-57s) were slow and clumsy bombers—not very accurate and not really suitable for the mountainous terrain. I'm not sure how many the Aussies had, but the numbers were small. I only worked with them a couple of times.

But the Aussies were good guys and always up for fun. Their camp wasn't very distant from us, and they invited us to a party and overnight stay with them. They feted us to good food and plenty of drink. Plenty. No one drinks booze like the Aussies. Fortunately, none of us tried. I'm forever amazed at the quantity of drink they put away.

The Aussies supported the ROK Army as we did with air power and close air support. The night we visited, a couple of them described the ROK Army's "pacification program."

Throughout South Vietnam the Viet Cong often ruled villages by fear and intimidation. We never knew which Vietnamese village was friendly and which wasn't. When the Koreans brought their forces into an area west of Cam Ranh, they ran smack into such hostilities in what was supposed to be friendly territory.

The Aussies described what happened at one village. The Koreans went into the village peacefully for an arranged meeting with the village chieftain, but while there they came under attack and were driven out. The Koreans returned the next day and again they were fired on from within the village. The Koreans warned the village chief it had better not happen again, but it did. So the Koreans killed the village chief and several elders. It was a brutal act and far different from American tactics, but the Koreans weren't attacked again.


## How Far Will It Go?

Al Moser had a question: how far would one of our 2.75 inch rockets travel? As FACs we carried eight of those rockets under the wings to mark targets, but we always fired them air to ground. How far would one travel if it was fired upward, ballistically?

This was a legitimate scientific question that lay beyond the scope of human knowledge (or at least beyond our knowledge), so Al and I set out to do some research.

Al and I were up at the 28th headquarters in Phu Hiep. We grabbed a rocket and took our jeep a few miles south of the camp. After removing the battery from the jeep we carried the rocket to the beach, propped it against a rock and rigged it to the battery with long wires. With the rocket pointed out to the South China Sea, we ducked down behind a dune and connected the wires to the battery.

The rocket was off in a flash, and we watched it launch rapidly toward the sun. The motor burned far longer than we expected, and it kept climbing. Finally the motor sputtered and we began to estimate where it would come down.

That's when we saw the fishing boat. We had seen something way out there but never considered it might be in danger, but it was. As we nervously watched, our rocket detonated a few hundred yards off the bow with its characteristic white phosphorous smoke plume. We carefully ducked down behind the dunes and slunk back to the jeep, our scientific research done for the day.

## R&R

With only two months to go in my tour I was told I must go on R&R. I told Personnel that the Rest & Relaxation vacation meant nothing to me at that time; my tour was nearly over, and I just didn't want to go. Send someone else. They said I had to. I was miffed. These were the same bozos who lost my assignment preference form three damn times. Now, just so they could fill a square, I had to take a vacation—under duress.

I chose to go to Tokyo. I figured that if I must take R&R, I could at least visit my F-4 buddies at Tachikawa while I was there.

Arriving in Tokyo I checked into my hotel and walked the streets of the Ginza business district that first night. A Japanese guy nattily dressed in a dark suit and carrying a briefcase scurried past and brushed me as he did. He seemed to be in an awful rush. He turned around, still walking ahead, and in slightly accented English apologized for his rudeness. Then he inquired if I might be American,

99

and I said I was. We struck up a conversation right there on the street. From there we went to a coffee shop. He explained that he wrote stories for the English-speaking newspapers in Tokyo, and he pulled from his briefcase a collection of newspaper articles he had written.

There I was, alone at night, walking the streets of Tokyo, speaking not a word of Japanese, and with nothing to do. He was quite friendly and didn't appear to be a threat. So I thought, "What the hell—here goes nothing."

We dined together. Then he asked if I had ever been to a Geisha House. I hadn't, so he suggested we go to one. He excused himself from our table, saying he promised his car to his sister that night and needed to call her to tell her where it was parked. I picked up the tab. We hopped in a cab and sprinted across Tokyo. When he had trouble fumbling for change, I paid for the cab.

Of course it was no Geisha House—it was just an ordinary hotel, but I didn't figure that out at first. We ordered food and drink served in the room, and of course I picked up the tab. And there was no entertainment, unless you call an ordinary room massage entertaining. Notably, he didn't get a massage, which would have required him to pay cash on the spot. We got sloshed on cold Saki mixed with some overly sweet orange drink. I guarded my wallet, but theft wasn't on his mind. I was full from dinner, but he ordered more food. That guy must have been half-starving, because he really packed away the food. I picked up the tab for everything.

I was a hapless "Innocent Abroad." In another city, another country, I might have been mugged. But instead, I met a little Japanese guy, bought him food, drink, and a place to spend the night, we both got tipsy, and that was it. It was kinda funny, really.

The next morning his hangover was bigger than mine. Boy, that Saki packs a wallop. I left him in the room and caught a cab to my hotel.

The next day I caught a train to Tachikawa where the Americans operated a fighter base with F-4s. The Japanese train passengers eyeballed me with friendly curiosity. No one spoke English, and I spoke no Japanese. All I could do was ask the engineer at every stop, "Tachikawa?" The passengers surmised my difficulty and kindly indicated when my stop came up, and I got off.

I was met by my old friend and roommate, Johnny Hobbs. Our other roommate, Bill LaFever, was there, too, along with other friends from Da Nang. I had a good visit, and it was nice to see them again. However, they lamented that they were all stuck in the F-4's back seat.

I stayed for a couple of days visiting old buddies, then returned to my hotel just as I came down with a flu bug that marred the rest of my trip. So much for R&R.

## Tet

I hadn't been back at the 28th very long when the massive North Vietnamese Tet Offensive hit. Tet made for a very tense week, filled with attacks, counter-attacks, and airstrikes across South Vietnam. Wartime activity rose to its highest pitch.

I was doing ground duty as the ALO all that week, working with the ROK regimental staff and coordinating air support missions. It was a grueling time—the toughest week of my life (except, perhaps, for a week spent on Mayo Clinic's cardiac ward years later). We worked all day and all night. I averaged around three hours' sleep each day taking catnaps. On the last night when it appeared the North Vietnamese regulars and the Viet Cong had been beaten back, I went to my room for my first night's sleep in six days. The next day was Sunday. My replacement was flying in and I'd fly the bird back to Nha Trang.

At that time I lived in a two-room, dirt-floored stone hut shared with a Korean major. Our only amenity was a wash basin between the rooms that was filled by the major's orderly—whom the major kicked or hit several times a day, usually for not shining his shoes well enough. We lived on "officers' row." Ours was one of five such stone

101

huts running north and south along the beach, housing the regiment's senior officers.

By that Saturday night the week-long fighting had finally subsided. I had just gone to sleep when a shell exploded 30 feet outside my room's wall. Thank goodness the hut was stone. The Cong had penetrated the base's southern perimeter, set up a 75 mm recoilless gun, and trained it on the officers' huts. Mine was the northernmost hut and received the first round. The VC walked their fire south, intending to wipe out the row of officers as they slept. Fortunately they had aimed a few meters too far left, and all the rounds missed.

Dazed, I threw on some clothes, scrambled to my jeep, and headed full speed to the headquarters building. The entire camp was under Viet Cong fire. The Koreans were in a panic, not knowing how they were being attacked. Shells were flying overhead, and tracers were everywhere. When the VC had broken through they had captured a ROK quad-barreled, 40 mm "Duster" and turned it back onto the camp. It was mostly the Duster's tracers that were lighting up the sky.

Apprised of the situation, I drove to our radio shack to get air support. My sergeant got our generator up and radioed our situation. A US gunship responded in about 15 minutes, and after showering its fire down for about half an hour, "Snoopy" drove the VC off. I had never seen the powerful gunship in action before, and it was impressive. Snoopy's other nickname was Puff the Magic Dragon—a very apropos name, because it surely resembled a fire-breathing, roaring beast that night. The Koreans were highly thankful because they had been taken completely by surprise and had no answer to the attack without US air support.

### Tet Isn't Quite Finished

The next day my replacement arrived, and I returned to Nha Trang. All returned to quiet at the 28th Headquarters again. The lesson was apparent: the Koreans had been too complacent, thinking the VC posed no real threat, and they hadn't established good perimeter defenses. In succeeding weeks they embarked on fortifying and camouflaging the entire encampment, top to bottom. We fortified our privy with sandbags.

Back at Nha Trang the Cutie FACs had heard of my week during Tet. I was greeted with pats on the back and admonitions that they hoped I hadn't brought those troubles with me to Nha Trang.

That night we were mortared. I had gone to bed, still exhausted from the prior week. I was fast asleep when the first shell came in. After the previous night's attack I wasn't going to get very excited over one shell. Lying on my cot I listened to the successive explosions and decided the mortars were walking away from us—not an immediate threat. I lay there, listening, when suddenly everyone else was up, running around, while someone yelled, "Get to the bunker! Get to the bunker!" I stayed there a few moments, thought about it, and reluctantly decided I'd go downstairs to the bunker. In the dark I got up, barefoot and wearing nothing but my skivvies. I stumbled, half-asleep toward the stairs and slammed my little toe into one of the room dividers. That really hurt. I hobbled down the stairs and sort of fell face down into the steel bunker. The other guys were all standing around, wondering why I was lying on my belly. The mortar attack stopped as suddenly as it began.

We toured the flight line in the jeep the next day. The main damage was to a C-130 Hercules that had melted down to nothing in its parking spot, its four propellers lying mangled on the ground. The rest of the damage was minor.

My pinky toe was broken and stuck out at an angle. I taped it back in. It was sore and purple, but I could still put on my boot and fly. As I looked at my sad little digit one morning I wondered if a busted pinky toe might qualify me for a Purple Heart.

I had spent the entire week of the Tet offensive on the ground, and to my surprise I was awarded the Bronze Star for valor. I'm grateful for the award, but on the dark side it officially marked me as a "grunt."

The Tet offensive was North Vietnam's biggest failure—US and ASEAN (Association of Southeast Asian Nations) forces had beaten back the VC and North Vietnamese Army regulars. North Vietnamese

103

losses were heavy—reportedly 20,000 killed. It was a huge miscalculation by Ho Chi Minh, who had expected their all-out attack would turn the tide of the war and prompt the South Vietnamese to revolt. That didn't happen.

Shortly after Tet my tour was finished, and I headed home. When I returned stateside, I read accounts in the newspapers that portrayed Tet as a US defeat, not a victory. Leading that charge was Walter Cronkite, the "Most Trusted Man in America." What a crock. American newspapers were misreporting many other events that I knew to be untrue—I had been there. It was another lesson learned— the vaunted American press wasn't to be trusted—especially Walter Cronkite, who eventually admitted he got it all wrong, but too late. The fiction endured.

## End of Tour

The Air Force didn't do me any favors for my return. During the last few months of my tour I had been on "permanent temporary duty" with the 28th ROK Regiment at Phu Hiep. I returned to home base at Nha Trang only occasionally. When I did, my first business was at the personnel office to inquire about my return assignment. With less than two months to go, it was highly unusual to have not received my next assignment. But each time I inquired, personnel said they had lost my forecast "dream sheet," and each time I'd fill out another before returning to Phu Hiep. In about a month I'd return to Nha Trang and get the same story. That happened three times.

On the last occasion I demanded an assignment and got one the very next day. That was just three weeks before my return in February, 1968. Although I had repeatedly listed my preference to fly fighters at one of the tactical air commands, I was instead assigned to the Air Training Command as a UPT instructor pilot flying the T-37 at Webb AFB, Big Spring, west Texas.

I was really miffed. Returning pilots were promised to get at least one of their choices for the air command, the base, or the airplane. I

104

got none of the above. They had really blown it, and I was their victim.

With only three weeks to go I had no time to lodge a complaint. When I returned to the States I flew to Air Force Personnel Headquarters in San Antonio and filed a complaint—in person, face to face with the administrative pukes who pushed pencils and had never been to war. I waited while a major investigated my case on the spot. I wasn't budging from that place until I got results. In about 30 minutes he came out and brought me into his office. He verified what was patently obvious: I was right and they were wrong. His apology was unequivocal and sincere, but it was too late to change anything.

For our wartime service we received a small stipend of combat pay—tax-free—and the opportunity for a follow-on assignment of our choosing. Well, I didn't get the assignment, but at least I had beaten the IRS for a while.

## The Last Time I Saw Charlie

Before leaving Vietnam I had one last flight in the Bird Dog. I was heading home the next day. As I flew north out of Nha Trang I was feeling happy to be leaving but strangely nostalgic, too. I wasn't scheduled with fighters that day. As I reconnoitered alone to the west of Tuy Hoa, looking at familiar places I would never see again, I saw a single black-clad man below trying to run and hide. But I had had enough of the war. I just watched and let him go.

# Big Spring

After 11 months in Vietnam I returned home. It was strange, like I didn't belong here. I went to visit my folks in North Carolina. Mom had kept every letter, every picture I had sent. She showed me an article in the local paper about my return.

I felt like a duck out of water. I awoke thinking I had no mission to fly that day, the next, or the next. I don't remember what I talked about. I just remember how difficult it was to relate to Mom and Dad what it had been like, and soon I gave up trying. I couldn't explain that I didn't feel regretful about my time in the war. The old adage, "War is hell," wasn't how I felt. I had survived an immense experience and had changed a lot, I think for the better. I was more confident and decisive in all I did. Sure, I was glad to be home, but part of me lingered over there.

I called long distance to that sweetheart who sent me a Dear John letter three months into my tour. She was engaged. I expected as much, but I just needed to bring it to closure.

I headed for Perrin AFB in north Texas for three months of instructor training in the T-37. Then I was off to Webb AFB at Big Spring, Texas, for the next three years. During my first year I instructed student pilots in the cockpit of a T-37. I spent a lot of time in the cockpit but didn't do much hands-on piloting—that was the student's job. My job was to instruct students and avoid grabbing the stick when something didn't go quite right, as was my tendency. Students learn best by fixing their own mistakes, but sometimes their mistakes tried my patience. Anyhow, as an IP at least I wasn't a GIB, but it was almost the same thing.

106

The first student I soloed, Ken, was afflicted with air sickness. He got sick on almost every flight. When he was ready to barf, he'd say, "Sir, you have it"—meaning he was giving up control of the airplane to me. I would fly while he retrieved the barf bag from the lower leg pocket of his flight suit, unhooked his oxygen mask, did his business, and stowed the bag. Then I handed control of the bird back to him. Once he had puked he seemed to fly okay. Nerves, of course.

There's a long story that precedes Ken's solo flight—too long to relate here. Let's just say that one of the most disgusting flights I ever had was because of Ken's air sickness problem, and I ended up wearing much of his lunch on my sleeve.

In the abbreviated version of the story, I'll simply say that despite his initial bouts of air sickness, he soloed just fine. The complete story is far from pleasant.

The second student I ever soloed started off marginally but became stronger throughout his year of UPT. Bill lived in the same apartments where I lived, so throughout the year I saw him occasionally even after he had he graduated from the T-37.

Prior to solo Bill always appeared very nervous, and I felt that fear was his biggest enemy. On the day of his solo, I decided to "play it cool." I sat in the right seat with my helmet's sun visor down, pretending not to pay him much notice. I hummed a tune and tapped out the rhythm on the instrument glare shield with my fingers, all the time watching carefully out of the corner of my eye. But he was nervous as ever, sweating bullets.

When we returned to the field, I was uncertain if I would climb out of the aircraft and let him fly alone, but I did, and he did just fine.

The year passed, Bill moved on to the T-38, and here came Bill's graduation day. Standing outside our apartments I congratulated him. When I told him how I had tried to soothe him that solo day, Bill was surprised. He told me that he had completely misinterpreted my nonchalance, thinking my finger-tapping was actually banging the glare shield in anger, and he couldn't figure out what he was doing wrong! My effort to ease his fears had entirely backfired, adding even more pressure on the poor guy. But he flew just fine anyway.

## It's Academic

Less than a year had passed since I arrived at Webb. I was teaching a tableful of students, as usual, when I was invited to become an instructor in the Academics Department. For the next two years I split the day by teaching students various aviation subjects in a classroom while also instructing a few students in the airplane.

I first went to academic instructor training school at Randolph AFB outside San Antonio for three months. Our first instructor was a gray-haired civilian who was totally blind. When he was a child an ice pick fell into his eye, and soon after his brother shot out his other eye with an arrow.

Standing on a platform at the front of our classroom, he was completely in command of his environment. The man was absolutely mesmerizing, a gifted teacher. He taught, and I absorbed his every word.

But he had a disconcerting habit. As he taught, he would walk around the small, elevated stage and occasionally make a beeline straight towards me with his blinded eyes looking vacantly ahead of him. The platform was one step up from the floor, and as he reached the front, he abruptly stopped with his toes hanging over the edge. I was seated in the front row just a few feet away, and every time he pulled that parlor trick I involuntarily leaned forward to catch him. But he never fell, and he did the same thing over and over again. I never got used to it. I also never fell asleep in his class for fear one day he'd actually fall.

Completely blind, he was occasionally seen on a nearby lake waterskiing behind a boat driven by his two boys. If I were ever looking for some inspiration, I had found it in this remarkable man.

108

Undergraduate Pilot Training was a great study of human behavior under stress. The human body didn't evolve all those eons with flying in mind. UPT introduces many pilots to flying high performance aircraft the Air Force way, which is far different from tilting your seat back on an airliner while sipping your favorite beverage.

Many people get physically ill when subjected to the motions of flight. Some UPT students never conquered air sickness and were eliminated for that. Some developed ulcers or showed other signs of unmitigated stress. One student pilot rode the flight line trolley out to aircraft parking with his IP and threw up when he saw his aircraft. The first student I soloed had to conquer his airsickness before I let him fly alone.

Yes, fear of flying is very real. And fear of Larry is real, too.

Captain Larry F____ was a check pilot who was particularly feared by the students. Larry had a gruff demeanor and he just looked mean. Students walked on the other side of the hallway when Larry came by.

Larry was giving a student a check ride, and his student was really, really nervous. On check rides the student flies and the check pilot observes and evaluates.

It was an extremely hot, summer day in the Arizona sun as they taxied out. The T-37's big, clamshell canopy was wide open, but the outside air gave them no respite from the searing heat.

As they approached the runway a long line of airplanes was waiting to take off, so they waited their turn with the sun beating down on them. They were enveloped by the hot exhaust from all those jet engines in front of them, and the superheated concrete taxiway radiated the summer heat. It was miserable.

They waited interminably as the lineup moved slowly forward. Larry was becoming agitated. The more he showed his temper, the more his student cowered. Fearsome Larry was feared even more when he was edgy.

Eventually they crept forward to the number one position for takeoff, but still they had to wait for numerous landing aircraft. Finally there was a break in the traffic stream. The tower controller said he could squeeze them in if they would expedite their takeoff.

Students don't know what expedite means, but instructors do, so Larry seized the brief opportunity. He immediately took the controls from his student and jammed the throttles full forward. As he did so, he asked his student, "Canopy clear?" The student replied, "Clear," and Larry motored the canopy down as the aircraft lurched forward. He quickly reached the takeoff position, jammed on the brakes, and gave the controls back to the student, saying, "Your aircraft—let's go!" There was a pause, and nothing happened. Larry repeated, "Let's go, let's go!" His student meekly replied, "I can't, Sir."

There was no time to stall—they had to take off immediately with other aircraft coming down to land. Larry was incredulous and yelled, "What do you mean? Take off, NOW!" The student said, "I can't. I can't reach the throttles."

In disbelief Larry looked over at his student. The student's left pinky finger was pinned under the heavy canopy with blood flowing out of his glove.

Isn't it remarkable that even with his finger smashed the student never said a word until he realized he couldn't reach the throttles.

That is absolute, raw fear. Fear of Larry.


## Ex-Student Byrne

Sometimes it's the IP who gets a taste of fear—from the student.

Tex was, of course, a Texas boy who happened to have been born in Pecos, which isn't far from Big Spring in Texas terms. Tex was an

110

amiable kind of guy who didn't get excited over trivial stuff. He also happened to be a pretty good tennis player who used to partner with Billie Jean King.

One of Tex's pre-solo students was a cocky guy named Byrne. Second Lieutenant Byrne was the type of personality who didn't take instruction very kindly. In fact, Byrne was downright snotty about it. Byrne's attitude had alienated all his instructors. He had just about burned all his bridges and was standing on his last leg before washing out of pilot training. Tex was in favor of giving Byrne one last chance and convinced his flight commander to let him try.

So Tex flew Byrne on a typical student contact mission. If Byrne performed well, he would stay in the program. Otherwise, he was getting the axe.

Tex decided to let Byrne fly the flight without any intervention or instructions unless absolutely necessary. They climbed into their "Tweet." Byrne ran the checklist, started engines, and taxied to the runway. He made some mistakes, but Tex let them go and stayed mum. When tower cleared them on the runway for takeoff, Byrne lined up and pushed the throttles forward. As they began the takeoff roll, Tex, who had been biting his tongue, pulled the throttles back, applied the brakes, and calmly said, "Don't you think you should close the canopy before we take off?" Byrne said nothing.

They took off and made the usual medium-bank turn away from the airfield. As was his bad habit, Byrne failed to apply additional back pressure to the control stick to compensate for the bank, and so the airplane began to descend. Byrne didn't perceive that they were headed toward the ground until Tex finally told him to roll out and get the nose up. Byrne was peeved that Tex had interceded and angrily told Tex, "I know what I'm doing." Tex began seeing red at this point but quietly let Byrne go on.

The mission profile was to fly to the T-37 auxiliary airfield (named "Peckerwood"—don't laugh) and practice landings, but Byrne got lost and headed south, straight into the T-38 student training area. Afraid they might collide with a T-38, Tex finally took control, dropped down below the training area, and turned back toward Peckerwood. Byrne was seething.

Tex entered the landing pattern at Peckerwood, which was staffed by two IPs who controlled traffic. Tex gave aircraft control back to Byrne, who began to fly an outside pattern to set up for his approach and landing. But in making his first turn, Byrne fell back into his old habit. He rolled into a steep-bank turn but failed again to apply back pressure on the stick. At 60 degrees of bank, the airplane rapidly began to dive.

Tex let things go as long as he could. When it became apparent Byrne wasn't going to pull out of the dive, Tex commanded, "I've got the airplane" and grabbed the controls. An instructor's command carries almost the same authority as God's, but Byrne said, "No you don't!" and wouldn't let go of stick or rudders. It was only moments before they would impact the ground.

Tex grabbed the stick harder. Byrne held on and resisted. Tex was a pretty strong guy, and he let his left forearm go full-force against Byrne's face. Byrne was stunned and let go. With both hands on the stick Tex pulled hard out of the dive.

Tex had pulled out of the dive just in time. Byrne's visor was split where Tex had hit him. Tex landed at Peckerwood and got out, shaken. The IPs in the tower had watched the whole thing, and they said that when Tex's airplane dropped from view they expected to see a fireball next.

Webb sent a vehicle to drive Byrne back, and Tex flew the bird home. Byrne was removed from the base the very next day and never heard of again.

## The Spin

A friend and fellow IP took off with his student one day and they didn't come back. A rescue helicopter found the crash site.

In instructor school we trained in normal spins and normal spin recoveries. We didn't practice inverted spins—they were too dangerous—but we were taught the recovery procedure. The only way to get out of an inverted spin was to first convert it to a normal spin, then recover from that. Spins can be very disorienting, and one of the first recovery steps is, "Determine the direction of spin." It sounds easy, but when an aircraft is pointed nose-down, spinning like a top on steroids, with your horizon twisting rapidly around you and the G-forces playing hob with your senses, it's not so easy to understand what's happening. An inverted spin is much worse—you're upside-down and everything is backwards.

When searchers reached the crash site it was apparent the airplane had impacted inverted, likely during a botched upright spin recovery that flipped over. There was a high cloud layer that day which likely caused the IP to become confused which way was up.

## Incentive Flights

Once a year during the Christmas holidays Undergraduate Pilot Training shuts down for two weeks. It's a time for maintenance to perform major inspections and repairs on the airplanes. But airplanes still must be flown periodically because certain equipment, like hydraulic seals, will deteriorate if not exercised regularly. A few instructors remain on base to fly the birds while all the students and most other instructors head for home.

It's a good time to reward maintenance workers and other support personnel for their hard work by giving some of them incentive rides. I had the pleasure of re-enlisting a maintenance sergeant for another term of duty, then flying him in the very airplane he had worked on. I asked him what he'd like to do on the flight, and he said he'd like to do some acrobatics.

We took off on a nice, calm and smooth day, but a cloud layer above prevented us from doing any acro. So we gently flew around the west Texas area, sightseeing. There was a break in the clouds, and I said we could then climb up and do some acrobatic maneuvers. That's when he blew his lunch. I flew the poor guy home. It reminded me of the photographer I had flown in Vietnam, and I began to wonder if this was my curse.

Another IP was flying an incentive ride with a nurse in the rear cockpit of his T-38. Of course he had briefed her on emergency use of rear cockpit equipment and how to eject, if necessary. As they taxied out, he told her to lower her canopy. Instead she fired the ejection system and blew off the rear canopy.

## Social Life in Big Spring

Big Spring was a small town of about 27,000 in the middle of west Texas cattle and oil country, far removed from real civilization. The nearest city was Midland, 40 miles west. Lubbock was 100 miles to the north.

This was the Permian Basin of west Texas, and for hundreds of miles around it was all flat. At one end of the Interstate running through town was an oil refinery that smelled real good when the wind blew just right. At the other end of town was a billboard saying, "Welcome to Big Spring, Home of Oil, Cattle, and Pilots." I wryly noted that pilots came in last on the list, just behind the cattle. Big Spring wasn't all that bad—after all it had a movie theater, a hotel, and a Pizza Hut.

I rented an apartment a couple of miles from the base. Soon after arriving I experienced a sand storm and a tornado. I took them to be omens of things to come. I always described my assignment to Big Spring as more of a "remote tour" than my time in Vietnam. Big Spring offered very little except what the base provided.

Living a couple of apartments away from mine was a fellow bachelor, Arnie Friedman. Arnie was one of the base flight surgeons (aviation medicine physician). Sometimes to kill the time we'd stay up most of the night either at his apartment or mine. Arnie was remarkably conscientious about his job, and we both liked classical music, so Arnie brought out a big paper cutter and would spend the

114

evening cutting current articles out of medical magazines while I recorded classical music on my tape recorder. That's entertainment, folks—living the dream in Big Spring, Texas, home of oil, cattle, and . . . whatever.

We bachelors were trapped on an endless merry-go-round. At first we made the most of the local scene. We went to the only place off base of any interest, a "private club" that served drinks under Texas dry-county rules. We had some local parties among ourselves and got to meet some local girls—the same ones, again and again.

When the local scene petered out we went to Phase 2. In that phase we flew weekend student cross-country training flights to Denver or El Paso, attempting to spice up our lives. That got tiresome fast. In Phase 3 we showed our desperation by driving 550 miles to Dallas on weekends. We'd return to Big Spring more discouraged than ever.

Phase 3 was the shortest phase of all. After trying Phase 3 a couple of times, it was time to try Phase 1 again, figuring maybe we had missed something the first time.

It was hopeless. That went on for three years.

Sure, we did stuff. I remember a Silver Gin Fizz party that began at eight A.M. on a Saturday morning. But we did more benign things like playing sports and having picnics. A rancher who owned a large part of west Texas hosted our Junior Officers Council. We drove miles to get to his ranch, then drove miles more after we passed the front gate. He set up a live country western band in one of his many barns and brought in his cowboys from off the range to put on a private rodeo for us. Pretty nice.

My married friends would invite me over. Harry and Gerry were particularly good friends, and I'd go to their place for dinner. With a full belly Harry was guaranteed to fall asleep on the couch after the meal, and Gerry and I would just talk for the rest of the night.

Friends got together to eat out at one of the two, small Mexican restaurants. They were family-owned and run, and by far the best

115

places to dine in Big Spring . . . except perhaps for Larry's BBQ restaurant. Larry served fine, Texas-style brisket.

But three years is a long time to live in Big Spring if you weren't born there. Arnie and I were sitting at my place one night and to break the monotony I asked, "What if we had a party?" Arnie asked, "When?" I said, "Right now." It was ten o'clock on a weekday night.

I started calling friends, and to our surprise they came. Everyone came, as if they had been perched by the phone waiting for the invitation. I kept a pretty good stash of booze and beer, and as everyone arrived I supplied them well. The party went on and on. I mixed and poured some vicious drinks. Hours later people wandered home in various states of consciousness. The party was a success except that the hedge in front of my apartment took a hit after someone disgorged their supper on it. But the hidden statement our party made was that Air Force people entrapped in Big Spring (or on the moon, for that matter) will do most anything to generate some fun.

One day my friend, Fred, took me down to the "Y" to teach me handball. We came back to Fred's house, and as Carol made us iced tea we assessed the damage to my body. My right hand and forearm were all red and swollen, already starting to turn black and blue. My left hand was only swollen a little because I couldn't even hit the damn ball with my very weak left. Fred laughed and said, "We'll give you a day's rest and try it again." I laughed back and said, "Nope." But Fred didn't kid about those things. He was relentless and had me back in the court right away. I got better thanks to Fred's persistence, and handball became my life-long favorite sport.

Decades afterward—after the base closed and the property had been relinquished to the state, Texas built a maximum security prison where Webb used to be. I always felt Big Spring deserved a prison. Actually they already had one . . . the Air Force just didn't call it that.

# Wichita Falls

Living in Big Spring was tough on morale. Several fellow IPs quit the Air Force to become airline pilots, and the supposed glamour of airline flying began to appeal to me, although shepherding people on transports didn't seem much different than herding cattle in west Texas. But airlines had stewardesses, which is more than Big Spring offered.

One of the guys quit the Air Force to attend medical school. Another went for the airlines but got furloughed and ended up selling vacuum cleaners in Minnesota—no kidding. I didn't know what I was going to do, but I had the urge to do something different.

The Air Force solved my dilemma. As I approached the end of my third year at Webb, the Air Training Command selected me to help start up a new pilot training program at Sheppard AFB in Wichita Falls. After three years in Big Spring, I was glad to be going to the "big city." Wichita Falls is just north of Fort Worth and at that time had a population of about 100,000. Today it still has a population of about 100,000.

The new school was going to be an undergraduate pilot training program for Vietnamese Air Force (VNAF) student pilots. The US Air Force was pulling out of Vietnam and we were going to train Vietnamese pilots to fill the void. I and three other instructors were tasked to design and teach the academics under leadership of our department chief, Major Davis. Taft Davis was a good man, and our small academic department became a good place to work.

The new UPT program operated alongside, but separate, from an existing pilot training program at Sheppard teaching German student

117

pilots. Our Vietnamese students would get their wings in only seven months—not the 55 weeks required in Air Force UPT. That abbreviated duration was a big compromise that I always thought was risky.

The Vietnamese students got all their training flying the T-37. After graduation they proceeded to England AFB in Mississippi for combat training in the A-37 Firefly—the beefed-up fighter version of the T-37. Then they returned to fly A-37s in Vietnam.

As a FAC during the war I had worked with Vietnamese fighter pilots flying their A-1E Skyraiders, and they flew very well. But those pilots had accumulated thousands of flying hours. Our students would graduate with less than 200 hours. I only hoped they could last and get through the war with as little flight experience as they were getting.

The Germans at Sheppard didn't like the Vietnamese. They resented that we were co-locating our Vietnamese UPT next to them. They protested to the US government, which I thought was very arrogant. It was our country, our base, our airplanes. The conflict was quickly put to rest when the US firmly told Germany they could put up with it or get out of Dodge—or Wichita Falls, in this case. The Vietnamese were staying.

I spent a year and a half at Sheppard teaching both in the classroom and in the cockpit. Our big problem was that no one really knew how to teach Vietnamese students in an American style, English-language pilot training school. It was definitely a challenge, particularly for our academic department.

The first problem we faced was that all our students—15 in each class—had been selected primarily for their English language comprehension, not their flying aptitude. Some simply didn't have the skills to fly.

Our first academic attempts failed dismally, and we had to re-tune our entire teaching methodology. We discarded the US textbooks we had used and designed our own. We learned to teach our students differently, based on what we observed. For instance, we came to realize the Vietnamese had difficulty visualizing three-dimensional objects from a two-dimensional graphic depiction, so we used three-dimensional models and cutaways extensively.

We encountered many cultural and educational differences, too. In Vietnamese classrooms the teaching methodology is mostly rote memorization where the class stands and recites from textbooks together. To them failure of one student was considered a failure of the entire class; class unity had been drummed into them. That was problematic because we were training them for individual performance, not class performance. It's hard to squeeze an entire class into a cockpit.

Our Vietnamese students would never allow any one student to be singled out. If a student stumbled over the instructor's question, other students who knew the answer would always interrupt before the student "lost face." During examinations we had to put two instructors in the room to prevent cheating—which to them wasn't cheating at all—it was just their one for all, all for one mindset.

There were myriad other problems that no one anticipated. Food was a big problem, for instance. The students were told to eat in the snack bar like everyone else, but American food was too greasy and they kept getting sick when they flew. We redesigned their quarters and put in a kitchen so they could cook their own meals, and that worked. There were many, many issues like that.

Just to illustrate the difficulties, one instructor told us this story. He was flying a Vietnamese student pilot and they were making an instrument descent. The student was descending too fast, so the IP told him, "Get your nose up." The student kept diving, so the IP told him again, "Get your nose up." Nothing changed. The IP looked over at him and saw that he had his head tilted fully back.

## Mister Coulibali

Our State Department, which never, ever makes a mistake, sent us Mister Coulibali—by mistake. Warrant Officer Coulibali was from

Mali—that land-locked nation in the northeast of Africa. Mali had an air force, sort of. It consisted of a two airplanes—old C-47 cargo airplanes remnant from World War II. The State Department figured we could use a man like Mister Coulibali in our all-Vietnamese pilot training program.

Yes, it was a mistake, and it was too late to rectify it, we were told. They had no place to put him, so Mr. Coulibali stayed. And it worked out surprisingly well.

Coulibali stood out among his classmates. He was a big, black man surrounded by the somewhat diminutive Vietnamese. What they shared was a knowledge of English, but Coulibali brought other assets, too. He was a quiet, friendly, smiling person who also spoke fluent French and other languages. He quickly took to his new role and learned Vietnamese. His understanding of western ways was another asset, and he helped the Vietnamese with their studies. They liked him. He was a leader.

I liked Mr. Coulibali, too. A very smart man. I particularly liked what he did for the class. I left Sheppard before that class graduated, but I felt like writing the State Department to send us more Coulibalis.

## Academic Chief

After almost a year I was appointed as the Chief of Academics when Major Davis came up for reassignment. I invited my class over to my house for dinner with our instructors. The students took over my kitchen and turned out a fantastically delicious meal. We had fun. It was truly an enjoyable evening, warm and friendly. There was bonding going on.

Some of the students just couldn't fly, but it wasn't for lack of effort. I sat on many flying evaluation boards, and it was disheartening to see the anguish of these fine young men when told they had failed. Funny, though—we had one warrant officer who had never driven anything but a bicycle, and he did quite well flying airplanes. Training them was always hit or miss.

120

The first class graduated and went to England AFB in Mississippi for their A-37 combat training. When they were finishing there, they invited us instructors from Sheppard to their graduation, and so we went.

The Vietnamese have a unique way to display true friendship. They hook little fingers with each other. As we got off the airplane, we were greeted by our former students. I was escorted in with my little finger fondly hooked. It wasn't exactly correct military protocol, but I felt honored.

I'll say this very loud and clear: these were the most motivated students I've ever had. I'll forever admire their desire and dedication. They were fighting for their country and the risks to them were extremely high.

We learned afterward that out of our first class, two-thirds were killed in action within a year of returning to Vietnam. Did we do our job in training them? I don't know if we could have done better given the circumstances.

# The Dragon Lady

After Vietnam I spent four and a half years instructing student pilots in the Air Training Command, the first three of those at Webb. I was becoming a permanent Training Command fixture. The year was 1971. I sensed I was coming due for some kind of assignment but had no idea what it might be.

One day a buddy passed me the latest Air Force Times newspaper and said, "Read this." It looked like an ordinary classified ad that said, "Wanted: U-2 pilots. Contact . . . ." How extraordinary. The Air Force doesn't fill their personnel needs via want ads in newspapers. The ad was certainly unusual, but especially because it pertained to the highly secretive, notorious U-2 "spy plane" that was the stuff of intelligence and classified secrets—another world entirely. I thought it might be a prank.

I had always been fascinated with the U-2. One day while flying over Texas I overheard a radio conversation between another aircraft and air traffic control. The pilot requested permission to enter into controlled airspace, which at that time went from 1,500 to 45,000 feet. The controller gave permission for the pilot to climb into controlled airspace. Then the pilot dryly informed ATC that he was requesting permission to <u>descend</u>, not climb, into controlled airspace. It had to be a U-2. I was inspired.

I called the ad's number and was connected to a lieutenant colonel at Davis-Monthan AFB in Tucson. Very brusquely he peppered me with questions and then hung up. He told me absolutely nothing. Nothing else happened, and several days later I put the matter out of my mind. Just then my boss said they received orders sending me to Tucson for a week.

So I showed up at Davis-Monthan ("D-M") where I had completed F-4 systems training years ago. I walked into the 349th Strategic

Reconnaissance Squadron and began a week-long process of personal scrutiny. It was far different from any interview I ever had.

I was approached and told right away that everything there was classified and to talk to no one about anything I saw or heard. My week consisted of interviews with everyone who had anything to do with the U-2 program, including the wing commander. They prodded and probed me with questions. One even asked, "What's your relationship with God?" I gulped at that one, but before I could squeak out an answer, he told me about his own relationship with God. His own answer seemed to satisfy him, and we moved on. I'm sure his answer would have been better than mine, anyway.

I flew three rides in the Lockheed T-33A trainer, including one ride with the squadron commander. I went through an astronaut-type physical. I was fitted with a pressure suit and spent two hours in an altitude chamber, testing me for claustrophobia. I spent time flying two different simulators.

When the week was over I walked out and flew back to Wichita Falls. I knew absolutely nothing about my interview results. Even if I did, I couldn't tell anybody.

The following week as I was walking down the hall at work, my wing commander passed by and said I was leaving. He had just received orders assigning me to the 349th SRS. He said they must want me badly—I was given only two weeks to move.

That was my first introduction to the high-powered authority wielded by the U-2 program. When mountains need to be moved, you call either God or the U-2 people.


A New Career

The 17 years I spent with the U-2 were the highlight of my life's work. As I sit here, reflecting and writing, I'm still amazed at my good fortune to have had such an extraordinary experience. I wouldn't be writing these memoirs if I didn't have this story to tell.

The U-2's purpose is high altitude reconnaissance—to gather intelligence at extreme altitude using various sensors installed onboard. High altitude provides a longer look over the horizon and a greater swath of coverage to obtain both images and electronic intelligence. High altitude also affords a measure of protection, flying where a U-2 would be relatively unseen and less vulnerable to enemy air defenses.

At first I was purely a pilot, flying the U-2 on worldwide assignments. Those assignments placed me at various locations outside the US for about four years. The U-2 acted as a "first responder" to international conflagrations of the Cold War. Wherever there were hot spots and emerging developments affecting America's defense interests, a U-2 was sure to go.

During my U-2 years I was assigned twice to the Pentagon, once to Strategic Air Command Headquarters in Nebraska, and for a year attending the Air War College in Alabama. I returned to fly combat missions in the Vietnam War on three tours of temporary duty spanning six months, flying from Thailand. I lived two years in England and a year in Cyprus commanding U-2 operational units. During the course of one year I spent nine months living overseas, no longer than two months in any one place. Here in the States I lived years at our home bases in Tucson and at Beale AFB, north of Sacramento, California. There were many, many short trips of all sorts. It's sheer understatement to say that I traveled a lot.

The U-2 and all its activities were—and are—highly classified and carefully guarded. While attending the U-2's 50th anniversary reunion, I learned of U-2 matters I had never known before—information recently de-classified by the CIA. Being in the U-2 program was always like that. The full U-2 story was like an immense jigsaw puzzle with the pieces scattered among many people and agencies, wrapped in compartmented secrecy. Getting the complete picture was nearly impossible, and that's by design.

124

My first challenge was learning to fly the airplane. That's what I was assigned to do, but it was by no means certain I would succeed. The U-2 was an exceedingly difficult aircraft to fly. The U-2's flying characteristics are officially described as, "Does not meet Air Force standards."

U-2 pilots are all selected from experienced pilot volunteers. Candidates are interviewed and carefully screened before being accepted into U-2 training. Air Force pilots are supposedly trained to fly any aircraft in the Air Force inventory, but that didn't apply to the U-2. In recognition of the U-2's difficult nature, there is a proviso that any pilot who fails to qualify will be returned to his former job or receive additional assignment with no recriminations. I know of two pilots who failed to qualify in the U-2 but went on to have very successful careers. They were each promoted to full colonel in other pursuits.

To achieve extreme altitude the U-2 has a powerful jet engine and long, straight wings like a glider. To save weight, it's stripped of many conveniences and safety features found on more conventional aircraft. It has bicycle landing gear, consisting of only a main gear and a tail wheel mounted along the aircraft fuselage. The wings are supported on the ground by removable "pogo" wheels that fall out upon takeoff. The tailwheel provides very limited ground steering. The U-2 is controlled by a yoke instead of a stick because the primary flight controls aren't hydraulically powered—again, to save weight.

In many phases of flight the U-2 performs like any other airplane with no abnormal handling traits. But at extreme altitudes and during landings it's difficult to fly. Its unusual design presents the pilot with some very adverse flying characteristics.

At its high cruising altitudes the U-2 encounters an aerodynamic phenomenon quaintly referred to as the "Coffin Corner." The Coffin Corner is an aerodynamic condition encountered at extreme altitudes, sandwiching an airplane between its maximum and minimum airspeeds. U-2 missions are normally flown within the Coffin Corner's restrictive airspeed range, and speeding up or slowing down by only a few knots can cause the airplane to go out of control. Altitude plus aircraft weight are the culprits. The ways to escape the Coffin Corner are to descend to lower altitude or gradually reduce weight by burning off fuel.

However, since the objective of the U-2 is to fly to its maximum altitude, throughout a mission the U-2 pilot climbs ever higher as the fuel weight is burned off. So a U-2 pilot purposely climbs into the Coffin Corner and stays there throughout much of the mission.

Most airplanes fly at much lower altitudes where the Coffin Corner isn't a problem, but the U-2 is different. The pilot has to be continuously attentive to avoid flying too fast or slow. Older U-2 models were particularly nasty about it. The now-retired C Model had that "bad attitude." Flying nicely along at mission altitudes it would sometimes pitch up or pitch down suddenly and without warning.

At high altitude the U-2 is negatively stable, meaning that if the pilot trimmed the aircraft and took his hands off the controls, it would soon either pitch up or tuck under, sending the aircraft out of control. The airplane's autopilot relieves the pilot from constantly hand-flying the unstable airplane. Whereas on most airplanes an autopilot is a luxury, on the U-2 it's essential equipment. Should the autopilot fail, the pilot is required to abort the mission. It's too dangerous to hand-fly the aircraft for very long.

In the rarified air of high altitudes, engine operation is very delicate. Any large or quick movement of the throttle will cause a compressor stall, and the engine will flame out. That would cause loss of cabin pressurization and heat. The pilot's suit would fully inflate, making the pilot resemble the Pillsbury Dough Boy and restricting his movements. The engine can't be restarted until below 35,000 feet, and the long-winged U-2 can't descend rapidly. Without heat and with an outside temperature of minus 65 degrees Celsius, the pilot would likely freeze before he could get down. Ejection is preferable.

So at high altitude the pilot doesn't touch the throttle; instead, he manipulates a vernier wheel next to the throttle that makes small, incremental changes to the engine fuel control.

Lockheed's chief test pilot and Air Force brigadier general, Ken Weir, said, "I have flown over 200 types and models of aircraft and helicopters, and the U-2 was far and beyond the most difficult airplane to land I have ever tried."

When I first entered the U-2 squadron at Tucson, I was greeted by a captain sitting at the front desk. "Sam" became a good friend. He was a fellow handball player and was quite good at it. But at that time he had been reduced to flying a desk because he had crashed a U-2 during his initial qualification. While attempting a landing he lost control of the bird, which climbed about 20 feet and then crashed to the runway, stripping off the airplane's landing gear. Sam was removed from U-2 training and was awaiting reassignment when I joined the 349th. He was a sharp guy, and in another career path became very successful.

Over the years there were a number of such landing accidents and incidents. The prevalence of such problems is why the U-2 squadron was assigned a full-time photographer to record videos of all domestic U-2 landings.

I was assigned an instructor and mentor, Lieutenant Colonel George "Hector" Freese. Our relationship and friendship would last for many years as George rose to become wing commander. Normally a U-2 checkout took about five months, but mine lasted nearly a year. The reason had to do with circumstances related to officer promotions, not my progress in training.

In those years U-2 pilots' duties were so highly classified that the descriptive section on their officer efficiency reports was left blank. With half-blank performance reports, the U-2 pilots were being passed-over for promotion through no fault of their own. Likewise, because their missions were so strategically important to the national defense, they weren't being released to attend the professional military education schools that also made them competitive for promotion.

The bottom line was that U-2 pilots were hand-picked officers but were not being promoted. The problem was being addressed at higher levels when I arrived, and I was the first to be affected. I had just begun U-2 training when I was told that my training would be interrupted to attend Squadron Officers School. SOS was a four-month leadership course at Air University in Alabama, and it was considered essential education for promotion to major. I dragged my heels because I was afraid of missing my U-2 opportunity, but professional military education was necessary, too. I headed off to Alabama for four months and essentially began my U-2 training from scratch when I returned. From start to finish it took almost a year for me to complete U-2 qualification. I held the dubious record for being the U-2 pilot who took the longest to train.

A U-2 checkout is, by necessity, long and arduous. First of all, the U-2 is a high-value, national asset, and to damage one in training would have national repercussions. Besides, I would be kicked out immediately. There were no two-seat U-2 trainers and no U-2 simulator in those days. Most of the U-2s were deployed overseas, performing their operational missions; only a few were kept at D-M for essential training and maintenance.

For those reasons U-2 pilots maintain their flying proficiency by also flying a companion trainer, and at D-M that airplane was the T-33 "T-bird." While home at D-M, pilots flew the T-bird about two-thirds of the time.

A new U-2 pilot began training with many weeks of ground study, flying other airplanes, and flying in simulators, all before ever cranking up a U-2. I studied reams of accident investigation reports, all classified with large portions of text redacted. I watched countless videos of U-2 landings with Hector. I practiced procedures in two simulators, but there wasn't a U-2 ground simulator so we used two others—adequate, but not quite right. We spent hours visiting U-2s parked in the hangars. I flew simulated U-2 maneuvers with Hector in the T-33. I simulated those maneuvers flying a light twin Cessna aircraft, too. We drove to a small civilian airport outside Tucson and I flew a rented Citabria—a light aircraft with tailwheel steering, such as the U-2 has. Everything possible was done to give me some

128

anticipation of what flying a U-2 was going to be so I didn't screw up and crash it.

Meanwhile, as my aircraft preparations continued I was preparing to wear a pressure suit.

## The Pressure Suit

Because the U-2 routinely flies at altitudes more than twice as high as the average airliner, pilots must wear a protective pressure suit. The suit pressurizes the body so that the body's dissolved gases don't percolate out of solution when you reach higher altitudes. It's similar to popping the top off of a bottle of a carbonated soda (or a beer, if you prefer)—bubbles come gushing out of the pressurized liquid.

The weight, bulk, and constraints of a pressure suit add considerably to the complexity and difficulties of flying an airplane. The pilot's peripheral vision is obscured by the helmet and it's difficult to turn your head without using one hand to help. The gloves give your hands fat fingers with no dexterity and no sense of touch. Continually breathing 100% oxygen in a pressure suit on missions over ten hours long is fatiguing and at some point becomes dangerous.

The difficulties of flying long hours at extreme altitude in a pressure suit make almost every mission an endurance contest. A returning pilot is in a state of physical and mental fatigue as he (or she—another story) attempts to land the Air Force's most difficult airplane to land. That's why all landings are accompanied by another pilot driving a souped-up chase car, providing radio guidance to the pilot as he lands.

The suits worn when I entered the program were all hand-made, skin tight garments like those the Mercury/Gemini astronauts wore. Over the years new pressure suit designs came around, and the U-2 pilots became pressure suit guinea pigs. Each U-2 pilot had a minimum of two suits. At one point as new designs came on board, I had six hand-tailored suits, and my personal wardrobe cost more than

129

$100 grand. I spent many, many hours testing those suits in altitude chambers.

That earlier suit design was called the MC-1. It was a skin-tight garment with laces and capstan tubes on the torso and sleeves. To apply pressure on the pilot's body, an altitude-sensitive regulator pressurized the capstan tubes, which inflated and pulled the suit's fabric tight. Under the suit pilots wore long underwear to prevent skin chafing. We wore the underwear inside-out so the seams were on the outside; continuous suit pressure against a seam or a wrinkle eventually becomes quite painful. Whenever I wore an MC-1 it gave me a shoulder-to-shoulder, black-and-blue skin bruise that lasted a couple of days.

It wasn't a perfect system, and the early suit design was only supposed to protect the pilot in event the cockpit air pressurization failed. Even then it would only protect the pilot long enough to leave a threat area to where he could descend to safety. Thus the "MC-1" designation: "Mission Complete – 1." You sure didn't want to be in that thing any longer than you had to.

Pressure suits are kept in the Physiological Support Division (PSD) where they're maintained and tested by technicians. To first get an MC-1 suit, the PSD techs measured every aspect of the pilot's body and sent the measurements to the manufacturer where the suits were cut and sewn to fit. When the new suit arrived, the pilot squeezed into it through a zipper opening in the back. PSD technicians zipped up the suit and tightened laces covering the entire body very tight to insure good protection. It was quite an ordeal and took quite some time.

One very large, burly sergeant had his own technique. He stood behind the seated pilot, grabbed the suit at the shoulders and hoisted the pilot up using his amazing strength. He literally shook the pilot down into the suit before the lacing began.

The fabric extended over the head, and then the helmet was added. Oxygen was fed to a face cavity covering the eyes, nose, and mouth and fronted by a clear, plexiglass faceplate. The faceplate was embedded with thin wiring connected to the cockpit electrical system that provided radiant heat to ward off fogging from the pilot's breath. The MC-1 suit of old was cumbersome and crude by the more modern "body bag" type suits that came with the advent of the new R Model U-2.

## Chamber of Horrors

Once fitted with a suit, it was into the altitude chamber to test it. During the course of my 17 years with the U-2, I was fitted for numerous suits and spent many hours in altitude chambers. My first such chamber ride was when I initially interviewed for the job. That was an endurance contest to see if I could take it, plain and simple. But each succeeding chamber ride was equally long and arduous. Not a favorite thing to do.

When my parents visited Tucson I brought them out to Davis-Monthan and gave them a show-and-tell. There was plenty for them to see that was unclassified. Dad got to actually go out on the runway with another pilot in the mobile vehicle to chase a U-2 up close during landings. It also happened that I was scheduled for yet another altitude chamber "ride" to test one of my pressure suits, and that provided a perfect opportunity to show Mom and Dad another aspect of the U-2 program.

I suited up and was placed in a cockpit seat inside the chamber, a reinforced metal room built to withstand tremendous air pressures. My chamber was connected to an adjacent chamber by a large evacuation tube. I was strapped into my cockpit seat, simulating actual cockpit conditions. A crew of four or five technicians manned the chamber from outside, and reinforced porthole windows allowed everyone to see in and out. When all was ready, pumps evacuated the chamber of air, providing the atmospheric equivalent of a U-2 climbing to higher altitude where there's less pressure. The pumps are loud, the valves make banging sounds, and it's all quite noisy—disconcerting for Mom and Dad.

The chamber mission profile took me up to 65,000 feet, then down to about 45,000 feet to perform a rapid decompression. As the chamber first "ascended," a technician remained inside with me until about 10,000 feet, then he left through the airlock. A beaker of water had been placed inside, and everyone could see that as we climbed, the water began to boil—exactly what would happen to my body fluids if I weren't wearing a pressure suit. It provides a very dramatic effect, but boiling water wasn't nearly as dramatic as what happened next.

I was connected to the chamber crew by intercom. We talked over our preparations for the next step—the rapid decompression. That involves opening a valve allowing the pressurized air in my chamber to suddenly escape through a large tube to the empty chamber next door. The sudden loss of pressure in my chamber is the equivalent of sending me in a matter of seconds to a simulated altitude above 60,000 feet. That's what would happen if I ejected on an actual flight.

The rapid decompression event happens suddenly and makes a very loud whoosh sound—almost a bang. The sudden loss of pressure instantly caused my suit to inflate as expected. The chamber immediately filled with dense condensation fog, and I disappeared from everyone's view until the misty fog cleared several seconds later.

For some reason no one—including me—remembered to tell Mom and Dad this was coming. A rapid decompression is sudden, loud, and shocking, and they were overwhelmed. Mom thought I was dead and almost fainted. Of course, it was routine stuff for the rest of us, but as Desi Arnaz might say, I had some "'splainin'" to do afterwards.

## Take the T-Bird

Before I ever flew a U-2 I flew the T-Bird. The T-33A was a relic of the Korean War when it had been a top-line fighter, the Lockheed P-80. In the early '70s we were the last Air Force unit flying the two-seat trainer version. U-2 pilots are dual qualified to fly both the U-2 and a companion trainer. Being a Lockheed aircraft, the T-33 had similarities in design and instrumentation that mimicked some of the U-2's characteristics. It was also good for conducting flying evaluations. Besides those justifications, the T-bird was also just fun to fly.

The airplane was quirky—it had split flaps, sloppy controls and a strange engine starting procedure called a gang start. It was even equipped with a relief tube. Strangest of all, it had no nosewheel steering, so to make turns the pilot just applied differential pressure to the left or right wheel brake. I have no idea what the designers were sipping when they came up with that brainstorm. It was probably a holdover—or hangover—from propeller-driven, tail-dragger days.

Ronnie Reinhardt and I were bringing a T-Bird back from Salt Lake City one day. I was in back, and "PF," as he was affectionately called, was flying it in front. We touched down at D-M, and Ronnie let the bird roll down the runway toward the far end. He was taxiing pretty fast, and when he turned off onto the taxiway he didn't make it—again, no nosewheel steering in a T-bird. It had rained recently, and our right main wheel went off into the grass and mud. Thinking quickly, he pushed the throttle full forward. We powered out of the mud and fortunately got back onto the taxiway before getting stuck.

The tower operator calmly—and sarcastically—asked if we needed any assistance. Rinehart sheepishly replied, "No—everything is okay," and we taxied to parking. The crew chief saw mud splattered all over the right side of the aircraft and asked what happened. PF sure didn't want the story getting around, so he looked at the chief with squinting eyes and said with a straight face, "Well, it was snowing up in Utah, and there was mud and debris all over the airfield . . . . " The crew chief said nothing, but just looked at him, grinning. PF then said, "Hey, Chief, do you mind washing us down?" The Chief winked and again said nothing. I smiled and said nothing, too.

A little while later I saw PF hauling a case of beer out to the crew chief's shack.

I flew a T-bird one day with Stan Lawrence. Every U-2 pilot in our squadron had some sort of quirky personality—probably a prerequisite of the job. When he wasn't an Air Force pilot, Stan was an entrepreneur of odd jobs. He was always looking to buy some piece of junk and sell it for a few bucks more. Sometimes Stan's ancient, beat-up pickup truck could be seen at the other end of the airfield where the customs and immigration guys kept assorted merchandise confiscated from the druggies. During the fall Stan took a couple of Mexican guys into the desert to cut mesquite logs which he'd chop and sell for firewood from the old pickup.

Stan and I took off in our T-bird. On these practice flights there was no prescribed routine—we just flew around to keep our skills up. Typically we'd go sightseeing over Arizona, visit a few favorite spots, return to the field, shoot a few landings, and call it quits.

That day Stan said, "Let's head south toward Sonoita." I knew what he was up to—winter was coming, and he's scouting for mesquite trees. That was fine with me—I liked looking around Sonoita.

Right after takeoff we dropped down low so the radar at D-M couldn't spot us. We flew down by Patagonia where placid ranches dotted the landscape. It's pretty down there in a part of Arizona where highlands and grassy hills give respite from the Sonoran desert landscape. I was enjoying the sights. We were flying just a couple of hundred feet off the deck as we leisurely wandered about.

Stan spied a town a little further south and we headed for it. We were circling it when Stan remarked that it had no paved streets. I agreed, that was strange.

We both woke up about the same time—we were in Mexico. We each let out an exclamation and ducked the T-Bird down even lower. The Fort Huachuca Army Base was just north of us, and we sure didn't want them to pick us up on their radar. The last thing we needed was to have a border violation on our records. So we wound our way through mountain passes and threaded our way back to the US. No one was ever the wiser.

A couple of weeks later, I saw Stan parking his decrepit pickup outside our squadron building. It was loaded with mesquite wood.

Our use of the T-Bird in largely uncontrolled Arizona was fun. Being a bachelor, I also volunteered to be on call weekends for any circumstantial flying. From time to time our pilots were called upon to fly someplace to deliver something—medical supplies, spare airplane parts, anything like that. It was hit or miss (mostly miss), but

134

occasionally I'd get a call to fly a T-bird elsewhere. I might fly to Colorado or go to Texas and back. It was like having your own private jet to fly around for free. Great weekend entertainment.

## Taxi, Please

My first U-2 flight wasn't actually a flight. Before you can fly a U-2 you have to learn to taxi one. Because of the bird's large wings, supported by "pogo" outrigger wheels, and because of its very limited tailwheel steering, the U-2 makes wide turns and has a very slow steering response. Many, many pilots have put a wheel into the dirt for misjudging a taxiway turn. When I commanded the 17th Reconnaissance Wing in England, the top brass in Europe would visit to get a ride in the two-seat U-2. Many were fighter pilots with a little bit of swagger who figured a slow recce bird with big wings and no guns shouldn't be much of a challenge. It was always a chuckle to see them humbled when they couldn't even negotiate the first turn on the taxiway.

On my first "flight," then, I taxied to the runway end, pulled onto the runway (which the control tower had kept clear of other aircraft), and used the runway length for several high-speed taxi maneuvers. Hector followed and instructed me by radio from the mobile chase vehicle. At his instruction, I applied just enough throttle and speed so the wings began to gain lift. That raised the wings enough for the pogo wheels to come off the ground (they were pinned to prevent them from dropping out). I had to be careful NOT to become airborne, like the very first U-2 test pilot, Tony Levier, did quite by accident. I practiced this a few times. Then I stopped, turned off the runway, and taxied back to the parking ramp. Mission accomplished. U-2 qualification training proceeded one step at a time, very carefully.

## Initial Qualification

Then came my Initial Qualification-1 mission. This was it—my first flight. The rules were simple: there'd be up to five of these IQ training flights. At the end of each one, I was evaluated by the wing commander; the squadron commander, the standardization/evaluation chief, Hector, and various other U-2 evaluator and instructor pilots. They all gathered in the small viewing theater, replayed the video tapes, and made a decision as to whether I performed well enough to be given another flight. I anxiously waited outside for their decision, which was given by a thumbs up or down, just like in gladiator days.

The U-2C model I first flew was based on the initial airframe that famed Lockheed designer Kelly Johnson built. It was later replaced by the larger U-2R model. The "C" was very light weight and was powered by a Pratt & Whitney J-75 engine—the same one used on the big F-105 "Thud" fighter, but without an afterburner.

My IQ-1 takeoff was restricted to using less than full power. The rapid acceleration of a lightly-loaded U-2 at maximum throttle can cause the aircraft to overspeed, so the aircraft was equipped with a mechanical apparatus, called the "gate," that prevented full-throttle application for light-weight takeoffs. At full power with a light fuel load, a U-2C will climb vertically to about 12,000 feet before the pilot has to push the nose over from vertical. Unlike with other airplanes, flaps aren't used for U-2 takeoffs; those big wings produce enough lift by themselves.

On that first flight I took off using only gated power; even with restricted power, I still reached 9,000 feet altitude by the end of the runway. Although I had been carefully coached about the U-2's rapid acceleration, I was still astounded. After takeoff I flew at low altitudes in the vicinity of Davis-Monthan's runway and performed various maneuvers to become familiar with how the aircraft handled. Two chase aircraft followed me with another IP in one of them. The IP gave me instructions from a chase bird while Hector waited on the ground in the mobile chase car for my return.

At intermediate altitudes the U-2 performs like other conventional aircraft. It has so much thrust that the landing gear is purposely left down and speed brakes deployed to create additional drag. With its long wings and unboosted flight controls, the U-2C is sluggish in turns. With so much excess engine thrust I had to keep engine rpm very low where throttle response is unusually slow.

Before returning to land, the pilot must assure the U-2's wings have a level fuel balance. Landing a U-2 with one wing heavy will induce directional control problems. There are no fuel gauges to display wing fuel (another U-2 weight-saving gimmick), so before landing the pilot must slow down in level flight to feel which wing wants to stall first—an indicator of a heavy wing. If necessary, the pilot operates a wing fuel transfer pump to move fuel from one wing to the other to achieve balance. It's mostly guesswork.

The underwing pogo wheels dropped out at takeoff, so I was landing an airplane with an unusual, two-gear wheel system for the first time. Without the pogo wheels, the aircraft literally behaves like a bicycle: you can steer it during the landing roll by tilting the wings. The airplane is particularly susceptible to crosswinds and has a strong tendency to weathervane or ground loop.

It was time for me to return to the airfield. The U-2 normally lands from a descending, 360-degree, race track pattern while gradually reducing speed. The touchdown procedure is quite unconventional. The pilot doesn't aim for a specific touchdown point; instead he aims to cross the runway threshold with his wheels ten feet above the runway and at a specific speed. From the threshold he reduces speed and altitude until the airplane loses lift and the wheels touch down in a two-point attitude. The airplane isn't finished flying until those huge wings lose all lift and start to droop. The C-Model also employs a drag chute, whereas pilots flying the newer R and S models press a switch that hydraulically raises lift spoilers just before touchdown.

As I and my chase planes approached the airfield on initial approach, I looked down and saw a lineup of about ten blue staff cars to the side of the runway. I had an audience. Apparently a new pilot's IQ-1 is a much-anticipated event for the higher brass on base. I had enough adrenaline pumping already, but seeing all those cars meant that I was on stage, front-and-center, giving a solo performance. I sure hoped it wouldn't be my swan song.

It happened that I was the very last U-2 pilot to check out single-seat before a two-seat U-2CT trainer was built. The U-2CT was fabricated from the bird Sam had crashed. Lockheed mounted a second cockpit sticking up behind the first. It sure looked ugly, but the "CT" drastically reduced training accidents. Once we got the CT, a lot of the drama of a pilot's IQ-1 went away. That ended all the fun for the spectators.

But there was no reprieve for me. My fate was lying ahead for all to witness. I made my first low approach, then another, then another—each time being guided closer to the runway. U-2s land under the guidance of another U-2 pilot riding in a hot, souped-up car called the "mobile." The mobile pilot communicates with the flying pilot using a UHF radio while driving onto the runway behind the landing U-2. That's what Hector was doing that day.

After crossing the runway threshold at ten feet the objective is to let the airplane land in a full stall in a two-point attitude or with the tailwheel touching just before the main wheels. If the airplane isn't fully stalled, those big wings have enough lift to get the bird flying again.

For a full-stop landing, just before touchdown the pilot pulls the drag chute handle with his left hand. With wheels on the ground, the control technique is to gradually migrate the stick and yoke aft as the speed slows. You must use the yoke (control wheel) to fly the wings and keep them level throughout the landing roll. Brakes are applied at a slower speed. Eventually the speed becomes too slow to maintain aerodynamic control, and the heavier wing falls to the runway onto its wingtip skid. For a touch-and-go, you apply forward throttle before that happens so you can take off again.

My first touch-and-go was okay. Not brilliant, not good, but okay. It was time for touch-and-go Number Two.

I climbed up and came back around for my second touch-and-go. It was winter, and I was wearing a bulky flight jacket. I came over the runway threshold, descended to just above the pavement, and gradually migrated the yoke back until it was in my chest—all standard stuff. But just then my jacket's left sleeve cuff tangled with the zero-delay lanyard retainer hook on my left shoulder and wouldn't let go. My left sleeve was pinned to my chest. I was then flying one-handed, unable to reach the throttle or anything else on the left side.

Not in a million years would anyone have seen this one coming. The zero-delay lanyard was a steel wire ring on the left parachute riser. It was conveniently out of the way except for the strange ways of landing a U-2. I was supposed to bring the yoke into my chest, and that damn lanyard came into play.

As I struggled to release my left arm, I was not doing a very good job of controlling the yoke with only my right hand. I needed to advance the throttle for my touch-and-go with my left hand, but I couldn't reach it.

It must have looked pretty bad to Hector and the gallery. I finally yanked hard and ripped the cuff away, causing the steel wire ring to stick straight out, waiting to snag me again. I advanced the throttle, took off, and came back around for my full stop, which went pretty well.

My one-arm antics had given the judges something to think about. They all filed into the theater room while I paced outside. Before Hector went in I explained what had happened, but I'm not sure it carried any weight. The wing had almost lost an aircraft with Sam's crash, and no one was of a mind to take any chances with me. I was being evaluated by video tape evidence.

It was a close decision according to Hector, but I passed. For my IQ-2 I saw the same number of staff cars making up the gallery. My IQ-1 had apparently given them the promise of more excitement. But my IQ-2 went smoothly, and after that the number of cars trickled down with each successive IQ flight. I was beginning to bore them.

I passed my IQ-5 check ride confidently and moved on to the Mission Qualification training phase. There were nine MQ flights, all flown at high altitude in the pressure suit.

Flying in a pressure suit at the U-2's highest altitudes is what the mission was all about. It was very demanding in all respects—

handling the aircraft in its other dangerous phase of flight, flying into the Coffin Corner with all its thrills and chills, day and night. The object is to put the aircraft precisely where it needs to be in order for cameras or electronic sensors to capture the targeted intelligence. I flew photo flight lines (PFLs, called "piffles") using the driftsight to navigate. The driftsight is an inverted periscope aimed and adjusted by a hand control [see the picture at the front of this book]. To navigate where there aren't friendly navigation aids in certain parts of the world, we navigated using a combination of Doppler navigation equipment, visual dead reckoning and celestial navigation. The C Model had a sextant built into the nose of the aircraft with pilot controls inside.

I completed all my mission training and joined the ranks of the other fully-qualified U-2 pilots, deploying to places around the world. I was still learning, gaining experience. But I felt great.

## The Pleasures of Flying High

Flying at those altitudes was simply exhilarating. The views, the earth's curvature, the blue-black sky at the fringe of space—gorgeous. The visual impact was surreal. At times I simply marveled that the earth was a true planet. I could see that it was. The view below encompassed numerous states, and large bodies of water looked like puddles. U-2s fly above the tropopause, so all the world's weather was below me (although one huge thunderstorm in Laos almost reached my altitude).

The first sunrise I witnessed was incredible. Sunsets and sunrises at 14 miles high became events imprinted in my mind for their overwhelming beauty. As the earth rotated I saw a distinct sheer line marking the difference between light and day. A sunset was like watching someone pull down a dark curtain, leaving myriad stars behind.

## Too Tall in the Saddle

Flying the U-2 was never boring despite long missions and the fatigue. There was always some new development affecting the mission, operations, or mission equipment.

I had completed my U-2C checkout when along came a new U-2 model. To perform its intelligence collection role in the digital electronics age more modern U-2 design was needed to replace the existing C Model, and so the U-2R was built. The "R" was similar in appearance to the "C" and other variants (the U-2A, B, CT, D, E, EP-X, F, G, J, N, RT, S, and ST). The R was one-third larger and had other modifications and improvements over the existing C Model. Gone was the drag chute, and instead were hydraulic lift and roll spoilers. It featured a new navigation system to replace the sextant for flying in places where radio navigation aids weren't available, and it had a much-improved autopilot. With its redesigned wing the Coffin Corner became less of a problem, and the R provided more fuel for extended range and longer endurance.

The R Model's larger size made it instantly recognizable when parked next to the smaller C. To preclude giving the Soviet Union knowledge that the US had built a new, larger U-2, we played an intricate game of "musical chairs," shuffling the Rs or Cs in and out of hangars so that both models were never parked openly on the ramp together when Soviet satellites came overhead.

The R's cockpit was large enough to accommodate a full pressure suit—an inflatable body bag rather than the skin-tight, partial pressure suits we wore in older models. It was heavier and bulkier, but far more comfortable (I no longer got skin bruises and my knee pain never returned). The bigger cockpit accommodated larger pilots—the pilot's maximum torso sitting-height measurement was a full inch greater. Instead of recruiting little guys, we now accepted oversized guys like "Tall John," "Big Al," and "Muff."

It was over this sitting height issue that I got into real trouble. Our physical exams were very rigorous, approximating the astronaut physicals. We were under constant medical scrutiny by special physicians. Prior to every high flight the pilot was examined by a doctor specializing in aviation medicine (the flight surgeon), and an Air Force flight surgeon accompanied us wherever we deployed.

My initial U-2 recruitment had been a week-long process involving numerous interviews with the wing's leaders, a couple of trial flights in the T-bird, a claustrophobia check sitting for a couple of hours in the altitude chamber, and a complete physical. During the physical I was measured for sitting height, and mine was exactly at the maximum. Once accepted, I never gave that measurement another thought.

I was fully checked-out in the C Model when I went in for a routine physical and found out my sitting height had jumped by one inch. To this day I don't know how or why that happened, but repeated measurements produced the same result. I was suddenly too tall for the C Model I was flying. But we were just receiving our first R Models, and my sitting height was okay to fly in that. But I was perplexed, and I'm sure the suspicion was that I had somehow faked my sitting height before and now I was using it to get into the nice, new U-2R. Exactly how anyone could fake a sitting height was never discussed. I sure didn't know how.

I was called up before the wing commander, Colonel Chuck Stratton, who asked me point blank what happened, and I had no answer. He said, "Okay, it is what it is, and we won't bring it up again." Colonel Stratton was a much-respected straight-shooter, and he certainly showed that genuine character to me. But to this day it's all still a puzzlement. I began my checkout in the R Model.

## Flying the Dragon Lady

So what was it like to fly this airplane? Certainly it was always a challenge. Landings and high altitude flying required the pilot's utmost attention. Landings were regularly botched by even very experienced pilots, sometimes resulting in the airplane running off the side of the runway or doing a ground loop. Airplanes aren't supposed to do that.

142

The cockpit was just big enough to accommodate an average-size man in a full pressure suit. On low altitude flights we didn't wear a pressure suit; it was only necessary for flying above 45,000 feet.

A high altitude ejection poses interesting problems. Pilots strapped spurs onto their boots that attached to cables from the ejection seat. Upon ejection the spur cables retract so that when the seat goes up the rail you don't leave your lower legs behind. Upon ejection the canopy is blown off by explosive thrusters, a rocket propels the seat up and away from the aircraft, and a drogue chute pops out to stabilize the seat and pilot as they free fall together to 14,000 feet. If the main parachute ever deployed at mission altitude and the pilot survived the shock, he would likely freeze to death during the slow descent. Temperatures at that altitude were around minus 65 degrees Celsius. In the seat are oxygen bottles for breathing and pressurizing the suit.

At 14,000 feet a barometric sensor triggers the next sequence. The shoulder harness automatically releases and an inertial real tightens a strap behind the pilot. This "butt snapper" separates the pilot from the ejection seat. One second later the pilot's main chute deploys.

The suit was designed to automatically inflate and provide oxygen for breathing and pressurization if you lost cockpit pressurization or ejected. If you parachute into water, a built-in life preserver automatically inflates and an anti-suffocation valve allows you to breathe ambient air after your oxygen is depleted.

That's what happened to a U-2 pilot flying over the Gulf of Siam. It was during the wee hours of the morning, and the pilot lost control of his airplane. He ejected and lost consciousness. When he awoke he was floating in the water with the sun coming up and a Thai fishing boat approaching to rescue him.

The term "Coffin Corner" connotes and describes the perils of flying the U-2 at high altitude flying quite well. Any description containing the word "coffin" should rightly grab your attention.

The U-2's autopilot helped keep the airspeed under control, but autopilots aren't infallible. As I described earlier, the C Model's autopilot was notorious for unexpectedly and suddenly commanding the aircraft to pitch up or pitch down, and if the pilot didn't immediately correct the condition the aircraft would likely fly out of control. I experienced two such pitch-ups but grabbed the controls in time.

Terry was flying a C Model over Germany when his aircraft suddenly pitched down and over-speeded. He couldn't pull the bird out of its dive and he ejected, safely. When he was on the ground a local German came running up to him. In his broken English he asked, "F-104? F-104?" The Luftwaffe's pilots in those days had a reputation for ejecting from their F-104s quite frequently.

Another U-2 pilot experienced a pitch-down like Terry's, but he had been a star weight-lifter and used his enormous strength to hold the control column aft and keep the aircraft under control until he could pull out of the dive at lower altitude.

Although long U-2 flights required the utmost of pilot endurance, I never found them boring. I always welcomed any flight, even those that required us to fly in orbits for hours. There's a thrill that accompanies flying and a special thrill that comes with flying a U-2. Being cooped up in a tiny cockpit, encased in a pressure suit while strapped into an ejection seat never produced any anxieties or claustrophobia for me. It was sort of like being in my own, private cocoon. I'll admit that the rock-hard ejection seat didn't make my butt feel too good, but those were the breaks. It would have been nice to maybe cross my legs once in a while.

## The Dangers of Flying High

High altitude physiology is still not fully understood. As U-2 pilots we took certain precautions before and after high flights, but I and the others certainly didn't realize the full extent of the dangers in those early years. We used to joke that all U-2 pilots were afflicted with high-altitude brain damage, but I doubt any of us really knew the underlying dangers.

Some hazards were well-known to us. For instance, we knew that at high altitudes solar radiation exposure was significant, and we wore dosimeters in our pressure suits. Records were kept about every condition, every malady. We were cautioned not to eat gaseous foods prior to pressure suit flights, and part of the pre-flight routine for both the pilot and his backup was logging a record of what food he had eaten the past 12 hours and how he had slept. And for operational missions, a doctor gave the mission pilot a medical examination.

But during the early 2000s very serious physiological problems began to develop among U-2 pilots flying modern U-2S Models over Afghanistan and the Middle East. Pilots began to suffer numerous cases of brain damage—in some cases permanently. In one case a pilot flying a mission over Afghanistan became so incapacitated that he couldn't fly the airplane back without the assistance of a chase aircraft. Another pilot returned from a flight and noticed red freckles all over his skin; they were his blood vessels rupturing.

Air Force experts discovered that the current U-2 mission of providing battlefield ground support required U-2 pilots to both fly longer and more frequently while also inducing more physical movement in the cockpit. Those factors increased the likelihood of releasing trapped body gases into the bloodstream which then migrated to the brain and other body organs.

Once medical researchers realized the cause of these recurring physiological episodes, the Air Force modified the entire U-2 fleet—at considerable cost—to reinforce the cockpit structure and increase cockpit pressurization, which gave the pilots added protection. It had been a very dangerous situation that caused at least nine U-2 pilots to suffer long-lasting brain damage.

## What's for Dinner?

To provide in-flight sustenance U-2 pilots are provided food in a tube. The pressure suit's face plate has a small feeding port that's sealed with a spring-loaded trap door. Food or drink is passed through a straw inserted through the feeding port. Tube food is simply softened food sealed inside an oversized toothpaste tube. The Gerber baby food company makes the stuff. We "enjoyed" food like Beef and Gravy, Turkey and Noodles, and Peanut Butter and Jelly. The pilot selects his menu before the flight and the PSD technicians stash the tubes on a shelf behind his seat. When time and appetite permit, the pilot grabs a tube and inserts it into a cylindrical hole on the lower left panel. That hole is an electric oven. The pilot presses a switch that starts the oven on a preset timer. When the timer goes off a flashing yellow light announces it's time to eat. He retrieves the tube and screws on a hard plastic straw that punctures the sealed tube. Using the cockpit's mirrors he guides the straw to his faceplate feeding port, pushes it in past the trap door, and squeezes the food into his mouth. Voila!—a delicious, warm, tube food meal!

Well, that's the way it's supposed to work. We should remember that the customer at this restaurant is sealed inside a pressure suit, wearing big, bulky gloves that encumber manual dexterity and sense of touch. It's not unusual for the pilot to drop the tube or straw while attempting to prepare his meal.

We also should remember that Lockheed's specialty is designing airplanes, not kitchen ovens. Many things did—very often—go wrong, like this:

1. The oven didn't heat. The yellow light never came on. The refrigerated food remained nearly frozen. Try as you might, it won't squeeze through the straw. Or, if it does, you wish it hadn't.

2. The oven heated too well and too long, and the food inside that tube is scorching hot. When you screw on the straw and puncture the tube, it turns into a bubbling geyser, sending hot tube food all over you and your cockpit. You brought nothing along to clean it up.

3. The food has been heated, but your fat, bulky gloves won't tell your hands how hot that tube is. When you squeeze it into your mouth, your mouth tells you what your gloves wouldn't—the food is scorching hot—and there's no place to spit it out. Mouth burns take a long time to heal.

4. The timer's yellow timing light doesn't come on. You think the oven didn't come on, but it did. In fact it came on and never shut off. As you stare down at the oven waiting for something to happen, the super-heated tube food explodes, sending a shower of baby food all over you, the instruments, the canopy, and everything else. You vow you'll never eat tube food again. But you do.

There are almost as many stories about tube food as there are about UCDs (Urine Collection Device, coming up next). I tried to sell the idea of offering kimchi in tubes, but nobody bought into that.

Years ago somebody experimented with a new culinary treat: stick food. Stick food was solid food packed into shapes resembling small licorice sticks. They were inserted into a rotating drum apparatus like the chamber of a revolver. The device injected a stick through the feeding port, one at a time. I thought it was a novel device, but it must not have caught on because after some weeks we just didn't get it anymore.

We consumed our liquids in much the same way as food. Plastic bottles with straws attached were filled with water or Gator Aid and kept on the shelf behind the ejection seat. Coffee would have helped on those long missions, but the PSD folks said coffee was too diuretic and too diarrhetic. We really didn't need any more diarrhea than we already got from eating ethnic food in countries we visited.

## Intake and Exhaust

It's important for the pilot to stay hydrated so he doesn't develop urinary tract problems. Lots of fluid must go in during those ten-plus hours, so it only makes sense that it must come out, too. No one goes more than ten hours without taking a pee.

That's where the UCD comes in. The Urine Collection Device is a diabolical contraption made of surgical rubber and Velcro. It fits over the male private part and attaches to special underwear briefs that have a round hole in front bordered by a Velcro collar.

Let me explain: the pilot stretches and pulls on the elastic UCD which fits snuggly over his you-know-what. The UCD is then threaded through the pilot's special briefs and affixed in place by the Velcro. A flexible tube is attached to the end of the UCD and held by a plastic clip. The other end of the tube attaches to a relief valve that's part of the pressure suit and located on the pilot's left thigh. Outside the suit another plastic tube is routed from the relief valve to a receptacle beneath the floor board that collects pilot pee. Pilot pee—a precious commodity—goes from pilot, through the UCD, through the tube, through the valve, and into the receptacle. The receptacle is emptied after the flight by some mysterious person without a name.

When you gotta go, you gotta go. It happens like this: first the pilot opens the valve. To help the pee flow, the pilot increases suit pressure slightly using the suit's adjustable pressure controller. Then he puts all his boyhood training aside and simply wills himself to do what Mom told him to never do: pee in his pants. That last part is sometimes the hardest part, because mothers taught their little boys too well.

As with any design, there are often problems, and the very simple UCD, with no moving parts, seems to have caused an inordinate number of cockpit incidents.

If you hold up a UCD and look at it (although you probably don't want to) it resembles a sausage casing. The UCD's top is cone-shaped with a hole in the center. To don the contraption the pilot stretches the hole apart with his thumbs and lets it snap closed over his penis. Very simple.

Through scientific observation we know that pilots—and pilot penises—come in various sizes. A brand-new UCD straight from the local hardware store is sized for a midget, and we all know midgets don't fly U-2s. So every pilot must snip off the top of the conical portion in order to adjust the size of the opening to fit his particular, uh, anatomy.

Since time immemorial every U-2 pilot knew to cut that hole to fit. Every pilot knew this—except Big Al. Big Al was a former All-State linebacker, and he was about the maximum size that could be stuffed into a U-2 cockpit. Somehow, no one told our biggest pilot that the little UCD hole had to be made bigger than the factory specification— or else.

Al was checking out for his very first high flight. It's a nervous time, even for a former linebacker. U-2 pilots preparing for a high flight are carefully attended as they prepare to fly in the pressure suit for the first time. But some matters are quite personal, and no one looks over your shoulder when you put on your UCD. And no one noticed that Big Al hadn't resized his UCD hole. Al figured if everyone else could wear this little thing he wasn't going to be the exception, so he said nothing.

Al stretched that little UCD hole as far as it would go, slipped it on, and let it snap closed. It didn't feel good at all, he said afterward, but with his football player's determination, he wasn't going to chicken out and ask the PSD technicians for help. He went to his airplane, got in, was strapped down by the technicians, and started up. By the time Al had taxied to the end of the runway, he knew something was really, really wrong with his UCD fitting, but off he went.

As pilots climb higher the atmospheric pressure decreases and the body expands. Al's expanding anatomy wasn't having any fun with his extremely tight UCD. It became painful—very painful—and Al finally had enough. He radioed back to his IP at that he was experiencing a particular physiological problem, and his IP immediately guessed what it was. Al declared an emergency and came home as fast as possible. Staff cars and an ambulance were standing by. He taxied to the end of the runway and shut it down right there. The cockpit was swarmed with the PSD and medical folks. They got him out of his suit and the flight surgeon cut off the UCD right there at the end of the runway. Al said he nearly fainted when the blood started flowing again.

Anyhow, there was no permanent damage, but he was pretty sore (and embarrassed) for a while. Some of Al's fellow pilots had the good will and presence of mind to call Becky at home to tell her what happened. They said Al was okay, but suggested she might want to perform a functional test upon the item of concern when Al got home.

UCD stories abound in the U-2 community, and we've all had personal encounters with that nefarious device. I remember preparing for a wartime mission in Thailand . . . .

A mission pilot suits up in the Physiological Support Division with the aid of two PSD technicians. They help him don the pressure suit and then run a series of functional leak and pressure checks on it. They also operationally check the UCD. The suit is inflated and the relief valve on the left thigh is momentarily opened. If all is well, the pilot feels a gentle flow of cool air upon his apparatus. That airflow check signifies that the valve is functioning, there's no blockage, and the UCD is properly secured.

On that day we were tight for time. When I opened my UCD valve for the airflow check I felt nothing. We repeated the check several times to no avail. Something was wrong.

With all the technology built into the U-2, its sensors, and the pressure suit, you'd think they would have designed a foolproof urine collection system, but it was anything but that. Sometimes the UCD didn't stay secure. Sometimes the hose clip at the end popped off. Sometimes the drain hose came loose.

I didn't know what the problem was, but I knew that if I had to climb out of my suit to fix it my takeoff would be late. These were quite important wartime missions, so I chanced that maybe the test was flawed and my UCD was okay. We proceeded. Once the pilot is strapped into the cockpit and his suit is mated to the aircraft's oxygen system, another airflow check is performed. We tried it again, and my UCD still wasn't working.

Everyone has personal body characteristics, and even on very long missions I usually didn't have strong urinary urges. So I said, "Let's go." I started up and launched. Wouldn't you know, I hadn't even gotten to mission altitude when I had my first bladder urge. It was going to be one of those days.

I resisted as long as possible, but I had to go. I was only two hours into the ten-hour mission when I became desperate. If you don't evacuate your bladder during these missions you're risking serious medical issues. You gotta do it, and so I did.

Normally the urine transits out of the suit and the pilot can see it flow through the clear plastic tube into the urine receptacle below the cockpit floor. I saw nothing. Soon I felt something warm and wet in my left boot. There was no escaping what had happened.

That day I had to void, and void again. I did my business several times, and my boot became my urine receptacle. Pilots wear long underwear to prevent skin chafing against the suit, and my long underwear became a wick. The urine slowly migrated up to where I was sitting. It was a long, long, uncomfortable flight, and the next day I was sporting a big lower body skin rash.

So what had happened? The damn little plastic clip that holds the tube and UCD together had broken, just like all little plastic parts break now and then. For a few pennies more they could have built a more substantial clip. After my episode the PSD guys routinely wrapped tape around the clip for me and everyone else—a good, low-tech solution for a low-tech device.

*[Author's note: Long after my U-2 days a few women have since become U-2 pilots. You'll find a discussion of their UCD issues in someone else's memoirs, not mine.]*

I suppose I'd better address the inevitable question, "What happens if you do a Number 2 in the suit?" The answer is if you do a Number 1 in the suit the PSD techs will clean it up, but if you do a Number 2 you clean it up yourself. Just ask Texas John, who against all advice made the mistake of eating local Korean food the night before his mission.

ALSS and Beyond

Before the new R Models replaced the C Models, the C was flying missions to test a new sensor system. It was called the Advanced Location Strike System, or ALSS. It was the forerunner of the Precision Location Strike System and succeeding technologies. The ALSS and PLSS trials eventually produced U-2 mission systems that are being used today, giving the U-2 a new role of locating ground targets with unprecedented accuracy, feeding target and threat location data to strike aircraft and their smart, guided weapons over a battlefield. The U-2 role in Afghanistan today is a direct result of those early tests.

During that early ALSS testing, we would fly a trio of U-2s over New Mexico, orbiting on six-hour missions before returning to Tucson. I didn't find any U-2 mission truly boring, but the ALSS missions came close. There was nothing adventuresome about circling New Mexico all day. But flying the U-2 was always full of surprises. The airplane was never to be taken for granted, and it was always ready to snap at the unwary pilot.

I was flying the ALSS pattern one day and was roughly one-third into the mission when my eyes started to water. I wasn't reminiscing about some sad affair; I wasn't doing anything in particular. But both eyes began to run tears, and they wouldn't stop. What was initially an irritation then turned into something more serious—I couldn't see. In the MC-1 partial pressure suit the faceplate served as your windshield, so to speak. My eyes were severely irritated, and the moisture was also clouding my faceplate.

I had to descend to lower altitude before I could open my faceplate, but I was already having difficulty seeing the cockpit controls and instruments. I told my fellow ALSS pilots what was happening. Very, very carefully I throttled back. Once I got to lower altitude the airspeed margin for error was bigger and gave me more leeway between the borders of the "Coffin Corner." At that point I increased my rate of descent because I was fast losing my vision.

When I descended to about 50,000 feet or so I opened my faceplate, and fortunately my eyes began to clear up. I continued to fly the orbit track for most of the remaining mission at the lower altitude but had to return earlier than the others because I had consumed more fuel.

On the ground I told the PSD guys what had happened. They investigated and found out my oxygen supply had somehow been contaminated.

On another ALSS mission I was flying comfortably when I began to feel a nagging pain in my right knee. It wasn't much at first, but it became more severe with time. There's not much a pilot can do about those things—aches, pains, and discomforts are all a part of flying in a very tight cockpit in a skin-tight pressure suit, sitting on a rock-hard ejection seat for hours. Have an itchy nose?—too bad, you can't scratch. How about an eyelash that turns under?—just live with it and press on. And so I let my painful knee go.

When I was descending into Davis-Monthan the pain went away, so I scarcely mentioned it to the PSD guys. But they were attuned to everything affecting the pilots, their bodies, and their behaviors. They picked up on my comment about having a "little knee pain" and were seriously concerned.

Sure enough, my knee pain was a case example of "the bends." That's precisely what happens to divers of the deep when they rise to the surface, and U-2 pilots are very susceptible to such "dysbarisms," as they're called—decompression sickness maladies due to high pressure differentials. These are potentially fatal occurrences involving dissolved gases that percolate out of the bloodstream and other body fluids. Nitrogen bubbles likely caused my knee pain precisely where I had a surgical scar from years ago. But if those bubbles migrate to the heart, lungs, or brain they can cause catastrophic damage. That's what pressure suits are supposed to prevent, but those older, MC-1 partial pressure suits were imperfect.

In any event, that old knee operation I had years before made the joint susceptible to such occurrences. I got the bends in that knee one more time while flying the C Model but didn't tell anyone. Job security. After transitioning to the R Model with its full body pressure suit I had no more physiological problems.

153

In U-2 terms, our home in Tucson at Davis-Monthan Air Force Base was just a stone's throw away from our ALSS orbits over New Mexico. We didn't have to carry much fuel since the ALSS equipment was light and we were flying so close to home plate. Depending on prevailing winds, a U-2's descent and landing requires 220-250 nautical miles distance and takes about 45 minutes. When leaving our orbits over New Mexico we had to begin our descents almost immediately or we would overshoot the base. Knowing this, and realizing that we could almost glide home, we sometimes remained on orbit a bit longer so the ALSS scientists on the ground could get more data.

U-2s don't fly their missions at constant altitude. During cruise flight they continually climb higher as aircraft fuel weight burns off. So by late in the ALSS mission we were extremely light weight and at our highest altitudes.

On one such ALSS mission we lingered longer than usual. There were only two of us that day, and Rich and I set our personal high altitude records. He finished up at 79,000 feet and I was a little lower at just over 78,000 feet. I'm sure our altitude was boosted by atmospheric conditions, flying above the hot desert floor and over a huge summertime high pressure air mass.

## Other Missions

Our missions were wide and varied, and a full description won't fit here. Besides, its classified.

One thing to note is that the US Navy also had an interest in the U-2. For several years the Navy put seed money into the U-2 development program with thoughts they would eventually buy some U-2s. To accommodate the Navy, our U-2R Models were wired for a tailhook and had a switch in the cockpit, although the Air Force birds didn't actually carry the tailhook—too heavy. The outer six feet of each wing could be folded up for carrier operations. The Navy's intention was to fly U-2s off of aircraft carriers, and they actually trial tested it. Rich Drake was the test pilot. I saw the videos, and it was pretty scary stuff to land a long-winged U-2 on a pitching deck.

Some things were quite different, such as when we entertained the entertainers. The TV series, "Call to Glory," starring actors Craig T. Nelson and Cindy Pickett was filmed on location at Beale. It was all about a U-2 pilot and his wife. The series bombed.

It seemed that every scientist wanted to try out some new piece of equipment on the U-2. One mission conducted out of Beale was for the testing the atmospheric distortion of laser beams. For that mission U-2s were fitted with a blue light laser package strapped onto the belly. The purpose was to shine the laser onto an array of sensors on the ground, miles below. The mission code name was "Senior Bounce." Pilots flew from Beale AFB over a sensor array at the Truckee airport in the Sierra Mountains, attempting to score a direct hit from over 70,000 feet high. It was tricky. One day I had a particularly good Senior Bounce mission, and the university professors conducting the test drove down the mountains to Beale to buy me beer at the end of the day. I liked those Senior Bounce missions a lot.

Essentially the U-2 was flown to be a smart collector of intelligence information. We carried a variety of sensors that scooped up electronic signals or captured images revealing what our adversaries didn't want us to know. The array of mission equipment was always changing, and every time I thought missions were becoming routine, something new came along.

There are many, many other developments that characterized the life of the U-2. Read all the books, go to the CIA's website, and then read more. It's quite a story.

## Time Passes

Back to the 1970s at Davis-Monthan . . . .

As some of the U-2 secrecy wore off I was selected to go to Air Force Water Survival School at Homestead AFB in south Florida. I was the first U-2 pilot to go through that course wearing a pressure suit. The purpose was to "test the waters" for other U-2 pilots to follow. Sergeant Prouty from PSD accompanied me to provide suit care and help me suit up. Prouty was a good guy, and we made the best of our Florida "vacation." I wore Don Webster's old suit. I was of a later vintage than Webster and never met him. He was apparently a little larger and his suit gave me some much-appreciated breathing room in the Florida heat and humidity.

In Florida's hot sun and high humidity wearing the suit wasn't much fun when I wasn't in the water. Much of the time I was either suiting up or waiting for my turn to practice survival skills. We informed the school that a pilot in a pressure suit can quickly overheat, and they accommodated us as best they could.

The school consisted of academics and water trials, and I didn't wear the suit except for those times when simulating water egress and survival. Our classmates were curious about me and Prouty, but we couldn't talk about why I was there wearing a pressure suit.

Most of the time the suit wasn't much of a hindrance—except when I had to climb into a life raft. We parasailed off the deck of a Navy LST, tethered to a tow boat, and I did that wearing the suit. When I reached about 100 feet above the water, I released the pelican hooks to detach boat's tow line, then parachuted into the water. (In the class just before mine, some guy got it all wrong; instead of releasing the tow line, he released his parachute risers and fell 100 feet without his chute. He was hurt pretty bad.)

After I was in the water, I found my waterlogged suit was really a drag, and it took a lot of effort to get into my one-man survival raft. I had to be really careful not to puncture the raft with my U-2 spurs on. Later, when I was doing the 12-man life raft drill, I needed help from the others to climb into that bigger raft, and I was really exhausted afterward. But it was nice in the water, and despite the instructors' warnings, we saw no sharks.

When I first interviewed for the U-2 program I was told I would likely have to deploy back to Vietnam and after the war I might not have a U-2 job any more. That didn't deter me from volunteering. I recalled how I had once been told I would upgrade to the front seat of the F-4, and that sure didn't happen, either. I had learned not to have much trust in such predictions. I figured time would tell, and I'd take my chances.

Sure enough, when the war came to a halt the mission needs for the U-2 changed dramatically. U-2Cs had been flying out of Bien Hoa Air Base near Saigon, but when the R Model came along the C Model was retired. By the time the war had ended I was flying the R Model with different equipment and a different mission. After the war the Air Force conducted a "reduction in force"—a downsizing—and several U-2 pilots were cut from the service. I remained with the U-2 program for 15 more years.

The U-2R gave the U-2 program new life—U-2 reconnaissance was no longer concentrated on principally obtaining wet-film, optical photography but focused instead on intelligence collection in the upcoming electronic age using new electronic sensors. An electro-optical slant range camera was developed that digitized imagery collected by a U-2. The R Model was also fitted with Advanced Synthetic Aperture Radar that took photographic images using radar energy—day or night, in all kinds of weather. The U-2's new electronic sensors captured signals intelligence from unsuspecting adversaries and instantly transmitted the data to analysts at a distant ground station. The R's intelligence collection array was formidable.

In the next several years, I deployed in the R Model to several operating locations we had established overseas. I mostly flew out of England, Cyprus, Korea, and Thailand. There were short excursions elsewhere, too. We typically deployed on two-month temporary tours of duty (TDYs).

When deployed a pilot flew on 4-day cycles. When first arriving at the operating location, a pilot spends the first two days adjusting to the time zone change and performing ground duties. On Day 3 he becomes the mobile pilot—the backup pilot who assists the flying pilot. On Day 4 he'd be the flying pilot.

157

Following a high altitude flight pilots are given a day of complete rest and must not perform strenuous activity because it could release nitrogen bubbles into the bloodstream and cause strokes, brain damage, lung embolism problems, etc. On the second day the pilot is given a day off, but could fly at low altitude if necessary.

At the end of a two-month TDY performing on this 4-day cycle you're pretty tired and ready to come home. One year I spent nine months out of country on various deployments, the longest being two months. Among the married pilots, the divorce rate was high.

I progressed in my U-2 work. I became an instructor in the T-33, then an instructor in the U-2R, then an evaluator in both, and within four years I became the U-2 Standardization/Evaluation Branch Chief in charge of all U-2 instruction and evaluation. I balanced those jobs with periodic overseas deployments.

The USSR was pressing the limits of détente by becoming adventuresome in Africa. There was some Soviet monkey business going on in Angola so we planned to deploy a U-2 to Ascension Island in the south Atlantic. Ascension was British territory, and we needed their approval. While waiting for that we sent a U-2 pilot and support crew in a KC-135 tanker aircraft to the US Naval Air Station at Roosevelt Roads on the east end of Puerto Rico. I was the pilot. Once we received British approval, another pilot would fly a U-2 to Roosevelt Roads and I would fly it on to Ascension Island, a flight of 5,000 miles.

Arriving at Rosy Roads I went into perpetual crew rest as we waited for mission approval and the U-2. But it never happened. Hector was commander of the deployment, and four times a day he checked Navy communications for our approval message. We set up a daily routine: Breakfast. Then handball. Lunch. Go to the beach (no one there except us). Sailing (the infamous "First and Last U-2 Regatta"). Afternoon cocktails (except for me—I was in crew rest). Dinner. Take in a movie. Go to bed.

For two weeks we waited. Leisure time in our tropical paradise wasn't much fun anymore. Finally we were called back to Tucson. It was late November, and we had trouble explaining our beach tans.

The Vietnam War was still on, and we were flying U-2s from U Tapao Air Base, Thailand. We mostly flew over Laos west of North Vietnam but sometimes to the east over the Gulf of Tonkin. They were long missions flown at both day and night. Through our own intelligence collecting, we learned that North Vietnam had selected its top fighter pilots to attempt to shoot down a U-2. They practiced simulated attacks against U-2s by paralleling our flights just across the North Vietnam border from Laos. Apparently they weren't able to solve the intercept problem and finally gave up.

I arrived at U Tapao for my second U-2 deployment shortly after Saigon fell. The refugees had poured into U Tapao by aircraft, and refugee encampments were set up all around the airfield. It was a sad sight.

## Nuclear Sampling

We continued to fly our missions out of U Tapao. These were designated combat missions because open hostilities existed, but when we U-2 pilots declared our combat pay exemption to the IRS, the IRS balked. The IRS declared the war was over; we knew it wasn't. A struggle ensued between the Defense Department and the IRS, and Defense won. We got our tax exemption.

With the war officially ended, the time had come to close down our operation at U Tapao. Just then the Chinese detonated an atmospheric nuclear test, and I was tasked to sample it.

The U-2 can carry equipment for the purpose of nuclear air sampling—the collection of particulate and gaseous samples from the cloud of radioactive debris resulting from an atomic explosion. The U-2's air sampling equipment consists of six filters and six collection bottles. The system operates by extending a filter into the airstream while simultaneously pumping ambient air into a collection bottle.

159

The collected debris samples were sent back to the US to be analyzed by technicians. From the samples they're able to determine the bomb's characteristics, such as the weapon's size, yield, construction, fusing, etc. U-2s had been used extensively for sampling both Soviet and Chinese nuclear weapons testing.

The key is finding the debris cloud. It may or may not be visible. Some have said it glows at night, but I don't know about that one. After the debris is dispersed into the atmosphere, fine radioactive particles and gases still remain airborne at high altitudes for quite some time. We depend upon meteorologists to predict where upper level winds will take the cloud.

I was nearing the end of my third deployment to U Tapao, my last tour of combat duty of the Vietnam War, when China's nuclear test occurred. My air sampling mission, code named Olympic Race, also served the purpose of removing a U-2 from U Tapao and delivering it to our new detachment in Korea.

The meteorologists predicted prevailing winds should take the debris cloud east from China across the East China Sea. I left U Tapao early morning, headed southeast over the Gulf of Siam, circumnavigated Cambodia and Vietnam, then headed northeast to land at Osan Air Base, South Korea, where my U-2 would remain. We hoped I would intercept the debris cloud while en route. It would be a very long flight.

My aircraft was fitted with a Rustrak radiation dosimeter with a cockpit display that would point me toward any radiation source. I took off long before sunrise. As the sun rose the Rustrak began detecting a radiation source and pointed to the sun above, as if I needed its help to tell me where the sun was. I flew on. As I approached the East China Sea east of Taipei the Rustrak detector began to steadily pick up more intense radiation, and I knew I had hit the debris cloud. I couldn't see anything except sunshine and the ocean below, although there seemed to be some glittering specks reflecting the sunlight.

I altered course and followed the needles. The Rustrak recorder points toward the most intense source of radiation, but upon entering a debris cloud its sensors become saturated and its directional information becomes useless. I sent a code over my high frequency radio that told our operations I had contacted the cloud and was beginning air sampling. To prevent radioactive debris particles entering my pressure suit I turned off the suit's ventilation. Without suit ventilation I was susceptible to overheating in my "body bag," and it didn't take much increased effort for me to begin sweating. To compensate I turned the cockpit temperature down quite low. However, that increased the likelihood my canopy would ice over whenever I began my descent. The outside air temperature was minus 65-70 degrees Celsius.

I flew a modified zig-zag pattern with six 30-minute legs, loitering in the debris cloud for three hours. That left me enough fuel to make Korea. It was a long time, but finally I finished the sampling and headed north.

It's necessary to preheat the cockpit for about fifteen minutes prior to beginning the descent from high altitude. If you don't, fog and ice will form on the inside of the cold-soaked canopy as you reduce power and decrease the engine airflow that provides cockpit heating and defrosting. Canopy ice forms first behind the pilot's head and then migrates forward, so it can become quite severe before the pilot notices it has begun.

If the pilot doesn't notice the creeping ice formation, it will eventually obscure the entire canopy. Just in case that happens, modern technology and ingenuity has produced the "swab stick." It's a two-foot stick of wood (painted black, of course) with a cloth swab at the end. It allows the pilot to reach the foremost part of the canopy and clear his forward vision. The swab stick rests on the canopy glare shield—standard equipment for every flight. But to remedy severe canopy icing, the only alternative is to stop the descent, increase power, and dial up the temperature and defrosting for about ten minutes to melt the ice. Until then, you're blind.

On this mission I had to preheat the cockpit longer than usual because I had been flying for hours with the temperature turned down low. During the preheating the cockpit got quite warm, and without any suit ventilation I began to sweat heavily. A U-2 descent from peak altitude to the ground takes about 45 minutes and covers a distance of about 200-230 miles, depending on winds. I was still very warm as I approached Osan. If possible I was supposed to fly through rainclouds to wash the airplane of radioactive particles, but there was no rain to be found. I landed at Osan after flying well over ten hours.

There was no relief for me quite yet. It took over an hour to complete the decontamination. I was directed to park at a remote part of the airfield where the aircraft would be washed and the radioactive water runoff collected to be disposed of later. I parked, shut down the engine, and was greeted by a gang of guys in yellow HAZMAT suits. No one could plug in external power and air until the bird was clean, so I had to remain in the cockpit with no ventilation or cooling while they began decontaminating the airplane. Finally they gave me the signal to open the canopy. Then they had to inspect the entire cockpit with dosimeters.

It was summer. I was really getting hot, and I was very fatigued. I figure it had been about 30 minutes before I got out and climbed down to the ground. They plugged in a liquid oxygen bottle and I got cooling air for the first time in many hours. I was walked to a special tent set up nearby to decontaminate me and my suit. I was a walking zombie at that point, in a state of complete exhaustion, and it was sheer relief to climb out of the pressure suit and shower down.

During the next two days that debris cloud split in two, one part heading northeast toward the Aleutians and the other part headed south. The southern portion got wrapped up by easterly winds in the horse latitudes. It reversed course, heading west. It crossed over India and the Middle East. Another U-2 pilot flying out of Spain sampled the cloud as it passed over the western Mediterranean. For some reason Don got a hot suit—radioactive debris in his suit exceeding the allowable dosage—and his air sampling days were officially over.

After my air sampling flight I flew some missions in Korea for a couple of weeks before redeploying back to Davis-Monthan in Tucson.

# California, Here We Come

I was enjoying life in Tucson and loved my work. Life was peachy right where I was when it was announced our entire U-2 operation was moving to California. The higher-flying, much faster SR-71 Blackbird was based at Beale Air Force Base north of Sacramento. It made sense to combine the two operations since both aircraft were doing the same reconnaissance work but in different ways. They were quite complementary in their operation and mission.

The high and fast Blackbird flew high-threat missions the U-2 couldn't, and the U-2 performed well in missions that called for continual surveillance, target revisiting, and loitering. The U-2 could stay up forever on a tank of gas and didn't require air-to-air refueling. It was far simpler to operate and was cheap. Both birds were high-flyers and needed physiological support, both required use of the companion trainer (the T-38), and they shared many of the same maintenance and mission support staff and facilities. The SR was far more expensive to operate with its need for a dedicated squadron of KC-135 tankers. Competition for its sizeable share of the Air Force budget eventually led to its demise.

I don't think anyone predicted the longevity that the U-2 has achieved. After being re-engined and continually updated, it gained new life with new sensors, a satellite data link, and a vital role in modern US battlefield support.

So we moved our U-2s from D-M to Beale. Soon after arriving I was given the job of Standardization and Evaluation Division Chief for the U-2, the SR-71, and the companion T-38 trainer, supervising instructor-evaluators for both the U-2 and SR-71. I was still an active flyer and periodically deployed TDY overseas.

The U-2 operating in Cyprus was due for full-body maintenance back at Beale, so in January of one year we deployed a team to fly a replacement U-2 to Cyprus and swap it for the Cyprus bird. A team was formed under the able leadership of Ron Williams. It consisted of maintenance workers, physiological support, a doctor, a navigator, and Don Schreiber and I as the pilots.

As usual, a KC-135Q tanker would accompany the U-2 to carry the U-2's fuel supply (the U-2 requires a special, thermally-stable fuel), the team, and support equipment. We flew from California to Washington, DC, then to England. While the tanker and team waited in England, Don flew our U-2 to Cyprus and flew the Cyprus bird back to England.

I flew the bird from Beale to Andrews AFB outside of Washington, DC. It was a long, coast-to-coast flight, but easily within the U-2's range. The team took off in the tanker just after me and, with its faster ground speed, landed at Andrews just before me to prepare for my landing. Don flew it on to Cyprus, got his crew rest, and then flew the Cyprus bird back to England.

The U-2 had a mystical aura as a "spy plane," and occasionally that reputation impacted our operations. In this case, the British Parliament approved staging our U-2 through England but restricted us to nighttime operations: we could take off and land only under cover of darkness. Furthermore, we had to change the tail number of the replacement bird and paint it the same as the Cyprus bird. That was to deceive British aviation enthusiasts into sighting one U-2, not two. I never knew why that was important, but that's what we did.

The weather in England is usually doggy, but in January it's particularly bad. After Don got back from Cyprus, the weather locked us in. It was either bad in England, bad in the US, or both. I was going to fly the bird across the pond to Pease AFB in New Hampshire, so I had to be in crew rest—eight hours uninterrupted sleep, no alcohol. Every night I'd go to bed early, wake up early, go to the chow hall for my U-2 meal (high protein, low residue, i.e., steak and eggs), and wait for Ron and the guys to give me the go-ahead. Every morning I did this, and every morning I'd watch those guys march into the chow hall with glum faces to say the weather was too bad to fly.

This happened each day for a week. But one morning as I was eating breakfast our guys came into the chow hall and announced the weather had broken and we were leaving. Just before dawn I took off, followed by the tanker and our team. As I climbed out the morning sun rose behind me, beautifully. But as I climbed, my suit began to inflate uncontrollably. The higher I climbed, the more the suit filled up, and I was beginning to look like a big balloon. A fully-inflated pressure suit gets hard and stiff, restricting the pilot's ability to operate cockpit equipment. Nothing I did helped, and I stopped my climb.

From the tanker below Ron was conversing with SAC Headquarters in Omaha. A decision was made: SAC didn't want me to fly across the ocean with the pressure suit malfunctioning, and we were returning to England. With the decision made, I pulled off one glove to deflate my suit. When I did that it released the suit pressure but also blew my body moisture into the cockpit, producing fog so thick that it took a couple of minutes to dissipate before I could see out again.

Then I faced another problem—the sun had risen, and the Brits wouldn't let me land until after sunset. The tanker could return to Mildenhall, but I couldn't.

That's the day I spent staring at Ireland. I set up an orbit just south of Ireland, flying at 45,000 feet, the maximum altitude allowed without a pressure suit. I stayed there all day long, drilling many, many holes in the sky. I watched the sun come up, pass overhead, and slowly start to descend. Fortunately England is at a northern latitude, and its winter days were relatively short. I was finally able to land in another six hours.

It turned out my pressure suit controller was defective. It was the only failure of a controller in the history of that pressure suit. To its credit, when it failed, it failed to the safe position, providing an abundance of life-saving pressure instead of deflating the suit.

Back on the ground in England, the weather turned sour again, and we returned to the previous routine. It was really frustrating. We remained in England for 2-1/2 weeks. At one point SAC Headquarters considered having me fly from England direct to California, bypassing the US east coast. That would have been a flight of more than 5,000 miles with a flight time well in excess of ten hours. They ultimately decided against it, deeming it an unnecessary risk. I applauded that decision.

I remained in perpetual crew rest, going through the same repetitive steps daily. One night the forecast looked particularly bad, and we had given up hopes of launching the next day. Our officers had rooms in the Officers Mess at Mildenhall, and that afternoon two Irish ladies set up a concession in the lobby selling Irish knit sweaters. I talked them up and learned they were transiting through with nothing to do that night. I was tempted to tell them how I had just stared down at their homeland for the entire bloody day and now hated Irish green with a passion, but thought the better of that.

Our flight surgeon was a full colonel and had a VIP suite in the mess, so after dinner the ladies joined us for a party in Doc Nash's rooms. (Doctor Nash was a noted brain surgeon, listed in Who's Who in America; he—and two other physicians I knew—left it all to join the Air Force in frustration over the current spate of widespread malpractice litigation.)

The party was a good time with all enjoying the company away from our homes. The Doc's suite had a furnished wet bar, and drinks flowed. But despite the dire weather forecast and no hopes of flying, I was still alone in my crew rest, abstaining from the booze.

It was considerably later than my usual bedtime when I was the first to call it quits. I went to my room and arranged for my usual wakeup call. That would give me but 2-1/2 hours sleep. The others didn't get nearly that much. Our navigator, Ned, stumbled into bed after arranging a call to wake him in 25 minutes.

166

I got up as usual, plunged over to the chow hall, ate, and waited. In they came, as usual. Ron sat down, looked me square in the face with severely bloodshot eyes and said, "We're going." Of course I didn't believe him. It took several minutes before I realized he was serious. The weather had inexplicably broken—so much for the science of meteorology.

Our team was really hurting. Ron asked me very seriously if I felt okay to fly, and I said I was fine.

I took off just before sunrise, followed by the tanker. It was nine hours to Pease AFB in New Hampshire. Ron kept calling me on the radio to ask how I was. I think he was worried. I really didn't get sleepy to the point of nodding off, but I was really tired. Ron's periodic checkup calls stopped coming. After quite a while I got another radio call, but this time it was from the tanker pilot, not Ron. He asked how I was, and I replied, Okay. I asked how things were down there and he described that Ron and the guys were in really bad shape, all sacked out in the back of the tanker. They stayed that way until we coasted-in at Newfoundland.

There's nothing to see crossing the Atlantic. I thought of Lindberg, briefly. I saw white things below, but at my altitude it was impossible to tell if they were icebergs, huge waves, or simply clouds. I was glad to finally see Newfoundland and head down the eastern coast.

I landed at Pease late in the afternoon, exhausted. It takes a while to bed down a U-2, so it was almost an hour before we left the flight line and headed to our quarters. I got into my room, stripped down and threw myself into bed. I fell asleep instantly. Not long afterward there was pounding on my door. The guys wanted me to get up for a handball game. Easy for them to do—they had slept the entire time crossing the Atlantic. I went along (I shouldn't have), but after trying to play for a while, I just gave up and slumped in the back of the court. I went back to my room and back to sleep, but not for long. There was pounding on the door again—Get up, we're playing poker. I got up. After poker it was off for an east coast lobster dinner.

I have no idea when I finally got to my room—I was obliterated. The next morning Don flew the U-2 and the rest of us hopped in the tanker, headed back to California with a cooler full of lobsters.

As I said earlier, the U-2 could fly forever on a tank of gas. The official description of the airplane's flying endurance says, "Limited by pilot endurance." I learned a lot about pilot endurance on that trip.

## It's Nice to Be Alone

Besides interminable flight endurance, the U-2 also flew above the area of positive control (the APC), which now extends up to 60,000 feet. The APC is that region in which Air Traffic Controllers direct and control most flying under FAA rules. It's noisy with all the radio chatter. To me it was always a pleasure to climb above 60 grand, leaving the APC below and saying good-bye to the controllers. There's nobody else up that high except for the occasional experimental airplane or rocket. The astronauts sure aren't flying there. (My observation is that astronauts are essentially space cargo, not pilots— but that opens an entirely different discussion.)

The airspace above 60,000 feet is uncontrolled. You go wherever you want, undirected. When climbing above the APC the controller assigns you to a special discrete radio frequency that is only used by us high-flyers. It's really quiet up there.

I took off from Beale on a routine training flight one day. Once I climbed above the APC, I was cleared by Sacramento Center to continue under "Visual Flight Rules on Top"—essentially saying to me, "Begone. There's no one else up there but you, and I'm busy."

I headed east on my practice route. I cut across Nevada, Colorado, and into Kansas. By now I expected Air Traffic Control to call and hand me off to the Denver Center, but no one called. I continued south into Oklahoma and Texas, expecting another hand-off to Fort Worth Center, but again no one called. I came across New Mexico, into Arizona and then entered southern California. Still no call from ATC. I turned north over California.

168

I was having a pretty good time—the view of the western states was stunning, all was dead quiet, and I was enjoying one of those surreal times that only U-2 pilots can experience—long hours of solitude and peaceful bliss, literally on top of the world with all the world's weather, people, and mayhem below me.

Unfortunately, it was time to end my reverie. My mission was about six hours in its entirety, and it was time to go home. So I called Los Angeles Center. They asked, "Who are you?" So I told them. They hadn't seen me on radar, and they had no idea I was coming. The controller quickly handed me off to Sacramento Center, who also asked who I was. These guys had completely lost and forgotten me— amazing! That was fine, though. I was perfectly happy to be out of their clutches above the APC, but now it was time to descend, return home, and join all the radio chatter and air traffic below. But what a pleasant flight that had been!

## A Visit to Japan

There are three things I hate: Pyorrhea, gonorrhea, and KO-rea— or so the old joke goes. I don't really hate Korea, although I have every reason to after a couple of disconcerting events that occurred while flying there.

After delivering a U-2 to our Black Cat detachment in Osan, I returned several months later for a routine, two-month temporary duty assignment. The detachment flew its U-2s from Osan Air Base day and night along the DMZ to gather intelligence against the always-mercurial and hostile North Koreans.

It was winter, and nothing is colder than Korea in winter. Absolutely nothing. Especially when the heat goes out, and that's what happened. The furnace in our barracks busted and it took two weeks to fix it. The outside daytime temperatures never got out of the teens, and at night it dropped well below zero. Inside it was hardly any warmer. To go to sleep I layered-up in long underwear, pants, two

169

shirts, a sweater, winter jacket, boots, multiple blankets, and a ski hat. With all that I still shivered all night.

The weather wasn't only bitter cold, it was snowy and unpredictable. Winter weather over the Korean Peninsula sweeps in from the cold, continental mainland of China, picking up moisture from crossing the Yellow Sea. That moisture is deposited as snow and ice upon reaching Korea. The Chinese weren't disposed to share their weather information with us, so we were often surprised by ferocious storms.

I took off in clear weather one morning before sunrise. The weather people hadn't predicted anything unusual. As the sun rose, I looked back onto the Korean peninsula and saw a blanket of white. A storm had hit sometime after my takeoff and deposited considerable snow. All day wave after wave of heavy snow continued to be pushed onto Korea by strong winds. The snow removal effort at Osan and other Korean air bases couldn't keep up. Detachment operations kept me informed of the progress—or rather lack of progress. As darkness came it became increasingly unlikely that I would be able to land at Osan. Even worse, all Korean airfields were in the same dilemma.

Decision time came. I couldn't land anywhere in Korea and I was nearing "bingo fuel"—the minimum fuel needed to fly to an alternate airfield. Our detachment commander told me to head for my alternate, which was Tachikawa Air Base in Japan where the US Air Force flew F-4s.

There were several problems with this plan. Of course, I had never flown there, and I was flying at night with no visual references and complete cloud cover below. I was tired—I had already been flying more than ten hours. Although the US and Japan had a diplomatic agreement in case of airplane emergency, it was untried and untested, especially for an airplane headed inbound from South Korea. No one in Japan's air defense system knew I was coming. To cap it off I was flying the notorious U-2 spy plane, and foreign nations had particular reasons for not wanting to have any association with the Dragon Lady. It was entirely possible the Japanese might refuse me entry into their airspace, as others have.

As I left South Korean airspace and headed for Japan, I signed off radio contact with Osan. I carried an emergency navigation card in my navigation package and dug it out. It had a radio frequency for Japanese air traffic control, so I called. An English-speaking Japanese controller responded. I gave him my call sign and explained I was an American aircraft headed for Tachikawa because of the weather in Korea. He was hesitant, but then seemed helpful. He put me on a heading toward Tachikawa and then asked me to identify what kind of airplane I was.

Alarm bells went off—I knew that to broadcast that I was flying a U-2 would likely cause international repercussions, so I said I was unable to tell him. He persisted, and I clung to my refusal. His voice was getting particularly testy, and although he now gave me permission to descend into Japanese airspace, I could tell he was getting very insistent.

As I descended in the pitch black I was getting low on fuel. I had no choices left. From the tenor of my Japanese controller's voice, I knew there would be armed Japanese fighters below waiting to intercept me. Whether they would shoot to bring me down or not, I just didn't know. They would certainly not be able to visually identify my black airplane in the dark, and besides the U-2 had no visible aircraft markings. To the uninitiated, an unmarked U-2 looks very sinister.

I was worried. My terse stalemate with the controller continued with long pauses between radio conversations. I knew that the entire Japanese air defense system must have been fully alerted to my approach.

But then there was an exceptionally long pause. When the controller came back up he asked me once more for the umpteenth time to repeat my call sign, which I did. With a friendly voice as smooth as silk, he gave me specific directions to the radar approach at Tachikawa and politely asked if I needed any assistance. This complete change in his voice and demeanor told me that the diplomatic breakthrough between our countries had finally come through. He now knew who I was and all was peachy. Whew!

I made a straight-in approach and touched down at Tachi. But when a U-2 lands the very first procedure is for the ground crew, waiting in a truck, to drive up and insert a pogo under each wing. Without those wing wheels, a U-2 can't taxi. I seem to recall leaving my pogos on the runway at Osan half a day ago.

Not knowing where to go, I stopped right away and waited. My heavier left wingtip fell to the runway. That causes more fuel to gravity-flow into that wing, making it super-heavy. Soon I was approached by a large assortment of vehicles and men that had been waiting for me on both sides of the runway. The people had no idea what to do with this funny-looking airplane with its bicycle landing gear, tilted with one wingtip on the ground.

The Tachi Wing Commander introduced himself on the radio; I'm sure my arrival had interrupted his sleep that night. I explained what had to be done—someone had to lift the heavy wing and weigh down the light wing while I slowly taxied to the hangar. Although I had very little fuel remaining and the wing tanks were relatively light, there was still a lot of weight in that left wing. It took several guys working very hard to carry that wing about a mile to the hangar as I taxied as slowly as I could. As wing-walkers got tired and dropped out, others replaced them. It was a terrible ordeal.

I pulled in at the hangar and shut down. Normally there's a crew chief to help the pilot in his bulky pressure suit, but no one at Tachi knew anything about that. I climbed down the shaky ladder they provided and was greeted by the wing commander. I was visibly fatigued and remember my difficulty in simply walking inside. He looked concerned and was very helpful. I told them how to bed-down the bird, and they were soon in touch with the folks back at Osan.

I really don't remember much about the rest of what happened. Immense fatigue does that. I just remember that the wing commander gave me one of his own flight suits to wear after I got out of the pressure suit. I looked at the rank on my shoulders—I was a colonel!

By the time I was taken to quarters I learned that Japan had only agreed to accept the U-2 provided it left the country by the next day. I

172

expect that decision had been made at the very top of government. Osan was sending a C-130 cargo airplane with pilot, PSD support, and a maintenance team to Japan the next day. The Japanese government directed that the U-2 be kept out of sight in a hangar. They wanted no publicity.

The next day I was standing around the hangar and saw a security team apprehend a photographer and strip the film out of his camera. The C-130 arrived, prepared the U-2, and pilot Jim B. flew it back to Osan while I flew back on the C-130. Afterward I learned that someone did photograph the U-2 and the picture made the front page of Japanese newspapers.


## Up in the Air With No Place to Go

After a couple days' rest back in Osan I went back to work. It was still winter, and it was still Korea, so I guess I shouldn't have been surprised at what happened next.

I took off one morning before sunrise, and as the day progressed the winds at Osan began to pick up. In fact they got quite strong. Even worse, the wind direction was all wrong, blowing 90 degrees across the runway. Far worse than that, it wasn't just Osan but the entire peninsula that was affected. The winds were gusting to over 50 knots, and since all of South Korea's major runways are pretty much oriented in the same direction, they were all experiencing exceptionally strong direct crosswinds.

The sudden storm caught everyone by surprise, emphasizing the unpredictability of Korean weather. The U-2's unique design—bicycle landing gear, tailwheel steering, large vertical tail, exceptionally long wings—makes it highly vulnerable to runway crosswinds. Its maximum crosswind limitation is a mere 15 to 20 knots. Detachment operations radioed to tell me that the Osan crosswinds had already reached 45 knots with gusts to 55.

It was too late. The crosswinds were already well beyond the aircraft's limits and wouldn't abate until the next day. All of South

Korea's airfields had the same condition. I didn't have enough fuel to go to Japan this time.

Jerry, our detachment commander, came up on the radio and gave me the inevitable news: there was no place for me to land. In a calm statement of my predicament, he said they had all evaluated the circumstances and I had a choice of either ejecting or attempting to land at Osan. He said to think about it and tell him what I wanted to do.

In all my flying life I've never had to consider ejecting until then. The pilot in command always has ultimate authority over his aircraft. What I would do was nobody's decision but mine, and Jerry made that clear. I had to decide which way I would encounter the least risk to myself. The high-value aircraft was of secondary consideration, but neither of us brought that up. First priority was to save the pilot, but there's no self-respecting pilot who wants to lose his airplane.

I hesitated only momentarily, then said I was coming back to Osan. I made a quick decision based on my instincts, but my thoughts included reasoning borne from years of flying. Ejecting during a horrific windstorm and leaving a perfectly good airplane to fall to earth God-knows-where didn't seem like such a good idea. I placed much more trust in my ability to land it—and land it where there would be crash and rescue support.

From years of flying the U-2 I had reasoned that in an emergency it could be landed in stronger crosswinds than the flight manual's restrictions. With the U-2's unique bicycle landing gear, the pilot actually balances the aircraft's wings during landing, but I figured if he purposely dragged a wingtip the friction and aircraft tilt would help counteract the airplane's tendency to weathervane and help keep it on the runway. Of course the wingtip would be damaged by doing that, but there was going to be damage no matter what I tried.

As I descended I dumped excess fuel and planned how to make the landing. The runway at Osan was all mine—no one else was flying, of course. The crosswind was coming from the right, so the airplane would weathervane sharply to the right and likely go off the right side of the runway. I planned to land using half flaps to reduce the weathervaning tendency. I'd pop up the lift spoilers and stall the airplane completely—removing almost all lift—landing very firmly and touching down the tailwheel first. I'd place the airplane on the left side of the runway, to the left of runway's crown. Immediately upon touchdown I'd crank the control wheel full left, using full roll spoilers and ailerons to push the left wingtip skid onto the runway with full force. I would use the friction of the dragging wingtip to help turn the airplane left and counteract weathervaning to the right.

It was a completely unpredictable maneuver. I knew there was a strong potential for going off the runway.

As I made my approach, Jerry and my mobile controller, Big Al, were waiting in the mobile chase car. Fire trucks and ambulances were lined up along either side of the runway and I briefly saw other vehicles, too. I'm not sure, but I think Jerry asked if I wanted the runway foamed for fire prevention, and I said no to that. I was afraid the slippery foam would neutralize the wingtip drag I was counting on. I told them that I was going to make a low approach first, then come around and do the real thing.

The winds were incredibly strong and gusty. My bird was bouncing all over the place, and it was a real effort to control it. I was already exhausted from my all-day flight. I had to use extra airspeed so I didn't inadvertently stall between the gusts.

As I approached the runway I took measure of the strength of the crosswind. It was every bit as strong as I was told. Winds are a little less as you fly closer to the ground, so I brought my wheels down to about ten feet above the runway. I made no attempt at that time to point my nose down the runway as I would for the actual landing. I was in a severe crab—flying almost sideways with the nose pointing about 45-50 degrees to the right of runway centerline.

That panicked Al. As my bouncing airplane came lower with its nose pointed far to the right, he feared I might land in that attitude, so he started screaming in the radio, "Go around! Go around!" That was ridiculous. I had no more fuel, no place to go, and I'm planning for a crash landing. There's only one guy in charge at this point, and it's me. I ignored him, of course, and continued to feel-out what the winds were like with Al still screaming in my ear.

I powered away, climbed, and came back around to make the landing. It seemed strange to be flying the airplane sideways in relation to the ground. On the short final approach I was severely crabbing to the right. I descended to where my wheels were within a couple of feet from the runway and raised the lift spoilers, which kill lift and cause the airplane to drop. As the airplane stalled and just before the wheels touched, I kicked in full left rudder, causing the nose to veer sharply left. For only a moment the aircraft was almost aligned with the runway's centerline before it began to swing back to the right. The wheels were on the ground, and at that moment I rotated the control wheel fully to the left, planting the left wingtip hard onto the pavement. The wing bent, but the wingtip stayed on the runway, thank goodness.

With the left wingtip dragging hard, the airplane skidded and tilted to the left of runway centerline, counteracting the crosswinds. As the airplane slowed I was suddenly presented with a problem I hadn't thought of—the possibility that my dragging wingtip would pull me off the runway's LEFT side. I was afraid to raise the left wing for fear the crosswind would grab me again and send me off the right side, so I just left it dragging until the airplane stopped, sort of sideways. It went incredibly well, and of course I'm very much here today, telling this story.

I never departed the runway, and there was no major damage except to the left wingtip skid and some scraped tires. Incredibly, the left wing didn't wipe out any of the left side runway lights, either. The fire trucks and ambulances surrounded the airplane until we determined all was okay and gave them a thumbs-up.

We were all sporting nervous grins at that point. One of our crew chiefs came up and beckoned for me to look at that left wingtip. The steel alloy plate on the skid bottom was completely gone, and most of the skid's support structure had been ground off.

The bird was saved, and I was relieved, spent, and still pumping adrenaline. The funny thing is that all along I really believed I could

176

do it—that the airplane could be landed that way. Now, when I relive that experience I remember two things in particular: First I remember proving that the U-2 could be landed in far worse crosswinds than were assumed. Second, I remember chewing Al's butt for screaming in my headset as I was trying to assess the situation.

Al worked for me as an evaluator at that time. Unfortunately, that ended when he lost his life in a U-2 crash within that year.

## Tragedy

Back at Beale I came to work one morning. Hector had been promoted to Wing Commander. He and Dave Pinsky, the Vice Wing Commander, drew me into Hector's office and told me that Al was dead. Moreover, others had died, too.

Al was flying at our operating location in Cyprus. Because of diplomatic sensitivities, our pilots had to make a left turn immediately after takeoff to avoid overflying Cypriot lands adjacent to the British base. Al had taken off and immediately made a sharp turn to the left—too sharp. A U-2 heavily loaded with equipment and fuel is not a sports car, and it must be flown with care. Al's turn placed the airplane in an aerodynamic condition peculiar to the U-2's long wing, fuel-laden design. His turn caused one wing to stall, and as the airplane further veered left, there was simply no way for it to recover. It hit the tower and then crashed into the nearby weather shack, killing Al and several Brits. It was a sad affair, made worse because it was unnecessary and avoidable.

Al's remains were returned to Beale. Following the memorial service downtown, a motorcade brought his remains out to Beale. With Becky and the two boys watching, I was given his ashes and placed them in the speed brake well of a waiting U-2. The speed brakes were closed and pilot Dave flew the bird high over the Pacific, popped the speed brakes, and Al's ashes were gone.

The history of the U-2 was often marred by tragic events. The risks were high, and many, many accidents occurred. The risks were especially profound in the early days when U-2 pilots were essentially flying an experimental airplane at altitudes no one had ever flown before, wearing experimental pressure suits and going where adversaries tried to shoot them down.

There are many stories of U-2 accidents, many of them fatal. When I began my U-2 training I studied all the prior accidents. They were compiled in a big binder several inches thick and were heavily redacted to hide the most classified parts.

I accepted those hazards as part of the job. Knowing the dangers, I still thoroughly enjoyed what I was doing. I knew what we did was a tradeoff between the risks and the importance of intelligence we collected. Our work contributed directly and importantly to the national defense, but that didn't always weigh on my mind. Even very special work becomes somewhat ordinary when you do it routinely and frequently.


## Showdown

Of course, U-2 pilots had a certain swagger. I never learned whether the ego came before the job or as a result of it, but whatever the sequence, a somewhat enlarged ego was a part of a U-2 pilot's uniform. It wasn't a boastful type of ego given to showmanship and ostentation; it was just a quiet sense of self-satisfaction that said to everyone else, "I can do this. You can't."

When the U-2s merged with the SR-71 Blackbirds at Beale there was a predictable clash of egos. Big egos.

The SR was the highest-flying, fastest operational airplane in the world. Its pilots and reconnaissance systems officers (RSOs) weren't just screened volunteers, they were hand-picked. But on the other side U-2 pilots flew solo, not as a two-man crew: "alone, unarmed, and unafraid," as the saying goes—with emphasis on the alone part.

U-2s didn't have a GIB. Their pilots didn't have split personalities, either. . . . Well, most of them didn't.

Each aircraft type was unique. Each was flown by volunteers, carefully screened for talent. Each program had a remarkable history and reputation, and the crews and support personnel all had pride in their aircraft and mission.

As it happened, the U-2 outlasted the SR-71. The SR-71s were retired from active service, victims of cost cuts to the Air Force budget and the onset of new satellite capabilities. The SR-71 aircrews and support people rightly hold their heads high because they, the aircraft, and their accomplishments are hallowed in aviation history.

Meanwhile the U-2 continues to fly in the Air Force today— thoroughly modernized and adapted to modern warfare and its reconnaissance needs.

But egos are egos. In the 1970s the U-2s and their operators moved from Arizona to California, merging with the Blackbirds at their home, the 9th Strategic Reconnaissance Wing at Beale AFB. Although each reconnaissance program flew and operated independently for the most part, they shared many common facilities—including the Officers Club.

The SR-71 and U-2 programs merged and the egos clashed. A face-off was coming, and it happened one night at Beale's Officers Club bar.

Officers and spouses from both camps were gathered there on a festive Friday evening. Somehow a challenge was issued and accepted. The weapon of choice was the yard of ale.

By tradition, when a pilot first solos the U-2 he's called upon to drink a yard of ale. The "yard" is a long glass tube that holds about 3-1/2 cans of beer. It was supposed to be downed in one continuous gulp; less capable gulpers had to pause for air or to uncross their eyeballs. In time it became a contest to see who could drink it the fastest. Bets were made and champions emerged. There were also dismal failures, like me (I think my throat was too small).

179

So on this night at the O Club the U-2 and SR sides squared off and selected champions to defend their honor. Everyone gathered around. Several one-on-one contests ensued, narrowing the victors down to our very best against theirs. We had Big Al, and we were confident. Amid raucous cheers they tilted up their yards, and Al won. Contest over.

But just to be sure no one would ever question the result, we put our biggest contender up for one more contest. "Muff" was even a larger body than Big Al, but Muff didn't drink alcohol. So in a bizarre contest, Muff filled his yard up with Coca-Cola and went up against the Blackbird champ, drinking beer. Everyone gasped as Muff simply poured the yard down his gaping throat without taking swallows. The contest was over in a flash, leaving everyone amazed that someone could actually consume a yard of Coca-Cola, let alone drink it that fast. It was like downing a jug of pure acid with sugar added for taste.

I'm not sure that night settled the contest of egos at Beale, but it sure established who was the King of Coke.

While at Beale I was given my first command assignment. The former Advanced Location Strike System (ALSS) program from prior years had morphed into the Precision Location Strike System which then became a mature intelligence collection system implanted in the R Model. The new system was intended for use in Europe should the USSR ever attempt a land invasion, so a single U-2 was deployed to RAF Mildenhall in England for an in-theater trial. It was a 90-day deployment, and a fellow U-2 pilot and I split the commander responsibilities. He took the first 45 days, and I took the second. I commanded about 65 people in all.

It was good experience, and I mark it as a bridge to my changing role in the U-2 program. I was acquiring other job responsibilities that slowly removed me from purely flying the airplane into greater leadership roles.

Nothing unusual occurred in the operation itself, but there was one personnel incident. Our navigator brought his wife over there at his expense for the 90-day deployment. That was fine, but he and she indulged in some heavy drinking. The previous deployment commander did nothing about it, although when I arrived and took over, others indicated to me their concerns.

One day after we finished up and locked up, we headed to the other side of the airfield to file our flight plan for the next day and check the weather. I drove my car, and the nav drove the station wagon. When we got to the other side and hopped out, I already smelled the alcohol on his breath. I noticed he had put a case of beer in the wagon. These were government vehicles, we were on duty, and there's no room for drinking on duty. I called him out on it. He admitted to "having a sip," and I gave him firm warning. He was under my spyglass for the remainder of the deployment.

I tell this story because it fits into my own story quite well. In my experience the largest concerns of commanders are the people themselves. Good people do good work; people problems undercut the organization and mission accomplishment. In succeeding years of multiple commands, I spent an inordinate amount of time and energy on people issues.

To finish this story, the navigator and his wife both drank themselves to early deaths. She died first, he went into heavy drinking and mourning, and not long afterward he died, too.

# The Pentagon, Phase I

I stayed at Beale a year and a half. I was a major, and the Air Force wanted me to take another position—a career progression move which is part of being a military officer in the "up or out" system. I was assigned to the Pentagon as a staff action officer in the Joint Reconnaissance Center (JRC) within the Office of the Joint Chiefs of Staff. It was reconnaissance work, but now I would be dealing with all the armed services and their reconnaissance aircraft.

The JRC acts as the link between worldwide reconnaissance operations and the Joint Staff in the Pentagon. Unarmed reconnaissance ("recce") vehicles—airplanes, mostly, but also submarines—patrol the world's hot spots and get quite close to our adversaries. If an adversary wants to indicate their pique at the US, there's nothing easier than picking off a recce airplane. That's how the first U-2 was shot down along with a number of other reconnaissance aircraft afterward. The JRC was established to cut through the layers of Washington bureaucracy for a quick response in the event of such an international emergency, and it keeps a 24-hour, worldwide watch on recce missions for that purpose.

I worked three years at the JRC. The first year was on the Watch, the next two at a desk doing staff projects related to recce projects. I spent a lot of time writing memoranda of various procedures for approval up through the Joint Chiefs. Like it or not, writing formal Memoranda of Procedure documents became my specialty.

The JRC was linked with the individual services, the intelligence agencies, and Department of State. I attended meetings at CIA, NSA, DIA and State on occasion. During the Iran embassy hostage crisis, I was JRC representative to the Joint Staff Crisis Action Team. Various episodes and incidents related to recce aircraft occurred, and I worked on those projects. For instance, when Libya attacked our RC-135 reconnaissance aircraft over international waters in the

Mediterranean, I became project officer for the resolution of that. While at the JRC I was promoted to lieutenant colonel.


## Sailing, Sailing

I was still the life-long bachelor, and when I arrived in the Washington area I roomed with Chuck Crabb, a fellow U-2 pilot who had preceded me in his assignment to the JRC. When I got there Chuck's first words to me were, "Where's your sailboat?" True, my big hobby back at Beale and in Tucson was sailing. I had owned several trailerable sailboats and sailed the lakes in Arizona (yes, there are lakes in the desert). After moving to Beale I sailed the Sacramento River delta region north of San Francisco. But rather than drag my sailboat coast to coast I sold it before moving to Washington.

Chuck was disappointed, and before long we agreed to go in together on buying a sailboat. I was the long-time sailor, so the deal was that I would find us a boat and give Chuck sailing lessons.

A new officer to the JRC is assigned as a Watch Officer for the first year. As Watch Officer I worked rotating shifts. Chuck and the other established staff officers did day work while a Watch Officer and NCO were teamed to staff the JRC watch console day and night. My shift schedule was two 12-hour days followed by two nights, then four days off. My days off gave me time to find us a sailboat.

Although Chuck was just learning to sail, he had definite ideas about what kind of boat we needed. I envisioned buying about a 15-foot, small daysailer to ply the waters of the Potomac River near Washington, but Chuck quickly established other requirements. First he said it needed an auxiliary motor because he wasn't sure he'd be able to get in and out of a marina under sail. I understood that—sure. Then he said we needed lots of deck space. I asked, "Why?" He answered, "For the ladies to lounge in their Bikinis, of course." My God, that made good sense—and I was left wondering why I hadn't thought of it.

183

And, he said, it needs to have a bathroom. Chuck was notorious for having certain "bathroom" needs when flying the U-2, so I understood his requirement—but I reminded him that on boats and ships it's called a "head," not a "bathroom." His first sailing lesson would be about nautical terminology.

Over the upcoming days, Chuck's list of "needs" was growing, demanding a more sizeable boat. It was apparent we were now looking for something to sail on the Chesapeake Bay, not the Potomac River. One day Chuck announced that we needed to have one of those big, colorful sails up front. I said, "Do you mean a spinnaker?" He said, "Yes, that's it. I want one of those." As I reminded Chuck it's called the bow, not "up front," I realized we're now talking about buying a bigger boat.

He dropped another bombshell the next day. He said, "Art, I don't think I could stand it if other boats passed us by. Our boat needs to be really fast." At this point I'm just nodding my head, wondering how I'm going to pull it off.

I figured we should set a budget. I certainly wasn't endowed with great finances, and Chuck was pretty parsimonious, too. When I brought up the subject of affordability Chuck said he could see spending ten thousand. I mulled it over and thought, maybe we could find such a boat if we each chipped in ten grand. Chuck quickly said, "I mean ten thousand TOTAL!"

So I set out on my quest, thinking it was nearly impossible. I looked at newspaper ads, personal ads, and inquired around nautical shops. No luck—not even close. I was seeing the futility of our project and decided to drive over to Annapolis. I walked the docks, eyeballing the many large, rich yachts that are quintessential Annapolis. There was nothing there for us, of course.

Discouraged, I turned my back on the place and headed for my car when I happened to notice a mast sticking up from off the side of a dock. I wandered over and looked down. Below was a neat, small sailboat with a For Sale sign stuck to the mast. The owner stood aboard, and I called down to him. He came up and we talked. He had been the sole owner of the boat from when it was first built. The boat was a genuine Alberg design (super fast), a 23-foot Sea Sprite, Hull Number 3. It was prim and sleek with classic lines and a fiberglass hull with nice teakwood trim. It had an auxiliary outboard motor, a red spinnaker, deck space, and—most importantly—a head.

The owner explained he was selling his boat because he had just bought a new 35-footer being delivered from Taiwan. He had just retired from the CIA. I told him I was a U-2 guy, and we connected. He said he was retiring because Jimmy Carter had sent Stansfield Turner to the CIA and Turner was axing senior CIA officials left and right. He said Turner was making an absolute mess of the place, morale was in the slop bucket, and he didn't want to work there anymore. "How much do you want for the boat," I asked. He said, "Ten grand."

So Chuck and I bought the boat. I arranged to berth it at a marina that was the shortest driving distance between the Pentagon and the bay. Chuck's sailing lessons didn't go as smooth as that Alberg we bought, but that's not a story for here. Still, we enjoyed our boat, the sailing was grand, and it provided a needed respite from that pressure cooker called The Pentagon. And when we first took it out we came up against a very speedy Cal 25 cutting across the bay. We beat him.

### It's the White House Calling

Twelve-hour watch officer shifts were brutal, but four days off were nice, even if one of them was consumed by just catching up on sleep. A year of that is just about enough.

My NCO and I were on duty one night, alone in the JRC. I had only arrived there a few weeks earlier. The watch console was equipped with myriad phones of all kinds and with scopes where we could visually monitor worldwide reconnaissance missions. If anything unusual happened we'd be among the first to know about it. Because we were intermediaries in this classified reconnaissance linkage, some of our phones provided secure, encrypted communications. We also had direct, no-dial hotlines going to all the pertinent intelligence and government agencies.

185

We were at a dull point during this night's watch when a phone rang. It was the secure hotline connecting us with the White House Situation Room. That got my attention fast. I picked up the phone and the other end introduced himself as David Aaron, President Carter's special advisor. He said, "Major, I want you to launch an SR-71 over Cuba tomorrow." I was new to the JRC, but I already knew that it would take an act of God to launch a Blackbird that quickly. However, I bit my tongue and said I'd start to work on it and would get back to him.

The head of the JRC was a rear admiral. Admiral Fuller lived at Andrews AFB in Maryland. He had recently arrived, and I knew he didn't have a secure phone installed in his home yet. So I stepped next door to the National Military Command Center where a brigadier general was in charge. I apprised the general of Aaron's call, and he began stirring the pot.

Before long he had arranged a secure conference call to discuss the matter. The secure telephone operator convened the conference call. She polled the conferees individually: the NMCC's general, the Secretary of Defense, the Commander-in-Chief of Strategic Air Command, the 3-star Director of Operations for the Joint Staff, Mr. David Aaron . . . and Major Saboski. I thought that was kinda neat. After only three weeks in town I'm on the phone with all the big wigs of national defense on a late night phone call. I had arrived!

This incident happened during the purgatory period between President Reagan's election and his inauguration. While in office Carter had unilaterally stopped the high-flying SR-71 overflights that had long monitored Cuba. He had thrown Castro an olive branch, and Castro had thrown it back.

The next day my boss came to work. During our morning briefing he grinned and said, "And here's Major Art Saboski, who last night told Jimmy Carter to go to hell." Not exactly, but I wish I had.

To finish the story, Carter was leaving office, and he was miffed that his good will overture to Castro had produced no results, so he was turning the Blackbird switch back on. Of course you can't launch an SR-71 overnight—so it launched two days later.

## Rear Admiral Fuller

An interesting side note: Rear Admiral Fuller had been a prisoner of war in Vietnam. He had been shot down flying a Navy A-4, and in the process both his shoulders were dislocated. His North Vietnamese captors denied him medical treatment. As a result, his shoulders were forever narrowed, and when he stood he kept his arms folded to relieve the chronic pain.

Admiral Fuller was hosting a delegation of Soviet Union admirals in his home for a Law of the Sea conference. Fuller had no love for the Soviets, our staunch adversaries, so the good admiral had some fun with them. Every day he'd come in and tell us of some little trick he pulled. It kept us in stitches. Like this one: The meeting was convened in his home's conference room that faced the sun all morning. Just for fun, he placed the Soviet delegation on the sunny side and raised the blinds so they faced blinding sun half the day. I think Fuller had learned well about subtle torture while he was imprisoned.

## Change of Life

All my Pentagon work paled when I experienced the biggest event of my life –I met Eileen.

I enjoyed the live jazz that abounded in the Washington area. My condo south of the Pentagon in Virginia wasn't too far from a nice restaurant that featured live jazz in their upstairs lounge. I headed there one night, ensconced myself at one end of the bar, and settled back to enjoy. I noticed a very pretty lady sitting quietly at the other end. My antenna went up even more when I observed that her date wasn't paying her the attention she deserved, leaving her to sit alone. I moved down there, introduced myself, and sat down to talk. The jazz was nice, but she was nicer. Her date was coming back, so I asked if I could call her. Eileen gave me her number, and that began the biggest change in my life.

Eileen and I began dating and I liked her a lot. She had been married before, and her teenage son, David, was living with her in an apartment not far from me. Our relationship grew, and I visited her family in western Pennsylvania—a fine family, nice parents.

My Pentagon assignment was coming to end, and I learned I was to be assigned as Commander of our U-2 detachment in Cyprus. I was to become the first permanent duty commander, succeeding previous commanders who had served on short-term, temporary duty (TDY) assignments. The operation was called Project Olive Harvest. I was assigned to be there on a one-year, unaccompanied tour of duty. Unaccompanied—meaning no Eileen, no David.

I had reached a turning point in my life. I had just met the finest lady I had known just as I was preparing to leave the country for a year. I had a decision to make. I might brag that I was firm and decisive, but I wasn't. It would have been easy to give in to my entrenched bachelor ways, but I knew this was different. It was actually Eileen who suggested we were right for each other. Her words made me think in a different way, and I sort of woke up to that reality. I proposed and she accepted. Then we faced the daunting obstacle of my upcoming year in Cyprus.

We made our plans. Halfway through the year I was scheduled to return stateside for two weeks to attend a Commanders' Conference at Beale. The conference was actually a pretext to give me a mid-year break. We planned to marry and honeymoon during that time.

I was also told that upon completing my year in Cyprus my return assignment would be to attend the Air War College for a year, so we would be heading to Air University in Montgomery, Alabama. David was of age and decided he wouldn't join us there.

It's not easy to plan an engagement and wedding when you're 6,000 miles and many time zones apart. It would be difficult, but we felt we could make it work. Off I went to Cyprus.

# Olive Harvest

Project Olive Harvest was spawned by Secretary of State Henry Kissinger's shuttle diplomacy to insure hostilities didn't rekindle following the Yom Kippur War of 1973 involving Israel, Egypt, and Syria. The US brokered peace agreements between Israel-Egypt and Israel-Syria. Key to keeping those peace pacts was photographic proof of the adversaries' actions and movements on the battlefields: the Sinai Peninsula and the Golan Heights. US reconnaissance imagery was provided to the belligerents to verify any claims of skullduggery. At first American SR-71 Blackbirds flying long distance from England by way of Gibraltar provided that imagery. But the complexity and costs of recurring Blackbird flights from England were prohibitive. The better answer was to station a U-2 at the British air base at Akrotiri, Cyprus. Olive Harvest was crucial to Middle East peace and Israel's survival, and it worked.

So began Project Olive Harvest. The two peace agreements— Israel-Syria and Israel-Egypt—were separate and distinct. For each agreement the U-2 had a window of opportunity to fly the agreed route over the Golan Heights and over the Sinai Peninsula. If cloud cover or other exigencies caused cancelation of the Olive Harvest mission during the window, we had to wait until the next window arrived on the calendar.

The Olive Harvest U-2 took off from Cyprus and approached the coast-in point. The pilot had to judge whether the route ahead was sufficiently clear of intervening clouds to allow photography. If the pilot judged there was too much cloud cover, he was to abort the mission before reaching a certain point and return to Cyprus. Once he crossed that decision point, the mission was considered complete whether the photography was successful or not.

All parties were suspicious of each other. All nations agreed not to attempt to shoot down a U-2 while flying within the schedule dates. However, our pilots were very cautious. We carried sensors on board that provided warning if an air defense radar illuminated us or a missile fire control radar locked-on, which was prelude to a missile launch. If that happened our pilots were instructed to take defensive countermeasures and abort the mission. I remember getting indications that they were tracking me on radar, but I was never locked-onto by fire control radar from a missile battery.

Keeping the Olive Harvest U-2 in Cyprus had attendant benefits: we also utilized the U-2 to fly other missions that gathered intelligence across the entire Middle East. The Cyprus U-2 was exceptionally productive, valuable both for its peacekeeping role and for its unique intelligence role.

Later on when the disengagement hostilities had tempered, Project Olive Harvest was ended. However, it was decided to keep a U-2 in Cyprus for the longer term, and our detachment was renamed as Detachment 3 of the 9th Strategic Reconnaissance Wing. I was its first commander. U-2s operating from Cyprus have since flown—and are flying—over the Middle East in support of US involvement in the wars in Iraq and Syria.

When I first arrived in 1976, Cyprus was a divided country following a civil war between the Turkish north and the Greek south. There were still anti-aircraft gun emplacements on the hilltops, and Canadians were guarding the Green Line that divided north from south under auspices of the United Nations. Cyprus was an uneasy place.

By the time I arrived as commander, the hostilities had subsided, but there was still reason to be cautious. The previous US Ambassador had been gunned down while skiing down Mount Troodos. The US Embassy in Nicosia had also come under attack. Every terrorist organization in the Middle East had an office in the nearby port city of Limassol, and there was heavy intrigue directed against the Brits and the Olive Harvest Americans.

We were told to be on guard. We wore civilian clothes and were advised not to advertise our presence. The US Ambassador directed Olive Harvest personnel to continue observing the curfew and other restrictions. We guarded our movements off base, never traveled alone, didn't stay away from base overnight, and didn't assemble more than five of us in one place when off the base.

As the new commander one of my first duties was to visit my civilian boss on the island. I drove alone the 100 miles to Nicosia to visit the embassy and meet Ambassador Ewing and his Chief of Mission. The drive was enjoyable, giving me my first opportunity to see a large part of the country. At the embassy I met and talked extensively with the ambassador. The Chief of Mission, an Army colonel, showed me the damage done to the embassy by the recent attack and briefed me on their new security installations. During that year I periodically visited the embassy and met with Ambassador Ewing for updates on the security situation affecting Olive Harvest.

A year later as my tour of duty was ending I made a last visit to Nicosia with my replacement, Jim Barrilleaux. Ambassador Ewing had invited us to meet him for breakfast at a hotel. Jim and I drove the 100 miles, arrived early at the rendezvous hotel and sat in the lobby. Aside from the desk clerk, we were alone. A man entered the lobby and took a seat on the other side of the room. I quietly pointed him out to Jim, and I was watchful.

Ambassador Ewing arrived in the embassy limo and came in alone. As the three of us headed into the café, I noticed the man from the lobby also came in. I was wary, not knowing if he was friend or foe. He sat alone in a corner table as we had a nice breakfast with the gracious and friendly ambassador. I had enjoyed a very good rapport with Mr. Ewing over the past year and always looked forward to our visits.

As we left the café the man in the corner followed. We said our farewells to Ambassador Ewing and he got into his waiting limo. The other man departed, too, and we got into my hire car for our return to Akrotiri. I pondered how the Ambassador must feel, having to be under constant guard after his predecessor had been assassinated.

There was a lot of attention focused on Project Olive Harvest. I was told that each OH mission was briefed in the White House Situation Room and the pilots were known there by name.

I had two, two-month tours of duty flying at Olive Harvest before I was assigned as the Olive Harvest commander during 1981-2. Whenever a U-2 pilot embarked from California to Cyprus he first stopped in Washington for a briefing at the National Photographic Intelligence Center of the CIA. There he learned of the latest Olive Harvest situational developments and the air defense threats he would be facing and reviewed photographs of the routes he would be flying.

For my visit I was told to wear civilian clothes and take a cab to a Washington street address. The NPIC building was surrounded by a guarded security enclosure and there were no signs or markings to identify it. I got out of the cab and gave my name to the entrance guards, and soon a man came out to escort me in. I stayed that afternoon, then left by cab to my hotel, leaving the next day for London, Rome, and Athens.

In Athens arrangements had been made for me to sidestep the usual customs procedures. I didn't know that. As I stood in the customs line, a man came up and asked that I follow him, which I did, of course. He took me out of the customs room through a locked side door. Inside were my bags. That was my first meeting with "Nick the Greek." During my travels to and from Cyprus I never learned his entire name or who he worked for.

Nick took me to the other side of the terminal where I boarded a waiting Air Force C-130 cargo aircraft that took me on to Cyprus. Upon reaching RAF Akrotiri, British Customs passed me straight to the Olive Harvest detachment. A new Olive Harvest arrival's passport was never marked—according to his passport, he was never there.

## The Joke's on Me

Working among a bunch of consummate practical jokers inevitably spawned an Olive Harvest custom: every new Olive Harvest pilot became the brunt of a practical joke. As I discovered, departing commanders heading for their wedding in the States were also easy prey for the jokesters.

I remember the arrival of one of our pilots who innocently blundered into an elaborate practical joke. Pilot John P. was a likable guy—a perfect target for a joke. John arrived on the "Charlie bird" from Athens, was introduced to me by our ops guys, and then escorted directly to British Customs. The customs guys asked for John's passport. Then they asked him why his passport hadn't been stamped in Athens. Of course John had no answer for that. Little did he know that the customs guys were in on the practical joke. Straight-faced and stern, they told John he couldn't enter the country.

Our guys marched John back to our hangar and up to me. John was perplexed and extremely apologetic, thinking he had done something extremely wrong. I expressed my dismay and said he'd have to return to California. John was crestfallen.

Our guys took him to the Charlie bird which was waiting outside our hangar with four engines running. They put his bags on the airplane while John said goodbye and climbed aboard. John never saw that another pilot had climbed through the C-130's rear ramp and removed his bags.

With John aboard, the Charlie taxied to the end of the runway and prepared to takeoff. But the Charlie's crew was in on the joke, as were the British tower operators. Just before takeoff our guys drove up to the airplane, the Charlie opened its doors, and poor John was extracted in bewilderment to the waiting car as the Charlie took off for Athens without him. Now that was an elaborate, well-planned practical joke—one for the annals.

You know, there's really nothing better than a well-conceived prank—unless you're the victim, of course. When it happened to me I never saw it coming.

Six months had passed since I left the States. Every Saturday Eileen placed an overseas call to me in my quarters (the call was cheaper that way). The long-distance calls were routed through an Athens switchboard and not always of the best sound quality, but it was our link together and hugely important to me.

As my mid-tour return to the US neared, Eileen told me of her preparations for our wedding. She's always been extremely organized and thorough, and although I rued that she had to do everything herself, I knew it was being done right. Among my people was an Air Force flight surgeon who provided medical assistance to the pilots as well as all detachment personnel. In preparation for the wedding I had provided him the required blood test to obtain the wedding license when I arrived back in Virginia. With that done, all I had to do was show up for the wedding.

The C-130 supply airplanes came from a squadron in Germany and showed up via Athens every Tuesday and Thursday. I planned to take Tuesday's Charlie to Germany, then fly a commercial flight to Washington DC and meet Eileen there. Our wedding was the following Saturday in Alexandria, Virginia, just outside Washington.

On that Tuesday morning I entered our hangar, prepared to take the Charlie when it arrived at about 1000. As I walked in my security guard at the entry said, "Sir, sorry to tell you the Charlie's not coming today." I was already on guard, and I smelled a practical joke coming. Despite the guard's insistence that it wasn't a joke, I knew better. I went into the Communications Room to make my usual check on messages, and my comm guy gave me the same story. He was about as straight-laced a human as God ever made, and I began to have doubts whether this was a joke or not. Walking into my office my sergeant repeated the message, and as the morning went on it became apparent it might be true. I called Nick the Greek in Athens, and he confirmed it—there would be no airplane coming that day. I surmised there was no way that Nick could be part of a joke, and I finally realized I was in trouble.

The aircraft had had a mechanical problem in Germany and the Olive Harvest flight was canceled. There wouldn't be another Charlie until Thursday. But my wedding was Saturday, and I needed to go to the courthouse in Virginia Friday with Eileen to get our license. Thursday's Charlie wouldn't get me there in time.

I began a frantic search for an alternative. The Brits tried everything to see if the RAF had anything that would get me off the island. Nothing worked. I was going to miss our wedding. Not

194

wanting to panic Eileen, I waited as long as I could to call her, but eventually I did, just to say there was a snag but we were working it out.

Then the miracle happened. Hearing that I was going to miss my wedding, the C-130 squadron commander in Germany put on a special flight, calling it a training mission. It would arrive Wednesday and I would arrive in Washington Thursday. I called Eileen with the news.

Wednesday morning came and I was wrapped up in last-minute things to do when I heard the roar of four big engines pulling up next to our hangar—the Charlie had arrived and began unloading supplies. Boy, was I relieved.

I busily gathered my things and prepared to leave. Just then my flight surgeon walked in holding a message. The former Marine doctor said, "Skipper, there's a problem. The Charlie just brought a message saying that authorities in Virginia won't accept your blood test because it was done at a British hospital."

He handed me the message, and that's what it said. I was floored—too wrought to notice everyone quietly gathering behind me, all grinning. The joke was on me, and I had bitten on it hard.

## My Change of Life

I was without sleep and on a different time zone when I finally arrived in Washington, but I brightened to see Eileen. After six months she looked better than ever to me, but I think my appearance shocked her. I had lost a lot of weight since she last saw me. My Cyprus job was all-consuming, and I spent long days and most evenings at it. I burned lots of calories. But a lot of that weight loss was from eating a Greek diet and exercising regularly—I felt great.

We took care of formalities at the courthouse and had a nice wedding on Saturday, getting to see my family and Eileen's. I wondered how David saw all this. On Sunday we left for California and the 9th Wing's commanders conference.

This Air Force business was quite new to Eileen, and I was still back on Cyprus time, trying to catch up. I really didn't relax until we were on the flight to California. We soon left California for our honeymoon in Arizona. It was over all too quickly. I flew back to Cyprus again and didn't see my wife for six more months.

## Back to Cyprus

The Strategic Reconnaissance Center at Strategic Air Command in Omaha was responsible for U-2 tasking and operations. The SRC wanted detachment commanders to fly the airplane on operational missions occasionally. Air Force commanders of flying units normally fly their mission aircraft, and I was no exception. For my situation I didn't see the sense in it and told them so. Because of the physiological effects of high altitude flying, U-2 pilots are required to rest with no duties for two days afterward and only ground duty on the third day.

My commander job was 7/24—I didn't have the luxury of taking time off. Besides, unlike previous TDY commanders, I was there for a full year, not three months. Over the course of a year purely occasional flying would make me seriously non-proficient—hazardous. I either had to fly more, which was impossible, or not fly at all. I won the argument, but not before I flew one more time.

Airplanes periodically undergo field maintenance tear-down inspections. Before returning the airplane to service it must be flown on a functional test flight by a qualified FCF pilot. That was me. I took off and put our bird through its paces. Everything went fine until I checked the engine fuel system. The test required switching to the emergency fuel system to insure it worked. It didn't.

My engine flamed out, which is always an attention-grabber. As the engine wound down I immediately turned back to the airfield while calling the tower. On an FCF I always made a point of remaining within gliding distance to the field just in case something like this happened. Fortunately I was able to air-start the engine using the main fuel control.

Each spring the Royal Air Force's Red Arrows limbered up for their summer season by rehearsing in Cyprus to avoid the bad weather in England. And where did they park their nine aircraft? Just outside my hangar. The noise of all those aircraft running engines came right through the hangar walls and reverberated inside my office.

Coming to Cyprus in springtime is pure fun for the Red Arrows team. They work hard, but they also enjoy the idyllic Mediterranean island with its temperate climate, a refreshing change from the dour weather back in England.

They quickly learned that the real action at Akrotiri was with the Americans. We were the only show in town, so to speak—certainly the only other flying show at Akrotiri except for two RAF rescue helicopters. My people lived in individual rooms within a "block," the English term for a long rectangular, single story building with a large, shared rest room and bath. At one end of the officers' block was our recreation room and bar. That's where the pilots mingled, and that's where the Red Arrow pilots came every afternoon. For two weeks the Red Arrows performed two aerobatic shows overhead each day. After two weeks of that everyone at Akrotiri walked around with a stiff neck.

When I first deployed to Cyprus on two-month duty tours I lived the life of the pilots—flying Olive Harvest missions and enjoying Cyprus when I wasn't. It was fun and interesting, particularly in mingling with our British hosts. Cyprus had so much ancient and historic culture to see. It abounded with Greek and Roman ruins and artifacts. We were confined to the southern, Greek-influenced part of Cyprus following the civil war and truce, but even under our curfew restrictions there was much to see and do.

Cyprus was serenely beautiful with its coastline, harbors, and resorts. We went to the nearby city of Limassol and sat next to the harbor, enjoying a beer at our waterside table. We went sightseeing to Kolossi Castle which was built by the Templar knights of the Crusade. We dined out on sumptuous Greek food cooked in quaint little local restaurants. One night a Scottish officer of the British regiment brought his bagpipes along to such a restaurant and played for us. Jamie was excellent, and neighborhood people congregated at the open windows to watch and listen.

My favorite thing to do was so simple, yet so enjoyable. Up on a hill between the two British encampments of Akrotiri and Episkopi was an ancient Roman amphitheater named The Curium. It faced the sea and had a commanding view of the southern coast. Quite beautiful. The summer sea breezes blew gently up there. Once a week the Brits set up large outdoor speakers and people from the bases brought up pillows and blankets. In the evening with the sun already down they played gentle classical music for three hours straight. The starlit night sky was usually perfectly clear, and there were no other sounds. It was magnificent.

## The Way We Were

The British Sovereign Base Area (SBA) consists of three major areas at Akrotiri, Episkopi and Dhekelia, plus some smaller military properties. All are under British ownership and administration, not the Cypriot government's. The Commander of British Forces Cyprus, a two-star general (RAF vice air marshal), also served as the governing official of the SBA. The SBA territory at Akrotiri covers the southern-most tip of Cyprus—a promontory jutting into the Mediterranean Sea. It consists of Royal Air Force Base Akrotiri and a British army battalion garrisoned at Episkopi.

As the Olive Harvest Commander I had several bosses. I was the senior US military commander in Cyprus, and our U-2 operation was the principle operation at RAF Akrotiri. Accordingly I was given an elevated protocol within the British military there. Yet, I was a lieutenant colonel and junior in rank to the RAF Base Commander who held full colonel rank—group captain. And all of us at Akrotiri worked under the auspices of Air Vice Marshal Davies, the Commander of British Forces, Cyprus. I also acted under direction of the US Ambassador, Cyprus, for all things diplomatic and international in scope. The Headquarters Strategic Air Command back in Omaha directed U-2 operations and tasking and I responded to SAC directives through its Strategic Reconnaissance Center. But my immediate boss—the man who wrote my performance reports—was the Commander of the 9th. Strategic Reconnaissance Wing (SAC) at Beale AFB in California, 7,000 miles away.

I was in charge of 90 people. About one-third were military and the rest were civilian contractors representing different companies. In some cases there was a single contractor responsible for a single system or sensor on the U-2, but the largest groups of contractors performed aircraft maintenance and operated our large satellite communications dish. Our military members performed flight operations, security, and administrative support. We also had a military flight surgeon. In keeping a low profile, everyone wore nondescript civilian clothes.

All the military members were assigned on temporary duty tours from two to six months. Members rotated in and out of Cyprus according to their assigned tours of duty. I was the only one on permanent one-year duty assignment. Civilian contractors were normally posted for a year but some had been there several years. The work everyone did revolved around the single U-2 and its flight schedule.

There were no American weekends or holidays observed on the Olive Harvest calendar. British holidays were respected, though, and none was more resplendent than the Queen's Birthday, with all the pomp of three marching bands imported from England and everyone dressed-out in full regalia on the lawns of Episkopi's soccer pitch.

My prime responsibility was the mission, but most of my time was spent managing people. Some performed admirably; some less so. I found that the contractors had the most quirky personalities. Some had lived on the rock too long, having family separation or other behavior issues that were particularly hard to deal with 5-6,000 miles away from their stateside homes.

The British Provost and Security Service (P&SS) kept watch on Olive Harvest people and informed me through the Station Commander of any aberrations or unusual circumstances they observed. Olive Harvest had a mix of mostly men, mostly civilian contractors who were living and working sometimes for years thousands of miles from home on an island, under curfew, and while performing a highly secretive mission. It was a frothy brew of personalities I dealt with, and of course there were conflicts and problems I had to confront.

Situations like these:

One of my best, most reliable contractors broke down in tears in my office because he had gotten a "Dear John" letter from his wife.

Through the British P&SS I discovered a contractor had married an Egyptian woman and had moved off base to downtown Limassol—a serious violation of our very strict curfew and fraternization policies. I had to terminate him and send him home.

Another got drunk and took our jeep off road, blowing out all four tires, then came back and threatened another guy with a knife. He went home on the next "Charlie."

A British RAF enlisted man was socially rejected by some of our people and decided to take revenge by pouring lighter fluid on one of our buildings and torching it.

My administrative sergeant brought her marital problems over from the States, started wearing provocative clothes and flirting with anyone and everyone. I reprimanded her, and she complied.

Then my own operations officer began to get a little too friendly with, of all people, the British Station Commander's young daughter. I warned him, too.

Our doctor approached me to discuss her troubled marriage and fears of returning home. She was an American-educated, non-traditional Muslim and her husband was a very strict Muslim who wanted her to quit her profession and become a traditional Muslim wife.

Just before my Olive Harvest tour was up, the Brits told me that our fuels guy was suspected of running guns for certain nefarious foreign groups. That case was still pending when I left Cyprus.

And the list went on . . . .

We were a small outfit performing a mission of very high international significance, and we were being observed very, very carefully by friend and foe alike. Our performance—our very presence there—had international significance.

Before I assumed command of Olive Harvest, I had attended a meeting about the operation and its significance at CIA Headquarters outside Washington. I specifically inquired whether it was necessary to observe strict protocol such as wearing civilian clothes, and I was told in very certain terms that our presence there was very precarious and those precautions were most necessary.

In Cyprus I sent a Lockheed contractor home for repeated curfew violations. The other Lockheed contractors thought I was being too strict. Some of them had been in Cyprus for two to three years. In fairness to them I visited the embassy in Nicosia and asked our ambassador whether it was possible to relax the curfew. He said no and then gave me several examples of threats and intrigue aimed at the Olive Harvest operation. British Provost and Security Services also told me how some of our people were being followed off base by some very dangerous people.

So I held an evening meeting with all the Lockheed contractors. I told them of my visit with Ambassador Ewing and related some of what he had told me. There was some dissention, but they appeared to mellow.

Their boss came up the next day and said my meeting with them was appreciated and they gained a better understanding of what was going on.

As commander I won some and lost some—that one I won. My entire year was like that.

My days began very early. I might take a break during the day after the bird was airborne and before it came back many hours later. I made time during most days to play some tennis or squash. I needed that. Squash was very much a British sport, and I played it with British friends.

Typically I'd show up at the hangar at dawn and work up to dinnertime, then take my officers to dinner off base in my hire car. After dinner I'd go up to "the Hill"—our satellite and communications station—and I'd spend the evening there talking through encrypted communications, coordinating with various functionaries back in the States when they were at work in their time zones. I'd get back to my quarters about 9-10 o'clock, then start over the next day.

I coordinated frequently with my RAF counterparts on base, but I also conducted business at the British garrison at Episkopi, about ten miles away. At Episkopi I occasionally met with my British boss, Air Vice Marshal Alan Davies, the Commander of British Forces, Cyprus, and Governor of the Sovereign British Area, Cyprus. He was most interested in Project Olive Harvest and very supportive. Davies was a good man and we had a good relationship. [I still regret that I was unable to bring him the Ping golf club he wanted when I traveled to the States for my wedding.]

The Brits were drawing down their aircraft and missions at RAF Akrotiri, and Olive Harvest had become the principle mission there. Our success was very important to both our nations and to peace prospects for the Middle East. When the British Minister of Defence, Sir John Nott, visited Cyprus he wanted to visit Olive Harvest. Sir John and Air Marshal Davies traveled unescorted to our hangar, and I spent an afternoon personally hosting and escorting them.

Also located at Episkopi was the British General Communications Office—the equivalent of our National Security Agency. Our U-2 intelligence missions were directly tied to the Brits through the GCO. When I recall the extreme security that surrounded our presence in Cyprus I think, with a smile, of the cloak and dagger circumstances governing my visits to the GCO.

Although I wore civilian clothes and was on sovereign British territory and surrounded by a Royal Army battalion, I had to observe a bizarre routine. The GCO building was entirely unmarked. It sat on a hill overlooking the Episkopi British Headquarters building. It had two guarded entrances, and I could use either one. But the protocol governing my visits required that whichever entrance I chose to enter, I had to exit through the opposite one. No kidding.

## British Friends

During that year in Cyprus I made numerous friends among the British. I was invited to social gatherings and into their homes and got to know many quite well. We played sports together, too, and there was nothing more hilarious than watching Americans playing the uniquely British game of Cricket.

Years later when Eileen and I lived in England we were more constrained by my job responsibilities and living on base, and I missed the opportunity to mingle more with British neighbors in surrounding communities. I genuinely like and respect the British. We have some different customs and protocols, but I admire the Brits for their values, their determination, and their courage under adversity.

I was in Cyprus during a period when the British economy and influence were in decline. I was saddened to see the Brits withdrawing from lands in the Middle East where they had maintained a presence for so many years. Britain was suffering economically at the time, and their overseas forces—military and civilian—were being pared down. Colonialism had no place in our modern world, but still it was sad to see an era of British influence crumble. I was in the control tower at Akrotiri one day and saw the last British Vulcan bomber come in from Oman, refueling at Akrotiri before returning to England to be scrapped. It was truly depressing for the Royal Air Force Brits in the tower to watch this event. Depressing for me, too.

Then the Falklands War broke out. Prime Minister Thatcher firmly said England would defend the Falklands from Argentine aggression. I watched the impact of her stand and the effect her words had on my British friends, and it was memorable. By digging in her heels she gave a much needed shot in the arm to everyone in British service. They were four-square behind her, and the lift in their morale was amazing to see.

## The Last Time I Saw Cyprus

When my year was over I was ready to return and begin my life with Eileen, yet I felt I was leaving part of me behind. With two, two-month duty tours as a pilot and my year's duty as the commander, I had spent 16 months at Olive Harvest. My work as commander had been all-consuming. I was involved in my job almost every waking moment. I lived a different existence there among British hosts in an ancient, beautiful land where its people struggled to maintain peace with Middle East neighbors.

Years later I was told by a British doctor here in Prescott that Cyprus was much changed. He said I'd be sorely disappointed if I returned there. His brother was living in Cyprus, and the doctor visited periodically over the years. Commercialism and tourism had taken root. He said idyllic Cyprus was no more.

I returned to the States, and Eileen and I finally began living our lives together. We were soon off to Alabama and the Air War College after visiting family in Pennsylvania and North Carolina. Although Eileen had no prior involvement with the Air Force or its ways, she obtained some friendly Air Force help to get us situated in Montgomery. I still marvel at all she did while I was away to prepare for our reunion and our lives ahead.

Our little joke over this was that in renting a house to live, my only stipulation was that I didn't want a large yard to maintain. On one of our weekly overseas calls she was quite pleased to say she had rented a nice home for us just outside Montgomery. Then she told me of its one drawback: the house had an acre of grass to mow. But she quickly added that the owners were leaving behind their riding lawnmower. But being game and knowing how busy I was at the Air War College, she spent as much time on that mower as I did.

# In the States Again

The Air War College is the senior Air Force higher learning institution. It's part of Air University—a sprawling campus on Maxwell Air Force Base, Montgomery, Alabama. Officer-students attend for a year and earn the equivalent of a Masters degree. Selection for residency is a privilege and an important gateway to promotion. However, there are other prerequisites for that promotion, as I came to realize on Day One at the AWC.

All attendees—Air Force officers plus some from other service branches and other countries—assembled that first day in the large AWC auditorium. Those who already had Masters degrees were asked to raise their hands, and I was one of the small number who didn't. I went home that day and told Eileen I'd have to get my Masters while attending AWC. There were convenient ways to do that because AWC had a matriculation agreement with Auburn University for just that purpose. I signed up for a Masters in International Relations. A professor dropped out of the faculty mix, and the degree was converted to a Masters in Political Science.

So that's what I did—I attended Air War College by day, my Masters classes by night.

Someone once published a list of the ten biggest pressures people encounter, and in that year Eileen and I experienced all ten of them. And there were others that didn't make it on the top ten list, particularly those that impacted Eileen—her rapid introduction to the Air Force—and me, following a year's separation.

The pressures were enormous, and it was patently unfair to Eileen. She was separated from David back in Virginia. She knew no one there except me. There were substantial activities with my AWC classmates and their families and we made friends, but I turned into a day/night couch potato with books open in front of me for that year. I never had a day off until one weekend when we decided enough was enough and ventured down to Mobile on the Alabama coast for a couple of days.

## Back to Beale

A year passed, and I graduated both from the War College and from Auburn University with my Masters—and with honors, which helped erase the memory of my woeful undergrad years. We packed ourselves into the car with our new puppy, hauling a popup tent trailer, and camped our way back to Beale AFB. We moved into base housing, which was old and cramped but really served us well. We were living in the foothills of the Sierras, and the back gate to the base led to the beautiful and historic California gold country west of Reno. So there Eileen and I were, pretty much enjoying ourselves and our new lives together, far more relaxed than in Alabama.

I was an Assistant Director of Operations—sort of a minister without portfolio. I did odd jobs for a while. Most of it was administrative—not exciting stuff. I was getting bored, but one day as I walked in from parking Phil Daisher came up and asked if I'd be interested in going cross-country. My eyes lit up—I hadn't flown an airplane since before the Air War College. I replied, "Sure, when are we going?" Phil told me he wasn't going along—I'd be doing this alone. I was puzzled, and asked who was flying in the T-38 with me. Phil said I wasn't going in a T-38—I was flying commercial. I asked when, and Phil said I'd go tomorrow. I perceived there was a lot more to this than Phil was divulging. "Where am I going, Phil?" "To Leavenworth," he said.

Okay, it was time to lay cards on the table, so I asked what was up. Phil chuckled and said I'd be escorting a prisoner there. Phil had strung me out pretty well. I had been suckered pretty good, and he was having a good laugh. But it was true. An airman had been convicted of a serious offense, and an officer was needed to escort him to prison. That would have been one of the cats and dogs I was handling, but other circumstances intervened, and Jim Rioux took my place. Jim's story about what he saw at the maximum security prison was eye-watering, and I'm glad he went, not me.

Ken Stafford was commander of our U-2 detachment at Patrick AFB in Florida. That detachment was responsible for flying the U-2 missions that have flown the periphery of Cuba since the Cuban missile crisis. Ken needed a vacation, so I replaced him for two weeks. Ken and Barbara let me stay in their nice home for that time. It was interesting to run a different detachment for a while. Ken had a good organization, so I had no problems at all. I focused on eating sumptuously good seafood.

Patrick abutted the Eastern Space and Missile Range at Cape Kennedy (now Canaveral). They announced the planned launch of a Delta rocket, so late that day I drove up to Cocoa Beach to watch. It certainly was spectacular, and I must say that after all the times of watching space launches on TV, there's absolutely nothing like seeing one in person.

Back in California, Hector (who had by then been promoted to 9th. Strategic Reconnaissance Wing Commander) called me into his office one day. He looked very serious and I was wondering what I might have done wrong. But then he said, "Congratulations. You've been promoted to full colonel."

I never saw it coming. I was both honored and surprised, of course. As a lieutenant colonel I would normally have entered the "primary zone" for promotion two years later and would then have two years to make it. What I received was a two-year early promotion—a "below the zone" promotion, as it's called—in the top one percent of all eligible lieutenant colonels.

I was assigned as the wing's Chief of Inspections. That job had very little to do with either the U-2 or the SR-71. My job was to evaluate all the wing's organizations for compliance with rules and procedures governing their portion of the mission. I and my assistant inspected everywhere—fire department, security police, supply, housing office—you name it. It was tedious work, but I learned a lot about what all those other Air Force people did—the ones who weren't flying airplanes. I was also our representative to the Chamber of

Commerce at nearby Marysville and Yuba City. Including families, we had 4,000 people at Beale and our presence was significant to the area economy.

Once every month I conducted a base Major Accident Response Exercise (MARE) to test the base emergency response forces in confronting sudden disasters. I ran a team of 35 evaluators who would watch, note, and critique each exercise. I graded the participants and then briefed results to the wing staff.

Aiming for realism and involvement, we planned very intricate exercises that tested the resources of virtually every major organization on base. In one exercise I perhaps went too far. In the accident scenario I decided to play the part of a deceased victim and enlisted Eileen as my bereaved widow (with her permission, of course). But when the mortuary people and chaplain arrived at our house, the realism was almost too much for her, and she came to the brink of tears in her role-playing. After that she had my promise I'd never put her through that again.

But the one MARE that proved most significant was a scenario involving a U-2 crash on takeoff. I had the wing shut down the runway and curtailed flying to play the exercise. Just two weeks later, a U-2 actually crashed under almost the very same circumstances. The airplane was a total loss, but the pilot ejected safely and no one else was hurt.

I happened to be nearby and drove to the crash site where crash, fire, and rescue forces were on scene. When the actual accident was debriefed, our Base Commander credited the MARE exercise for giving his responders exactly the training they needed to handle the accident. He said their response was flawless because, "We had just done this." Practice makes perfect.

# The Pentagon, Phase II

We had been at Beale just over a year when I was assigned to the Pentagon—again. For Eileen it meant going back to the D.C. area where she had first begun her employment years. I was less enthusiastic in my memories of Pentagon work and living around crowded, congested Washington. We set out to find a place to live. We didn't know how long this assignment might be, but we opted to buy instead of rent. We bought a three-story townhouse located within the Beltway, which meant a shorter commute to work and greater sanity over time. Returning to her old abode Eileen decided to go back to work, and so she returned to the Immigration and Naturalization Service where she had worked before.

In conjunction with my promotion I was assigned to Headquarters Air Force as Chairman of the Reconnaissance and Intelligence Panel. At that time the Air Force budget was divided into 14 functional slices, and I managed that portion allocated to reconnaissance and intelligence programs. I also held the titular position of Assistant Division Chief of the Air Force Reconnaissance Division.

It's no exaggeration to say the Pentagon was splitting at its seams. The 1940s-vintage building wasn't built to accommodate modern growth and the sizeable number of service staff who oversee and run today's large, full-time armed forces. That's particularly true of vaulted rooms that are wired and proofed to protect the highly-classified work of intelligence and reconnaissance operations.

The Reconnaissance Division was at the very bottom of the Pentagon's two basement floors, adjacent to the Government Printing Office and the famous purple water fountain. The purple water fountain—an iconic landmark known to everyone who has ever lost their way in the massive building—was just outside our door. Our offices were inside a vault, and there were at least twice as many people assigned as could reasonably fit. We literally had desks backed up to desks, nudging other desks that competed for space with shelves of classified archives. There was absolutely no privacy, and we just had to make do. As panel chairman, most of my work occurred in a conference room six stories above on the outer E Ring. I took the stairs.

My work was very involved, governed by due dates and deadlines on the budget and legislative calendars. I faced long and arduous days. My duties fingered out to various agencies both within and outside the Pentagon walls. Besides my own panel's work, I served on two other intelligence committees. I attended many meetings around the DC area and often visited the three-letter intelligence agencies, as well as the offices of Department of Defense officials. My panel had responsibility for a $1.7 billion annual chunk of the Air Force budget.

The year-long federal and military budget cycle is fraught with deadlines, meetings, and conferences of all sorts. I learned many things about budgets and program costs that I'm only too happy to have forgotten since then. Beyond doubt, this was the least-favorite job I've ever had in my Air Force life. Yes, I accomplished some things of considerable importance, but I can't say I felt any great satisfaction for it. They don't call it a budget "cycle" for nothing—it keeps spinning around and around, year after year. Air Force panel chairmen are usually reassigned after one year, just before they have to be institutionalized to an asylum. One of my panel chairman colleagues was unfortunately tapped for a second year due to exigencies; when I last saw him his eyes appeared to be permanently crossed.

I was ready to bail out. It was only the second time I had considered finding another Air Force job on my own. I investigated air attaché positions.

Air attachés are military assistants to US ambassadors located in various embassies, worldwide. They span the worlds of international diplomacy and intelligence. It's a responsible position, but it means spending more years overseas. The job is one-half voluntary—you opt to get in, but you can't opt out.

I spoke with the Air Force assignments chief in the Pentagon about it. There were two such positions open at the time, and I was eligible. One was air attaché to Saudi Arabia and the other was to India. Saudi was out—no way I'd ever volunteer for that. India was the alternative, and that seemed like a possibility. Eileen and I talked it over and started to lean that way.

I arranged a long distance call with the current air attaché in India. He described the position and duties to me. He said we would live in a sizeable mansion just down the street from Prime Minister Indira Ghandi's residence. We'd be provided funds to completely redecorate the house to our taste. We'd have a household staff of thirteen Indian civilians including a driver, cooks, servants, groundskeepers and—get this—a dung picker-upper (for the sacred cows in Hindu culture). I'd also have an American military driver. We'd be expected to entertain parties of 300 people in our home every two weeks or so.

Then he dropped the bombshell. The tour of duty had just been increased from two years to three. As he candidly told me, two years in India is tough—three is tantamount to suicide.

I changed my mind about an air attaché position and waited out my luck at the Pentagon.

There are two things I remember most about my panel chairman job. I remember working for a two week stretch without ever once seeing daylight—each day, all day, and into the night. And I remember the day I called Eileen to say we were leaving.

I was walking the hallway of the always-dim lower basement, stepping around someone's week-old sandwich lying on the floor, when I passed by our personnel director. He said, "Art, I'm working your assignment." I would have shed a tear of delight just then if he hadn't been looking, but instead I tempered my joy it by asking where I might be going. He said I'd know by the end of the day.

I didn't venture far from the phone the rest of the day, and sure enough he rang me up. I was being assigned to Strategic Air Command Headquarters, Omaha, Nebraska. I was going to become something called the "SAC Senior"—the Senior Controller of SAC's underground Command Center. I didn't quite know what that was.

He dropped the other shoe when he said, "You'll be leaving in February." Christmas was two weeks away.

After we hung up, I called Eileen to tell her the news, which was really, really stupid. In my enthusiasm for leaving the Pentagon I forgot to think how this news might impress her. It didn't.

It was another very long Pentagon day when I finally got home, and she greeted me nearly in tears. It wasn't the kind of news she needed. It hit her with force that we would be making our move in the dead of winter to cold Nebraska and facing a household move and a home sale in only two months and over the holidays. Additionally, living in the DC area had put us near David, her family, and mine; with the upcoming move we would never again live that close to family.

We scrambled to make the move. Luckily our townhouse sold quickly to a Navy captain and we headed on to Nebraska. And our brief time in Omaha worked out well for us, too.

# Then to Omaha

Just outside of Omaha we rented a nice split level home from a friend of mine, and I began this new job of being Senior Controller of the SAC Headquarters underground Command Center. When I arrived I really had no idea what that entailed. I certainly had no idea that it meant I would have responsibility for launching the nation's land-based nuclear forces—bombers, tankers, and missiles. To this day I'm still awed to have held such responsibility.

I went through special psychiatric and medical evaluations. Hence forth I could only receive medical care from certain designated Air Force physicians. My medical folder was specially marked and colored to denote my nuclear responsibilities. My folder grew to twice its normal thickness and was kept in a special vault. I was restricted from taking certain drugs. If I required surgery, an approved observer with nuclear credentials had to be present.

I worked deep in the bowels of the Strategic Air Command Headquarters. SAC's underground Command Center was the reinforced, vaulted and guarded locus of SAC's worldwide operations and forces. It's the hub of all SAC's activities, where senior officers and staff would manage operational control of the world's largest nuclear force in event of unmitigated war.

The senior officer who controlled the nuclear orders and managed the Command Center—the Senior Controller, or "SAC Senior," as he was called—was one of five colonels holding that job on rotating shifts. The SAC Senior managed shift-working team members who staffed the Command Center at all hours, under all conditions. These team members linked via secure communications to their counterparts throughout SAC headquarters and outside agencies.

214

As airborne backup to the underground Command Center, SAC continuously flew a command and control aircraft. The "Looking Glass," as the aircraft was called, was an EC-135 (Boeing 707) fitted with a mass of electronics and communications equipment, fully staffed and commanded by a general officer. It was the SAC Senior's job to insure that a Looking Glass aircraft remained airborne at all times of day and night. As part of my initial orientation I flew a mission on the Looking Glass.

I also attended executive-level orientation courses at both the US Space Command in Colorado Springs and at the Western Space and Missile Test Range at Vandenburg AFB, north of Santa Barbara, California. In Colorado I was given a tour of Space Command's vast complex inside Cheyenne Mountain, buried deep under the Rocky Mountains. At Vandenberg I was taught orbital mechanics and briefed on US satellite capabilities, given a tour of an ICBM silo, and witnessed an ICBM test launch.

SAC's Command Center used satellite technology to detect what the Soviet Union was doing with their nuclear weapons. The most immediate threat was their Yankee class nuclear subs. Should we detect that the Soviet Union was getting a little too close with their Yankee subs, we would increase the response posture of our nuclear alert forces. Increasing our nuclear alert status was the within the authority of the SAC Senior, and I've had occasion to direct an increase to our nuclear alert posture more than once.

The SAC Senior sat at a long, elevated console in the large, vaulted, underground Command Center. Other team members sat at the long console or at tables on the floor below. A glass-enclosed balcony was directly above the Senior's position. In time of war or crisis, that's where the Commander-in-Chief of SAC (CINCSAC) and his key general staff would be.

The mass of communications at the SAC Senior's console was arranged in color-coded panels to help sort out its complexity. The Senior's principle duties were to act as the crisis manager for SAC worldwide forces, to physically launch the SAC nuclear response force upon the President's decision, and to keep the Looking Glass airborne and viable at all times. Additionally, he was personal representative for SAC's Commander-in-Chief, a four-star general, and was the focal point of communications for the SAC general staff.

Essential persons with a role in America's nuclear plans had to be readily available to answer a call within two minutes at all times. SAC's general officers were particularly important, and it was the SAC Senior's job to maintain close communications with the SAC general staff and track their locations. As each general came to work, went home, or went elsewhere he would call the Command Center to report his position and we would note where he was. That's just another part of nuclear command and control.

Over time I got to know those generals through those phone calls. A familiarity developed between the SAC Senior and the headquarters generals that often made for interesting ad hoc conversations.

When CINCSAC—General Chain—decided to impose new personal behavior guidelines aimed at improving the health of SAC's members, he initiated those rules in stages beginning with his top generals. First he informed them they could no longer drink hard liquor. Then they had to give up smoking. To solidify his new policies, General Chain hosted them in his home one night. No booze was served and no smoking allowed. The resulting commentary from the generals was funny. Over the next few days many made a point of commenting to me about it. They were really miffed. Over time little snippets like that gave me insight into the lives the generals led.

The SAC Senior also gave orientation briefings to dignitaries and other visitors who viewed the Command Center. Everyone visiting SAC wanted to see the storied underground command center that figured in Hollywood's doomsday movies. Eileen got the tour, too.

## Nuclear Deterrence

The Command Center was an investment in national security during the Cold War, and it certainly lived up to all descriptions as a worldwide crisis nerve center. Throughout all my daily activities, I was always mindful that the keys to nuclear launch were just five feet away from where I sat.

Day after day we practiced nuclear scenarios, linking via secure voice communications with the White House Situation Room, the US Space Command, and others. These "Night Blue" exercises were rehearsals for what might happen. I and our team took them very seriously—it was impossible not to.

I'll describe here one notable exercise not only because it reigns high in my memory but also because it illustrates the seriousness of our nuclear preparedness efforts. I wish everyday citizens knew more about our jobs, but layers of secrecy and obscuration prevent full public disclosure. But perhaps this one example may reveal the extraordinary precautions we took in guarding the nation.

For this exercise, under cloak of darkness and extraordinary secrecy we uprooted and relocated the entire Command Center to a remote Nebraska location, simulating what might be done under an actual attack involving enemy insurgents on American soil. I and others dressed in civilian clothes and worked for days at this secretive location. Others played the role of the "red force" and attempted to find us. For this exercise I could tell Eileen only that I was going to be away for some period of time—no more than that. It was a genuine display of SAC's ability to control its nuclear forces and discharge its responsibilities under hostile circumstances, and it was quite successful. The degree of planning and involvement was massive.

Emergencies and crises occurred throughout SAC's worldwide command, and we in the Command Center handled them as they arrived using the network of headquarters experts available to us. Some events are more memorable than others, and some were very serious. Some days there were no crises or emergencies that made it to the SAC Senior; other days were much more interesting. SAC had tens of thousands of people operating around the globe. Of course stuff happened—it had to—like fire in a missile silo, a massive fuel spill, a bomber's emergency landing on a dry lake bed, and . . . Mike Wallace.

I was on duty when a call came in one day from F.E. Warren AFB in Wyoming. Warren was responsible for a widely-dispersed array of Minuteman nuclear missiles scattered throughout Wyoming. The call reported that "Plowshare" political protestors were attempting to attack and vandalize an underground missile silo. Following behind the small mob of protestors was famed celebrity correspondent Mike Wallace and a CBS "60 Minutes" film crew.

Warren's security forces were aware of the situation almost as soon as it started. Using various sensors and security devices embedded in the missile field they knew exactly what was transpiring without ever revealing themselves.

As the protestors and "60 Minutes" crew made their way, they cut through security fences and destroyed what they could. Eventually they reached a missile silo, which is built to withstand a nuclear blast. Using sledgehammers, they tried to beat up the place and then splattered containers of blood around. Mike Wallace and crew filmed it all, never once attempting to intervene. It made no difference that they were themselves US citizens and—just maybe—they should have interceded to prevent destruction of their government's property. But they just wanted a story, even if it required abetting a criminal act.

Warren's security forces had seen and recorded it all through their cameras, and they moved in and arrested everyone.

Back in Cheyenne a judge brought Wallace and crew before him and severely admonished them. For "60 Minutes" the prize was that precious film, but the judge confiscated it. They were all fined substantially.

To this day I refuse to watch that damnable TV show.

218

# England

When we first moved to Omaha, I was told I would be there fifteen months, and that's precisely how it happened. One morning when my two-star boss left home and called in to the Command Center he said, "Art, call me in the office around mid-morning—I've got your assignment." When I did, he said, "You're going to be the next commander of the 17th Reconnaissance Wing in England." The 17th was home of warfighting U-2s—re-designated at TR-1s—for the European theater. But, he said I couldn't tell anyone except Eileen for the time being. I understood the reason; with senior officer assignments there's a daisy chain of notifications, and some of them are delicate, such as when someone has been fired but hasn't been told yet.

But first we had to get there. Not being able to disclose the news proved to be problematic. I would be moving soon, and I started getting phone calls from the personnel people who needed to arrange the overseas move. Eileen and I each needed two kinds of passports, our shots, and we needed to arrange shipment of the car. We had to send hold baggage overseas quickly to tie us over until our household goods could arrive. There would be a large change-of-command ceremony with the three-star Commander of 8th Air Force presiding. We needed to set up our quarters in England. We had to get British drivers licenses, security processing, etc. But we could do nothing until an official announcement was made. We waited patiently day after day with time to do everything running short.

With only three weeks remaining until the change of command General Johnson gave permission for the personnel people to start some of their machinery, but there was still no official announcement. I set up our household moving dates. Meanwhile, Eileen had a medical issue that required surgery before we left—out patient stuff, but still a huge bump in the road. Movers would be coming in for three separate household goods shipments. We had to pack, move out, drive two cars to North Carolina, leave the dog with my parents, drive to Norfolk, drop off the car for shipment to England, catch the last flight out of Norfolk to New York City, and catch the last available airplane to London. It was going to be a tight squeeze with no time to spare.

Soon there were only two weeks remaining to do all that. I called Major General Johnson and said I was simply out of time. He understood and put me on hold. He called back in fifteen minutes and gave me the green light. Then the real scramble began.

Eileen's surgery went without a hitch, fortunately, and she had a little time to recover before the movers arrived. There were three separate shipments of our household goods, but fortunately the big move was handled by three ex-marines, who proudly told me there's no such thing as an "ex-marine." They Hoo-rahed their way through that move with zeal and efficiency I had never seen in a moving team before. They were hardly out the door when we put our little Shorty in the car with Eileen, I got in mine, and we hit the road for North Carolina. We arrived at the folks', left Shorty with them, and then we were off the next day for Norfolk. We dropped the car off and sped to the airport to catch the last flight to New York.

We had arranged to stay at the Kennedy Hotel nearby the JFK Airport. It was a cockroach-infested flea trap, with a beer bottle and other paraphernalia lying on the floor and a filthy bathroom. Fortunately we only had six hours there before catching our international to London Heathrow. We were met by a civilian driver who drove us 50 miles to Royal Air Force Base Alconbury. As we arrived late evening we were greeted by the outgoing commander and his wife, Jim and Deanna, and others we've known who extended their greetings. Through the evening we were briefed on the ceremony and upcoming events. We didn't get to sleep until well after midnight, then got up early and were briefed some more as we dressed for the change of command. We were still on Omaha time, seven hours earlier.

Lieutenant General McCarthy and his wife had arrived from Louisiana, and we all met at the big hangar for the morning rehearsal. Fortunately, the incoming commander doesn't have to do much except stay awake and avoid falling off the reviewing stand. Eileen was holding up remarkably. Then we went to the Officers Club for the pre-ceremony receiving line. Jim, Deanna, and we shook hands with guests for an hour, then went back to the hangar where wing personnel and guests had assembled for the ceremony, about 400 people. A military change of command ceremony is a fine, precision, formal affair with lots of choreography. Sharp, uniformed squadrons and a marching band are assembled. There's nothing quite like it. I felt like I was floating—half of me was still asleep back in Omaha.

All went without a hitch. As the ceremony concluded, staff cars pulled up and we were taken back to the Officers Club. Jim and Deanna bade their farewells—their jobs were done, and tradition requires the departing commander to leave immediately. Then the next receiving line began for just Eileen and me. It lasted two hours—no kidding. After it ended we stepped into another room to have a farewell chat with Lt Gen McCarthy and his wife along with my new boss in Europe, Brigadier General Astorino and his wife. For the next two years, Astorino was my nearest boss, the 7th Air Division Commander in Germany.

That night General Astorino took Eileen and me to dinner in nearby Huntingdon. He informed us of our working relationships, pledged his ready support for whatever we needed, and, with respect for our exhausted state, kept his remarks brief. It was a most friendly evening. I liked my new boss.


## The Mission


Royal Air Force Alconbury is located west of the famous university town of Cambridge. It was in the countrified East Anglia region of northeast England, about an hour's train ride north of London. The 17th was home to the TR-1—a U-2 in every way except by name. (When I had been the R&I Panel Chairman in the Pentagon, General Johnson and I met with an Assistant Secretary of Defense and designated which aircraft coming off the Lockheed assembly line would become U-2s or TR-1s.) When I arrived the 17th was only five years young and growing.

In commanding the 17ᵗʰ I had responsibilities to the European Command, Strategic Air Command, and NATO while operating from a Royal Air Force base in England. I was reminded of my multiple responsibilities a couple of times each year when we got the loan of a U-2RT trainer from California to meet our pilots' annual training requirements. Having the two-seat U-2 was like waving a flag before Europe's top brass, and they climbed over each other to get a back-seat ride in the famous U-2. The spectacle of all those VIPs coming to Alconbury to fly in a U-2 was far different from when I had to stealthily fly a U-2 in and out of England under cover of darkness years before.

The "TR" in TR-1 stands for Tactical Reconnaissance, meaning (importantly) that the operational command of those airplanes belonged to the European Commander-in-Chief (CINCEUR), not US national authorities. This significant distinction meant that if the Soviets invaded Europe, CINCEUR's ownership and control of our TR-1s would give him a significant warfighting weapon, whereas if they were U-2s, they would likely be recalled to the States in time of war to protect them. In other words, the TR-1s were warfighting U-2s intended for use in fighting a European battle, and I was responsible for bringing our growing wing up to warfighting readiness in support of NATO.

In the course of my two years in command we accomplished that. Our TR-1s were performing in a new role, and our success in that new role ultimately extended the U-2's useful employment in active service until present day. The TR-1's systems provided wartime battlefield intelligence and precision targeting for allied attack forces. It was the culmination of what began for me 12 years earlier when I first flew those experimental ALSS missions over New Mexico. The U-2/TR-1 had become a critical asset for the European or any other allied battlefield plan—what's known as a "force multiplier."

## The Organizations

RAF Alconbury in 1987 was a British-owned, American-operated, two-wing base. The host wing was the 10th Tactical Fighter Wing

(TFW), and the 17th Reconnaissance Wing was the tenant wing. When we first arrived the 10th was flying RF-4Cs under command of Colonel Ken Habedank. Soon afterwards the 10th converted to flying A-10 Thunderbolt fighters—the "Warthogs," the "tank busters."

The A-10 is an impressive ground-attack aircraft—ugly and mean-looking. Two-thirds of the fuselage houses a big Gatling gun. Upon the arrival of the A-10s Ken Habedank was succeeded by Colonel Mike McGinty with his wife, Karen. Mike and I were associates and became good friends, as did Karen and Eileen. Some years later Mike presided over my retirement ceremony in Texas.

Mike was responsible for all the base support functions as well as his operational flying mission, whereas I was responsible just for the 17th's operational mission. Some of the A-10s and the base support buildings were on one side of the airfield, and all the TR-1s and their facilities were on the other along with the remaining A-10s. Mike was truly as supportive of our operations as he was of his own, and I'm forever thankful for his professionalism and friendship. Mike and Karen were fine people and by chance we got to see them again in San Antonio just a year ago.

Several miles to the south was a new Air Force wing of ground launched cruise missiles, the 303rd Tactical Missile Wing. Like the 17th, the 303rd. was also working to achieve NATO operational readiness status for NATO. The 303rd. was commanded by Colonel Ken Harbaugh with his wife, Cathy. Mike, Ken and I were the triumvirate of American wing commanders in that part of England.

I won't delve into the many responsibilities and activities of my job in this missive. Too lengthy. The brief description is that the TR-1s of the 17th had both peacetime intelligence collection and NATO wartime battlefield targeting missions over Europe. The 17th RW was a SAC organization performing a job for NATO and the US European Command.

I thought our two wings worked together at Alconbury quite well. Mike expressed in both words and deed that the 17th's mission was also his mission, and he and his staff were very supportive. The 17th continued to grow during my two years in command, and when I left

223

we were at full strength with about 650 people and 13 TR-1s in 13 brand-new, hardened shelters and support buildings.

## Day One

So we began our two years with the 17th RW in England. Jim Wrenn had left the 17th Wing in very good shape, and George Freese had commanded the 17th quite well before Jim. I was pleased to not have a basketful of headaches facing me.

On my first day I arrived at my headquarters building and parked in my reserved spot. My office was large and furnished with a conference table. I was assigned an Executive Officer—a captain who provided mostly administrative assistance—and a British civilian secretary who worked in the outer office that separated my room from the Vice Wing Commander's office.

On my first day I began to open some of my mail, but Captain Julie Tepe admonished me that it was her job to open my mail—a security precaution so that if there was a letter bomb her head would be blown off instead of mine. I thought it might be nice to have her taste my food, too, but that would probably be overreaching a bit.

My first day was filled with back-to-back informational briefings by various officers on my staff—the "fire hose" treatment. That day was a long time "in the saddle," and when it drew to a close and my last visitor had left, I was bushed. I was on information overload. As I was ready to wrap things up I asked Julie if there was anything else, and she asked, "Did anyone tell you about the murder yet?"

One of my sergeants had knifed and killed a fellow NCO at an off-base party two months before my arrival. It was a fit of jealous rage over his wife. Under the US-UK Status of Forces Agreement, he was punished under our Uniformed Code of Military Justice instead of under the British courts since no Brits were involved. He was tried and convicted of premeditated murder, then taken for imprisonment at Fort Leavenworth.

My involvement was relegated to dealing with his wife. She was an NCO working in my headquarters building on the second floor above me. I was told she was a very good NCO and a good worker. I had her come in to see me. She seemed to be handling things as well as could be expected. I asked what I might do to help her, and she said she just wanted to be near Leavenworth so she and her children could make family visits. I was able to arrange that.

## Superb People

Eileen and I were surrounded by very fine people. At the top of the list was my good friend, fellow U-2 pilot, and very accomplished Chesapeake Bay sailor Colonel Chuck Crabb who was my Vice Wing Commander. Chuck and Soyoung helped us in many ways. Chuck was always the model of efficiency and capability. Soyoung was an Air Force major specializing in mental health and worked at the area military hospital nearby Alconbury, but she found time to help Eileen with her new spouse duties. When Chuck and Soyoung were reassigned, John Sander stepped in with his wife, Sharon. John eventually succeeded me as wing commander.

The U-2 had always attracted very competent people, and the 17th was full of them. I was in very, very good hands.

Another member of my staff was the Senior Enlisted Advisor. Air Force units operate on the strong backs of the enlisted force, and the non-commissioned officers make things work. The man advising me about those people was a chief master sergeant, and during my two years I had two excellent men in that position, Chief Bruno and Chief Saurage. I don't know if any wing commander ever arranged an aircraft flyby for a retiring Chief Master Sergeant, but I did that for Chief Saurage. I thought it was fitting for him and fitting to recognize the wing's enlisted force.

## Dale

When Chuck left and John moved up from Director of Operations to become vice wing commander, I needed a new DO to replace him. I knew exactly who I wanted—Dale Hudler. Dale was a top performer, and really smart. For work he did for the Defense Intelligence Agency in the Pentagon, Dale received a very special personal commendation from the Chairman of the Joint Chiefs of Staff.

The problem in getting Dale was his cancer. After working years in the Pentagon, Dale had been anxious to get back to flying operations. He finally received orders to do so, but as he flew to California a birthmark on his leg started to throb. When he arrived he sought medical attention, and the diagnosis was melanoma. He had an operation and was returned to the Defense Intelligence Agency in the Pentagon. Dale's cancer was in remission when I told General Astorino I wanted him as my DO. I explained Dale's cancer circumstance, but Astorino approved and I called Dale. Dale had been climbing the walls in the Pentagon, and he readily agreed.

Dale was very sharp as my DO, just as I expected him to be. But shortly before Eileen and I were scheduled to leave, his cancer returned. The cancer had spread to vital organs. Dale was operated on in the States and returned to England after Eileen and I had already departed for our next assignment in Texas.

Dale was medically discharged from the Air Force and pronounced terminally ill. He and Janelle moved to Austin, nearby us. With no other alternatives, Dale successfully applied for an experimental cancer treatment at the National Institutes of Health in Washington.

The short story of all this is that Dale became the star of the NIH treatment program and was actually cured. But the treatment weakened him tremendously, and it took him a year to recover his memory function. The Air Force toyed with bringing him back onto active duty, but they relented and let Dale retire to recuperate. Dale resolved to stay away from high pressure, executive-level work. He got a job in the paint department at Home Depot.

Dale's reticence didn't last. As he recovered, he craved more involvement. Already with one Masters degree, Dale got another in his love, archaeology. That wasn't enough for him, so he got a Ph.D.

in archaeology and became a successful professor at the University of Texas, Austin.

We were fast friends all those years. But cancer was Dale's nemesis. Tragically, Janelle died of cancer first, and Dale recently succumbed to still another of his several cancers. Colonel Dale Hudler, U-2 pilot, faced those prospects for much of his life—stoically, resolutely, and very bravely.

## Our Home on Base

Beginning with my succession, the 17th's wing commander was required to live on base at Alconbury in newly renovated base housing. The rest of the 17th's wing staff could live in the British community if they chose, as many did. RAF Alconbury was close to several small, quaint British villages. Eileen and I would have enjoyed living in a British community and regretted that we couldn't enjoy that opportunity.

Our house was half of a duplex and rather small, built decades ago to British standards at the time. It was at the end of a row of officer homes and adjacent to a farmer's field that abutted the base.

We arrived in July, and the field was glowing with bright, golden-yellow blossoms. I didn't recognize the crop, and when one of my officers was visiting, I remarked to him about the brilliant blossoms and asked what that crop was. Just then an F-4 fighter flew low overhead and drowned out our conversation. Over the din from the passing jet I heard Lee yelling, "Rape! Rape!" I had no idea why he started yelling, "Rape!" After Lee left, I remarked to Eileen how strange that was, and I had some doubts about this officer. It wasn't until a month later that I learned that the field crop was rapeseed—commonly called rape.

Our house on base didn't meet size standards for a colonel, let alone a wing commander. Just before my tour was finished, contractors began to expand and renovate the home, but it was too late for us. Without sounding pretentious, let's just say our house was far from sumptuous and woefully inadequate for meetings and entertaining that accompanied my position. I particularly loved the house's plumbing system, with its water tank in the attic and gravity providing the only water pressure. In each room we plugged in a small transformer to give us 110 volt AC power for our American appliances.

While waiting for our Jeep to arrive from the States we rented a "hire car." So the new commander and his wife could be accommodated quickly, Eileen and I were exempted from driver training and simply issued our military and British driver licenses. I had driven right-hand-drive cars on British roads in England and Cyprus, but Eileen hadn't, and she would have benefitted from some driver's ed.

The Brits drive on the "wrong" side of the road, of course. That was new to Eileen as well as contending with England's old, narrow streets, the traffic markings, and the notorious roundabout intersections. So every day after work we'd take our hire car out to give Eileen some practice. The nearest roundabout was not far from the base's front gate, and we drove endless circles there before suppertime. And I do mean endless—more than once we got stuck in the roundabout and couldn't get out.

Eileen stepped into a brand new role, assuming both official and unofficial roles as the wing commander's wife. Back in those years, a wing commanders' spouse did much semi-official work for spouses and families, acting as an ambassador and participating with the many support agencies that provided care for family needs.

Behind the formal Air Force organization lies an informal one made of spouses and volunteers. Ever since I joined I've heard repeated reference to "The Air Force family." It truly exists. The concept of command is far different than management. Command includes management, but a commander's responsibilities are far more encompassing and extend to responsibilities for the civilian families of service members. In wartime, commanders are responsible for the very lives of service members.

Military family members must contend with many adversities that civilians don't usually confront: sudden or prolonged family separations; short-notice and frequent long-distance household moves; uprooting children from schools and friends; destabilizing an otherwise stable home environment; disrupting courses of medical treatment, education, civilian occupations, or even careers. All these matters put enormous strain on both the military member and the families.

Various support organizations and agencies are established to support Air Force personnel and family needs, and Eileen assumed formal and informal roles working with them. There's no training, education, or practice for what she did. It was just another thing that wasn't written on the back of our marriage certificate.

## The 17th At Work

When I assumed command of the 17th our wing had nine TR-1As, and over the two years of my command we grew to thirteen. My job was to bring the 17th to full operational readiness for NATO participation. To do that, the TR-1 had to prove its ability to perform its wartime mission, but it also had to endure. That meant providing defenses for our aircraft, support facilities, and the wing's people.

During my command NATO's largest-ever construction project was started and finished: the construction of 13 hardened aircraft shelters to house and protect 13 TR-1s, plus attendant hardened support buildings and a crosswind runway improvement to accommodate the notoriously poor crosswind performance of the TR-1/U-2. The hardened shelters were unique—the largest hardened aircraft shelters ever built, and these were specifically designed to protect the TR-1s of the 17th. Each shelter was built to withstand a direct hit by a 500-lb. bomb. When the project finished, we passed the NATO Operational Readiness Inspection and were certified as combat-ready. Mike McGinty used to joke that if I relinquished just a single shelter, he could stuff four of his A-10s in there.

With the hardened shelters and support buildings built, the final step was to expand and refurbish the crosswind runway. That put us temporarily out of business at Alconbury. To the northeast about 60 miles distant was an air base in caretaker status, RAF Sculthorpe. US Air Forces in Europe and the British opened it and partially reconstituted it for us to use until the crosswind runway construction was finished.

I moved our entire operation to Sculthorpe, placing most of the wing's people in temporary quarters there while families remained in the Alconbury area. I, too, spent time living at Sculthorpe and spent considerable time driving back and forth to Alconbury to cover all my responsibilities. When we first set up Sculthorpe's operations I invited the local Mayor, Town Council, and other dignitaries to visit. They were all very gracious and welcoming, and we had good relations with them during our stay. We operated out of Sculthorpe for six months and still flew all our missions with hardly a ripple in our mission success rate.

From time to time we got the temporary loan of a two-seat U-2RT trainer from Beale to conduct proficiency checks and training for my pilots. Having the two-seat U-2 was like a magnet to every Air Force general in Europe. Everyone wanted a shot at flying in a U-2, and we accommodated a number of VIPs for "gee whiz" rides. Every visit was a drain on me and the staff, but that was a consequence of being in the TR-1/U-2 business. However, there's no one who's ever flown in the aircraft who hasn't come away duly impressed and wearing a huge grin, and flying the dignitaries paid dividends in good will and mission support. And for those who thought they could fly anything, I remember only a single general who said it wasn't hard to fly, and he was lying. Most of them immediately ran into trouble just trying to taxi the bird.

I was the only SAC wing commander who didn't fly his own wing's aircraft. Operational commanders were required to fly their aircraft— except for the 17th's commander. The single-seat TR-1 was considered too valuable and too testy to risk having the wing commander ding one, especially since this wing commander hadn't flown anything in ten years. I wasn't bothered by it, but my pilots were. I was told regularly and candidly of their disappointment that their wing commander didn't fly.

Near the end of my two years, I broached the topic with General Astorino prior to the upcoming visit by Lieutenant General Shuler, the 8th Air Force Commander. Astorino said I could mention it to Shuler—carefully. The 17th had done well on our Inspector General inspection, and generals Astorino and Shuler expressed their congratulations. As I drove Lt Gen Shuler to his departing aircraft I asked him about my flying the TR-1. He was ready for the question and said, "Go ahead and fly, but with two provisions: be safe, and don't hog flying from your pilots."

So shortly before Eileen and I left England, I flew a couple of flights in the visiting U-2RT, then flew a solo in the TR-1. I was all grins. I knew that would be my last time to fly a TR-1 or U-2, and it marked the end of my 17 years flying that airplane.

During operational readiness exercises we turned Alconbury into an armed camp, playing "war games." Our exercises were very intense, involving everyone on base. The leadership of both wings hunkered down in the hardened command post bunker, wearing our chemical gear. These exercises were very necessary. They simulated what we would do in actual warfare, and each lasted several days.

In war our base was protected by a British Rapier anti-aircraft missile unit. After one particular exercise, they invited me to view their Rapier live fire training in Scotland. They picked me up at Alconbury and flew me north to the Outer Hebrides islands. It was so starkly primitive there, yet wondrously beautiful, too. After landing we hop-scotched by military armored car from one tiny, rocky island to the next until reaching the larger mainland. There were no trees that far north—just rocks with some grass. The few scattered homes were all made of rock, and it was cold and damp even in the summer sun.

The Rapier live fire was impressive. A Canberra bomber towing a target flew over, and the Rapier crews scored three hits with three missiles—two under the missile's own guidance and the third under manual crew control. The Rapier is a speedster—it's already flying at

Mach 2 by the time it exits its launch tube. I stayed the night and flew back to Alconbury the next day, well-treated and very respectful of those RAF Rapier people.

For Eileen and me our lives were full of ceremony and protocol—formal and semi-formal events of all sorts occupied our lives. Through the Anglo-American Committee we met British dignitaries and neighbors. Our wing received official visitors and VIPs regularly from England, elsewhere in Europe, and the United States. We hosted and were hosted for fetes and dinners several times every week. It seemed that we ate half our meals seated at head tables.

We were invited to various British activities, always with considerable formality, as the Brits are apt to do—and which they do quite well and often. We joked how we got tired of eating cucumber sandwiches and sipping sherry at these things, but still we appreciated the consideration. The British were polite, hospitable, and friendly. I've always had great respect for their traditions and culture, and I'm particularly fond of British humor.

The contrast between British formality and their earthy humor is quite remarkable. The transformation happens fast—it's as if they're cruising along in third gear with typically starchy formality when suddenly the clutch slips and they become completely unhinged. Lurking behind every Brit with a limp handshake is someone who will "go Monty Python" in a heartbeat. Love 'em.

My Director of Maintenance, Jim Deal, and his wife, Maryanne, really got the most out of their tour in England. They lived in a small English village with English neighbors, and they absolutely threw themselves into the English way of life. I was envious—because of my position we had to live on base, and our intermingling with our hosts was always accompanied by ceremony and formalities. When the Deals returned to the States, their daughter wedded a Scotsman, and back to Britain they went. Thanks to Jim's heritage and his Scottish ways, at his retirement party I was compelled to eat haggis while he paraded around in a plaid skirt.

Many gatherings were socially inspired, often associated with British holidays. At nearby Huntingdon we attended a social affair with English community leaders, many who wore regalia displaying their town or community official standing. Some events we attended were less formal, such as when we gathered at a local doctor's manor home.

When Alconbury opened its gates to host an airshow for the English public, VIP hospitality tents and viewing chairs were pitched just a few hundred feet from the runway. I didn't think it was safe to put us that close, and afterward Mike agreed it was too close for his comfort, too—especially when a Swedish demonstration pilot flying a Viggen fighter came extremely close to hitting one of the hangars.

Up the road from Alconbury was an RAF base, and the English wing commander invited all local area wing commanders and wives to dine there one evening. His wing operated Harriers—single-seat fighters with vectored thrust that enabled them to land and takeoff vertically and hover like helicopters.

Our group had the entire Officers Open Mess to ourselves that night. After the meal was over the commander asked us all to step onto the front steps. One of his Harriers appeared, and we were treated to one of the most impressive aerial shows I've ever seen. It was a one-man, one-airplane performance of the remarkable, acrobatic, vertical-thrust Harrier directly over the parking lot just a few hundred feet in front of us. It was incredibly noisy, but quite a thrill.

Another invitation we received was to an outdoor party thrown by the Lord High Sheriff of Cambridge. Eileen was sick, so I went alone to that one. It was a party for 3,000 guests and featured a receiving line for the sheriff and his wife. I really wonder the wisdom of shaking hands with 3000 guests, but that's what they did. We were all accommodated in numerous, huge tents, each of which housed a complimentary wet bar and food for all. Who pays for this stuff?

Nostalgia

The 17th RW is aligned under 7th Air Division in Germany which is aligned under 8th Air Force in Louisiana. Eighth Air Force gained renown from its bombing campaigns in World War II. When a group of World War II veterans of the Mighty Eighth traveled to England to revisit those days, they were aged men and women with memories rekindled by returning to places where they had lived and fought. Eileen and I accompanied them to airfields where graveyards and a small church service commemorated those left behind. It was vivid and touching for us to relive the experience with them. After the veterans had returned home, we received warm letters thanking us for sharing that time with them.

Sometimes we were asked to attend events because we were American and represented our armed forces. That's why we traveled 90 miles to Sheffield one day. It was because of a singular event that captured the essence of those World War II days—remembered dearly by the British who lived through it, often forgotten by the Americans of today.

During the War, an American B-17 bomber had been shot up badly and was returning to land at Sheffield. Realizing they couldn't make it back to the airfield, the crew purposely crash-landed into a hillside so as to miss the populated city. The citizens recognized the sacrifice that had been made for them. Every year the townspeople assembled and walked to that hillside for a small ceremony to commemorate the American crew.

Preceding the ceremony we met with Sheffield citizens at a town hall. It was just a gathering of ordinary people, most quite elderly—simple and without formalities. Many had been there at the time of the crash. They remembered, and they weren't going to let that memory die.

I was introduced to an English gentleman who was obviously older than the others and couldn't hear very well. I learned that he was a World War I veteran pilot who had joined up as a teenager. He had flown SE-5As, and in his early 20s had been promoted to flight commander. When I asked how he had become a flight commander so young, he smiled and said, "Because I was the only one left."

When we returned again the following year I didn't see him and inquired about him. We were told he had passed away. When I think about meeting him, I think of all of us who went through our own wartime experiences. Among my fondest memories, I reflect on meeting and talking with a man who actually flew, fought, and survived in World War I.

\* \* \* \* \* \* \* \* \*

Mike McGinty arranged a dinner for his 10th Wing officers at the Alconbury Officers Open Mess. The featured speaker was a local Member of Parliament who talked to us about that famous, historic English document, the Magna Carta, which produced the modern British governmental system.

Try as I might, I just couldn't garner any enthusiasm for his talk. I'm sure the Magna Carta must interest someone, but it sure didn't seem to excite the crowd that night. As I looked around I saw yawns in the American audience.

At the end of the talk, Mike stood, thanked the speaker, and asked if anyone had questions. Deathly silence. I thought, Uh-oh, this is going to be a huge embarrassment. Eileen and I were seated directly in front, and when I realized, fearfully, that no one was going to ask a question, I stood and asked the speaker if he would please tell us how he had acquired such a deep and interesting knowledge of the Magna Carta. I think my nose grew at least an inch when I heard myself utter those words.

The gentleman smiled and gladly responded, giving us his background in such studies. Then someone else asked another question, and the moment of pregnant pause had passed. Whew!

Afterward Mike motioned for us to come up to meet the speaker. We were introduced and then engaged in small talk for a while. His name didn't mean anything to me at that time.

Months afterward, John Major became the Prime Minister of England.

After the dinner guests had dispersed, Mike thanked me and said how worried he was that no one was going to ask Mr. Major any questions.  Hell, if I had known the guy was going to be prime minister, I would have asked a lot more—and gotten his phone number, too.

\* \* \* \* \* \* \* \* \*

My highest-ranking boss was General Jack Chain, four-star Commander-in-Chief of Strategic Air Command.  When I was SAC Senior Controller back in Omaha I was General Chain's designated personal representative, but I had only talked with him on the phone a couple of times.  He endorsed my officer efficiency report, though.  We were told the general was embarking on a visit to all his overseas wings, and his first stop was to be Alconbury.

His personal visit to the 17th was a big affair.  His past protocol for visiting overseas units was to arrive early morning so that he and his large entourage could embark on an all-day visit.  But coming to Alconbury would require a night flight from Omaha through the time zones, arriving with little sleep.

His protocol office advised that he was going to try something different this time.  He would travel instead with a smaller contingent and arrive at early evening so as to have a night's sleep before touring our wing's facilities.

Because of his late afternoon arrival time and smaller numbers, we decided to host him that evening in our home.  We made catering plans and hired an employee from the officers club to provide tray service.  However, just a few days before his arrival his protocol office called to tell us that instead of an accompanying party of twelve, his group had grown to thirty.

Eighteen additional people changed everything.  Our house was far too small for his thirty plus ten of mine.  It was too late to book the officers club or get more help—our modest home would have to do.  They all arrived, and we squeezed everyone in, but it was literally a shoulder-to-shoulder affair.  The waitress could hardly move through the crowd. It was stuffy and horribly uncomfortable, but no one complained—at least out loud.

The next day I escorted General Chain for his inspection of the 17th while Eileen gave Mrs. Chain a tour of family facilities and took her to lunch with the wives of enlisted members. His visit went well, but that night of hosting a four-star general plus 40 in our home is a memory I wish would go away.

## Pride and Sadness

For me our most memorable ceremony was a heartfelt one. I wish every American would attend one of the memorials commemorating the tragedies of two World Wars held at one of the large gravesites that dot Europe. So much of today's internal bickering would fade away if Americans who have never been deprived of anything could cast their eyes on the remnants of those wars that brought all together at one devastating period in history.

The British never forget to honor those who sacrificed the most. They have a day called Remembrance Day, the equivalent of our Memorial Day.

Eileen, I, and American military leaders from all over England were invited for Remembrance Day ceremonies at the American Cemetery at Cambridge. Many, many hundreds were assembled for the most stirring ceremony I've ever attended. We military were in our best uniform and everyone else wore full attire. The most elaborate, precision military outfits in England paraded in tribute to Americans who fought on soil, air and sea to protect British citizens.

As I said, the British never forget. That day Britain's flag flew beside the Stars and Stripes. Perhaps all Americans should be more respectful of who we are, what we fought for, and what we gave.

## An Accident Isn't All It's Cracked Up to Be

I was attending a meeting in the 10th Wing conference room one day when the secretary came in and handed me a note. It said one of my TR-1s just had an accident.

There's no worse news a wing commander can receive, but as I exited the building and got into my car, I called ahead and learned that no one was injured and the bird was intact, resting on a taxiway. I drove across the airfield to the crash scene, expecting the worst but receiving far better news. As I pulled up, I was approached by several officers including Stormy Boudreaux, the pilot. Stormy began by saying he had done everything he could, and then the story unfolded. In all my aviation years I've never encountered such a bizarre accident.

Stormy had landed from a low altitude training flight, had turned off the runway and was taxiing in to park. Meanwhile, a British construction worker was working to the side of that taxiway. He had been using a jackhammer that was connected to the running engine of his parked tractor. As he hammered away, his tractor somehow slipped into gear. It pulled away from him, dragging the attached jackhammer with the driver in pursuit. The tractor jumped the lip of the taxiway and skipped up onto the pavement. When the trailing jackhammer caught the taxiway lip, it yanked and turned the tractor, pointing it straight toward Stormy's approaching TR-1. Stormy saw it coming and could do nothing except stop. Just before impact Stormy has presence of mind to release his brakes in hopes it would lessen the impact. The tractor hit the airplane at the left wing root and kept churning away until the driver finally caught up and shut it down.

Stormy was quite upset, but it was evident he wasn't at fault, and there was nothing for him to fret about. He was a victim of circumstance. Stormy was one of my best, and my job at that point was to simply reassure him.

SAC sent an accident investigation team to Alconbury. As I met the lead investigator, a colonel, in my office, he was grim and all-business as I related what happened. I could tell he was skeptical— nothing that strange could really be true. I chuckled to myself as he left my office to begin his investigation. Putting the damage aspect aside I saw a vein of humor in such a bizarre circumstance. In a couple of hours the inspector was back, and his demeanor was much more relaxed.

For the 17th Wing it was a no-fault accident—the best kind, if you're going to have one. The airplane was sent back to the States for a one million-dollar repair job. My maintenance guys pulled the wings off the bird as you might pluck them from a fly, and they fit the entire airplane inside a C-141 transport aircraft bound for the States. We got our TR-1 back several months later. I don't know what became of the British worker. Probably took him out back and shot him along with his tractor. With a camera, of course.

Fortunately, that was the only serious operational incident or accident that happened to the wing while I was there. Our operational performance was quite good, and we passed our NATO operational readiness inspection—the ultimate goal. We grew, and the 17th was fully prepared for its successful engagement in the Gulf War that came within two years after I had left.

Well, there actually was another accident, but it was a personal one.

After more than a year at Alconbury I actually took a vacation. Vice commander John Sander took over my commander responsibilities while Eileen and I left to have a good time in London. Eileen had already taken some trips with the officers' wives—to Holland, Russia, and sights in the U.K. But this was my first time away from duty, and I was looking forward to it.

We took a train to London and booked into the Columbia Club Hotel which accommodates American service members. We took taxis and a double-decker bus to sightsee around London, enjoying it very much. We got tickets to hear the Royal Philharmonic Orchestra for an evening concert. When we left the performance hall we saw it had been raining, as usual. We hailed a cab, and I remarked to Eileen that it didn't have seatbelts—a modern, 20th-centruy innovation that was slowly finding its way to England. Ten minutes later we were smashed by another car in a roundabout.

Eileen and I were sent head-first into the plexiglass partition separating us from the driver and ended up on the back seat floor. I don't think we lost consciousness, but we were stunned. As we regained awareness, she got up and I noticed blood splattered all over her raincoat. When I asked, she said she was okay, but I was intent on trying to see where she was bleeding. Something was obscuring my vision. That's when I realized she was wearing my blood.

After treatment at the hospital, Eileen was released but they kept me overnight. The driver was treated and released, and he came by to see how we were, very concerned. We reassured him we would be fine, and he left. The police cited the other driver who turned out to be a foreign national without a driver's license.

I called to the wing and one of my pilots volunteered to come to London and assist us home. As we walked through the Kings Cross railway station like a couple of bandaged zombies in our bloodstained clothes, we met local Alconbury citizen Lady Emily Blatch, a Member of the House of Lords, coming off a train headed toward us. We must have looked pretty bad because she looked horrified when she saw us. She offered to help, but we were okay and just thanked her. We were busted up and bruised, but the worst part was cutting short our "vacation." I had cervical damage and had to undergo therapy for quite some time. It took almost a year for British authorities to finalize the case, and the settlement netted us a huge, whopping $5,000. British common law.

## Other Happenings

During our two years in England my life was very full. Days were involved with work and many evenings were filled with official and semi-official affairs with the Brits, the people of the 17th, and our counterparts from the 10th Wing. I also attended duties and functions at nearby air bases. At RAF Lakenheath I played handball with an old War College friend who was wing commander there, and at RAF Mildenhall I saw SR-71 friends and a general I knew from the Pentagon. Sometimes the Air Force family can be quite small.

Our wing hosted a lot of visiting dignitaries, military and civilians. For many such visits we took guests to dinner at local restaurants, usually in the company of the wing's top officers and wives, most of them friends from our previous U-2 days. I think how fortunate I was to have such good, competent people around me—it's so much easier when you have personal confidence in the wing's leaders.

One night we arranged for a visiting general to have dinner with our wing's senior officers and wives at The Eagle, a local restaurant and pub. British food wasn't always to our taste (e.g., unsweetened desserts), but The Eagle's service and atmosphere were quite nice. That's why we were completely floored by what happened. We were just conversing when the dinners were brought to our table on a big tray. As the waiter squeezed between other tables, Eileen and I were astounded when a nearby patron simply reached out and grabbed a piece of meat off of the general's plate. No one else saw it happen, so we kept our mouths closed and enjoyed a laugh afterwards.

Eileen and I got away when we could, traveling locally to enjoyable places in East Anglia. We remember nice dinners with Chuck and Soyoung at an unusual restaurant that was made from a barge anchored in the Ouse River. We went to a favorite French Restaurant in a 500 year-old building where you had to stoop low to miss the ceiling beams. The owner served tables and his French wife was the chef—they argued incessantly. One old place with beautiful gardens and an expansive lawn had once been a girl's school. We took our little Westie and spread a blanket on the grassy grounds. We drove there through a tiny village that quaintly posted signs for a duck crossing, and we actually had to stop one day while a duck hen and chicks crossed single file to reach a nearby pond.

These outings took us to castles, manor houses, private residences, and even a race track where the horses ran around clockwise. In one place tradition held that marks on the banister were Queen Ann Boleyn's nail scratches made as she was dragged to her execution. We visited the huge cathedrals at Peterborough and Ely and toured the campus of Cambridge University while rowers skimmed the quiet waters flowing nearby. We had afternoon tea at The Swan, a very old hotel in Lavenham, the Flemish mill town given fame for the rhyme,

"There was a crooked man who lived in a crooked house." The old houses really are crooked there.

We had many pleasant memories like these.

## More Stuff

Some memories weren't pleasant. One of my sergeants attempted suicide one day. She stepped outside and slashed her wrists. She was okay after medical attention, but the incident revealed a much deeper problem that involved racial issues, collusion among senior NCOs, and poor performance by an officer. It was very complicated, and it involved much of my personal attention to rectify problems that had festered within my organization.

There were other unsavory issues I had to deal with. That's what commanders do, as I had learned long before. With 650 people in the wing problems always popped up. But the 17th was a good organization, and I've got to admit that I had relatively few such issues, in large part because my vice wing commanders, Chuck and John, dealt with such matters very well. Regrettably, though, during those years I had to remove and replace two of my key officers.

But our wing did well. Thanks to a top commander, my supply squadron won the Best in SAC award, and Colonel Jim Deal led his maintenance squadrons to win awards for excellence, too. We had an abundance of good people, we got our jobs done, and we did them pretty well, I'm pleased to say.

\* \* \* \* \* \* \* \* \*

Most of the generals and higher echelon officials I've met were truly gifted leaders, but not all impressed me so. When the 2nd Air Force commander, a two-star general not in my chain of command, visited the 10th TAC Fighter Wing, I was invited to dine with him and the colonels of the 10th. The general was making an inspection of the 10th Wing, and I was invited along purely as a courtesy.

At dinner I had little to say and even less to do, but there was no shortage of conversation because the general supplied it all. The guy must have thought he was destined for glory because he gave the entire table enough personal philosophy to last a lifetime. He was the life of the party, or so he thought, and his colonels politely nodded to his words of "wisdom."

It was a very droll dinner for me. However, I remember one of his philosophic, homespun remarks to this day: "Them who can, do. Them who can't, teach." I suppose that comment was made to denigrate and discourage those like me, who later enjoyed many years in academia.

Just before I left England SAC sent over a Senior Span U-2 for test and evaluation. The Senior Span equipment featured a satellite dish mounted in a tear-shaped pod above the fuselage. Senior Span was built to give the U-2 the ability to beam its digital intelligence to a satellite which would in turn relay it to ground-based intelligence analysts elsewhere around the world. It was the end product that began with those ALSS missions I flew over New Mexico some fifteen years earlier. It sure was an ugly-looking configuration of the U-2, but it looked nice to me.

As I mentioned earlier, toward the end of my last year we moved the 17th's flying operation and people to RAF Sculthorpe at the northeast coast of England's East Anglia region. Our new, hardened aircraft shelters and support buildings were mostly completed, and construction to widen and refurbish Alconbury's crosswind runway had begun. We moved to Sculthorpe, and Mike moved his A-10s to other Tactical Air Command bases around England.

## Time to Leave

The relocation to Sculthorpe went well, and our flight operations were soon up and running smoothly with very few problems. And then I realized the clock had run out on my tenure as the 17th's commander. It came time for us to leave England and Alconbury.

Eileen and I had talked over our future, and together we decided I wouldn't seek another "onward and upward" assignment. I may have been burned out from our very involved lives during those two years. Eileen was certainly ready to end the very demanding Alconbury way of life.

Perhaps it was time to leave the Air Force, too.

We knew that my next assignment would likely be to a headquarters staff, probably at SAC Headquarters back in Omaha. After years of staff and headquarters assignments, I didn't want another. I suspect I would have been competitive for promotion to general officer, but no one made any promises or assurances of that.

I had really gotten all I ever wanted from the Air Force and much, much more. I didn't think I'd enjoy a general officer's life with all the meetings and protocol, working in an office someplace within some large organization. General Astorino said he would support whatever I wanted to do, but my decision wasn't all that difficult. I had simply come to a point where there was nothing else I really wanted to do. Sure, I wonder if I would have been promoted if I had tried, but I wasn't motivated enough to endure the necessary tribulations. With the decision made, next I had to find a next assignment to finish my Air Force life.

Military service always meant that eventually you had to leave it for something else—there are no stodgy, doddering old officers occupying the quiet corners of the room in today's active forces. I had enjoyed my years in the Air Force, but it was over.

Our departure change of command ceremony was on a far smaller scale than the first one. Most of the wing's people were working at Sculthorpe, so necessity reduced the change of command in size and scope. Lieutenant General Schuler and his wife had just visited, so General Astorino flew in from Germany to preside over the downsized affair. We assembled a couple of squadrons inside one of the new hardened shelters—the scale was small enough and the shelter large enough to do that. John Sander became the next—and last—17th Reconnaissance Wing Commander. The 17th was disbanded when the first Gulf War began.

\* \* \* \* \* \* \* \* \* \*

And so we left. A car with civilian driver pulled up to the house and we loaded our bags. Coincidentally, he was the same driver who had driven us from London to Alconbury two years before. Eileen, I, and our little British Westie pup headed for London Heathrow Airport. We gave up "Mini" to go into the cargo bay for the flight to Dallas, hoping she would do okay. She did. Once back in the US, we cleared customs, got in our rental car, and headed for San Marcos. I managed to avoid the urge to drive on the left side of the road, and we made it onto Interstate 35 heading south. It wasn't until we put the car on cruise control that we truly sensed we had left England and were back in the United States. We were tired, but uplifted. Our car came with a built-in cell phone, so we called all our family as we drove.

We were fulfilled by two memorable years in England, but as we looked upon spacious Texas on that warm summer day, it felt really good to be home.

# In One Career, Out the Other

Years before when I had returned from Vietnam as a captain I was tendered a regular officer commission, which I accepted. I signed on for an active duty service commitment with the expectation that if I passed successive promotions leading to lieutenant colonel or above, I would earn a retirement. The Air Force is a pyramidal, up-or-out system, meaning that if you don't earn promotions your time on active duty is limited. Most Air Force members must make the change to civilian life while still in their working years.

I had intended my last Air Force assignment to be a stepping stone to prepare for our civilian employment phase of life. I had no idea what my civilian employment might be, but commanding an AFROTC detachment at a university seemed to be a good way to ease out the door rather than face transitional shock head-on.

Again I wondered if I had made the right decision. Would I have been promoted to general if I had tried for it? It would have meant seeking a more competitive position upon leaving the 17th. My credentials were excellent, and I'm confident I would have competed well before a promotion board.

But before even weighing the odds, I made my choice based on more fundamental reasoning. I simply didn't have the desire.

Once I had made up my mind—and Eileen made it clear she would support me either way—the decision to ask for a career-departure assignment became much easier. And it wasn't all just about me and my personal aspirations—our two years in England and my preceding assignments were as demanding on Eileen as they were on me. I think

246

she thought I really wanted to stay in service and compete for general officer, and she gave me every opportunity to say so.

But I really didn't have the ambition. I had reached the end of the line. The time was approaching for me to leave the Air Force. I—and we—were ready to begin our transition to civilian life, and our last assignment would get us there.

## Civilian Life

Southwest Texas State University is now the University of Texas at San Marcos, but in 1987 it was known by its former name and had earned recognition for having graduated President Lyndon B. Johnson. SWT was a sizeable institution with a 22,000 student body. It's located on the edge of the scenic Texas Hill country and along Interstate 35 with the cities of Austin and San Antonio serving as bookends.

Air Force Reserve Officer Training Corps Detachment 840 had an enrollment of about 100 cadets. Running the detachment with a cadre of seven officers and NCOs was far different from commanding a wing of 650 Air Force members and operating airplanes with a wartime mission. I had to really unwind over the first weeks, but the calm of campus life was most welcome.

I led two lives at SWT: one as an Air Force detachment commander and the other as a university department chair and professor. My job was to select qualified students as cadets, train them as officers, and ultimately commission some as new second lieutenants.

Students were genuinely motivated and very enthusiastic; they were an enjoyable group of young people. The detachment's staff of three junior officers and two NCOs also led roles as both Air Force instructors and as mentors to young students coming of age. The cadre was carefully selected from other non-rated (non-flying) Air Force specialties. Stella Brecher was our civilian secretary but was also a key figure to the detachment and a mentor to students. They were all really fine people.

I commanded Det 840 for two and a half years. Campus and faculty life were laid-back. Minor issues—mostly involving people and personalities—came up, but none of them were very problematic. The most interesting circumstance was when my senior NCO got married.

My position as a department chair and professor involved me in official university activities. My university boss, the Dean of Applied Arts and Technologies, Gene Martin, was a fair man and friend. My Air Force boss, Colonel Rich Buickerood, was also a good boss, a most capable guy and a long-term friend. We're still corresponding after all these years.

Eileen had a role to play in cadet activities, too. Part of introducing young cadets to the Air Force way of life was in social gatherings that previewed officer roles and responsibilities. Eileen found herself in the role of senior spouse and mentor to the young ladies who were either dating cadets or were cadets themselves. Fresh from Alconbury, it was a more relaxed atmosphere for her, too.

Living in San Marcos was pleasant. The Texas Hill Country has a sublime, peaceful quality. We envisioned that we might come back someday, perhaps in retirement. San Marcos was certainly convenient. The town was just the right size for us. The two large cities, Austin and San Antonio, were far enough away but not too far to drive occasionally. For our Air Force needs, Randolph AFB was just south of us, 45 minutes away. Dale and Janelle Hudler had moved to Austin, and we visited them often. Dale was recovering from his rigorous, experimental cancer treatment that proved to be successful.

In 1989 the Cold War was ending, and the Air Force was drawing down. After the Vietnam War ended there had been a reduction in force that terminated active duty for several U-2 pilots. Likewise, in 1989 there was another reduction in officer strength. The Air Force announced that colonels were to be screened for selective active duty termination. I thought I might be vulnerable since mine was an end-of-duty assignment, but I was retained.

It was pleasant to work at the university as both an Air Force commander and a university professor—sort of one foot in the door and one outside. My position as a university Department Chair gave me an insight into university governance and culture that I would use later when I became a professor once again.

University governance was far different from military organization. I recall visiting with the university president one day. Dr. Supple was a very good man. He and I mostly discussed matters affecting my detachment, but then we just talked for a while. I think he welcomed the opportunity to chat with someone slightly outside his campus purview.

At the time he was facing tough times with the faculty senate over several policy concerns. It seemed extraordinary to me how much power and influence a faculty body had over the university president. For example, one of the issues was over the use of rodents for laboratory testing. There had been some vandalism in university laboratories. He was having a difficult time placating the unrest and he commiserated how no one wanted to compromise. I listened with sympathy while taking some private solace that I was still in the Air Force. I never had to deal with a faculty senate, thank goodness. However, in later years as a professor at Embry-Riddle I would become a member of the faculty senate.

# From Air Force to Airline

After Two and a half years at SWT it was time to prepare for my retirement and civilian afterlife. Mike McGinty was now a Brigadier General and the Director of Air Force Personnel just thirty miles away at Randolph AFB, and he came up to SWT to preside over my retirement ceremony. With Mike came my former executive officer at Alconbury, Captain Julie Tepe. It was sad to leave the Air Force after nearly 27 years, but my two years at SWT had given me time to prepare. Eileen and I were given a warm send-off by Dr. Supple, Dean Martin, and my staff.

I had decided to seek an airline pilot job. I began flying light airplanes at the aero club at Bergstrom AFB in Austin. As it happened, I became president of the Aero Club, but only because they needed a ranking officer to fill the role. I built up flying time and airplane currency, then got my Airline Transport Rating. It was only light airplane flying, but I thought it might be enough to burnish my credentials for the airlines.

I woke up to reality when I realized I was too old to be hired by a major airline, and the little flying I had recently accomplished didn't make me very competitive. I looked at a couple of management job possibilities that were decidedly unattractive. Everything was a step down from the Air Force responsibilities I had held, and I would certainly have to adjust to that. I had no particular civilian, foot-in-the-door connections, although I might have looked to Lockheed or such. A former SR-71 back-seater I knew was employed with American Eagle, and he said he'd get me a pilot job at that regional affiliate of American Airlines (AA). I took a deep breath and went for it. It was a mistake.

I should never have tried to go back to the cockpit. As a first officer at Eagle I was too old to fit in. I was a fish out of water. I trained in Dallas, then flew out of Albany, New York. We moved there and rented an apartment. The airline business was like nothing I had ever encountered. Although it involved flying and aviation, it was a far cry from the mission, the camaraderie, the dedication, and the people I had known in the Air Force. The airlines were strictly union territory, and everything was governed by union contract. I had become just a number on a seniority list. I quickly became disenchanted by union dominance in the airline industry. Later on in my airline management positions, I would truly detest how unionism suppressed everyone's ambitions and stifled innovative thinking.

After several months in Albany, I bid for and got the Raleigh, North Carolina, domicile (RDU), and we moved again. One of the attractions of Raleigh was that it was near my home. My parents lived in Hickory, about three hour's drive from us. But Mom's health was failing. I was at work in Raleigh with Eileen helping with Mom and Dad the day Mom passed away. Dad decided to live on in the house alone, but later he came to live with us in Tennessee.

I wasn't happy with airline work at all, and I started looking for other employment. I got my real estate license and worked part-time for a real estate company, but sales work wasn't for me, either. One day I went into the RDU chief pilot's office, introduced myself, and offered to help. I was flying standby lines that gave me considerable time off. I struck a friendship with the chief pilot and helped him with various matters.

A domicile chief pilot is the bridge between management and rank and file pilots. The pilots' union is dead-set against relinquishing any power it has over its members and had an adversarial relationship with management. The RDU chief pilot walked a tightrope much of the time. On the occasion of an impending strike he made a decision to side with the union and not enforce a company policy against wearing union badges on the uniform. He got canned for it. The company advertised to fill his position. I applied and got the job. I was surprised—I had flown as a first officer for 18 months and had never been a captain.

Domicile Chief Pilot

I was now supervising 320 pilots at the Raleigh-Durham International Airport, one of our four hubs with American Airlines. But in an airline those pilots are forever flying to other cities. They're seldom in the domicile, and when at home they were usually waiting to fly out again. In more than a year as chief pilot, I actually met or got to know very few of those who worked for me.

On my first day I went into the crew room and was approached by the union's domicile president, Marty. As we shook hands in greeting, he looked at me and boldly stated that he could make or break me. Nice introduction. That pretty much set the tone for my 18 months as chief pilot.

It was a rough and tumble job in a company structure very different from any Air Force organization. Pilots did what was required and nothing more. There were relatively few managers to oversee many pilots and flight attendants. To most crew members airline flying was a job, not a calling. For managers in the face of union adversity, trying to build trust and unity was a hapless effort.

One day I wanted to talk to two pilots who were returning to Raleigh from a multi-day trip. I sent word to their airplane for them to stop into my office when they finished their post-flight procedures. Instead they bolted and were last seen scaling the perimeter fence.

As in all managerial positions, I spent much time putting out fires and soothing dispositions. But a great deal of my time and effort was also spent trying to keep airplanes flying on schedule. At an airline the schedule reigns supreme. Every day we four domicile managers— representing field services (customers, ticketing), flight attendants, maintenance, and flight operations (pilots)—would meet to discuss and resolve flight delays and cancellations during the previous day. There we'd decide which organization was responsible for any flight aberrations. Airlines live or die by those publicized on-time success rates, and it was a daily finger-pointing exercise.

The Allied Pilots Association made sure the relationship between the union and management was formal and antagonistic. Although union officers would occasionally arrange to meet with me behind closed doors, those times of consultation were very rare, and cooperation was even rarer. At those times the mood was more congenial, but they'd never allow us to appear that way in public.

Initially the Allied Pilots Association formally complained that I had become chief pilot without having been a captain, but they had no say in that matter. Informally, we worked most things out, but the APA's domicile president at RDU, Marty, was all mouth and distinctly a horse's ass. He had earned his spurs as a staunch union guy at Eastern Airlines before they went bankrupt.

I learned much about airline structure, management and union employee relations as time went on. I repeat that the airline business is and was a far cry from the Air Force. People issues, complicated by union entrenchment, dominated much of my time—in that way there wasn't much difference. Regional airline pilots were young and often immature or undisciplined, and they gave me much to do. Unlike the Air Force, civilian airline pilots aren't carefully screened and selected for officer qualities, and there were far more behavioral problems to deal with in the airline business.

With 320 pilots it would have helped to have some more staff assistance, but my entire staff consisted of a single administrative assistant—a former flight attendant—whom I shared with the flight attendants' manager who had half the people and complexity that I had. That was the regional airline way. For approximately 1200 pilots there were just four domicile chief pilots. I was stretched pretty thin.

I regularly read the Raleigh Observer newspaper and noticed that the editorial staff frequently hammered a Raleigh city councilman who was a retired Army colonel. The paper seemed to take pleasure in faulting him for his "military ways." It was clearly anti-military, biased reporting by the paper, and I wrote a critical letter to the editor in his defense.

He called at home to thank me. We talked, and he asked about my background. The next day he called again to ask if I would be willing to take membership on the newly created Airport Noise Abatement Committee. I said I would and was soon appointed by the city council. That brought me into a working relationship with the RDU airport authority and the former mayor, and I got to know some of the airport authority staff quite well.


## The Crash

I had been chief pilot over a year when an American Eagle airplane crashed five miles off the Raleigh runway. A Raleigh-based crew was making a night landing approach when an engine ice warning light came on. The warning should normally be no big deal, but together they mishandled the situation and crashed five miles from the airport with crew and passenger fatalities.

I was attending a Noise Abatement Committee meeting at the airport that night when I was paged and told of the crash. I didn't get home until almost dawn the next day. The ensuing investigation dragged me deep into the legal world as lawsuits were filed against the company—and me, as the chief pilot.

For years afterward I met with company-appointed lawyers as those lawsuits played out. There was no doubt the company was legally at fault for the crash, but aviation lawyers and families wanted to pin negligence on the company. American Eagle was part of American Airlines and AMR Corporation, and their pockets ran deep. I became the target for a negligence lawsuit, holding that pilot error was at fault and implicating me as chief pilot. My name appeared in the New York Times, USA Today, and the Raleigh Observer. Charges were levied that the captain had training and performance deficiencies that somehow I should have known about and addressed. The fact that his training records were 1000 miles away in Dallas made no difference. The fact that some earlier training deficiencies had already been addressed appropriately by Eagle's Manager of Aircrew Training in Dallas made no difference. It also made no difference that I had only met him once and had never met the first officer who was the real cause of the accident.

Shortly after the Raleigh crash and because of corporate marketing decisions, American announced the Raleigh hub would close. With that announcement Eagle's pilot union was thrown into chaos.

254

Raleigh pilots (and flight attendants) were going to be displaced to other locations, and some might lose their jobs. The union was desperate and without any leverage or information despite all their promises that they had the "upper hand" over management.

Their desperation led them to invite me to an APA meeting. I accepted—the first breakthrough in relations in all the time I had been chief pilot. When it was announced that I'd be attending the pilots' meeting, the flight attendants attended, too.

It was sad to see the worry everyone showed about their jobs, their homes, their lives. Most of their worries stemmed from uncertainty and disinformation—information that would have been forthcoming if they hadn't created such barriers against management. Union leaders had stupidly breached a confidentiality agreement they had made with Eagle's management and for that they were banned from further inclusion in management's planning meetings. Now they were in the dark and had no clue what was happening.

It was in that atmosphere of desperation that I attended the Raleigh union meeting. I wasn't there to levy recriminations for their many missteps; I just wanted to provide information to help them manage their personal situations.

I was well-received. I didn't do anything except try to breach the void of misunderstanding and give information about company movement and consolidation plans. Afterward I was approached by numerous pilots and flight attendants simply thanking me for attending. On the ride home I thought how different it all was from the Air Force where such communications and common planning were expected, not the exception.

We had two more such meetings before the domicile closed, and I was always given enthusiastic thanks from the attendees. It was a shame that sheer pig-headed unionism had stood in the way of better relationships for so long. Why couldn't we have met like this before?

I closed and locked all our doors that last day of Raleigh's operations. No one else was there—just me with the keys. It was a sad occasion. That was the end of RDU's American and Eagle hub for many years. More recently Eileen and I have had occasion to fly into RDU, causing me to think back to my early days.

Just a week before we closed I had a knock at my office door. It was Marty, the domicile union president. He asked to talk and closed the door. He seemed nervous. He was a man without any union title now, wondering what he might do next. To my surprise he asked if I would write him a letter of recommendation. I never liked the guy, but I consented. I wrote the letter carefully. I commended him for his staunch union loyalty, but nothing else. Anyone who read my words could clearly see that Marty was a union guy through-and-through who put union goals before company loyalties. No manager I know would ever hire him after reading my letter, but Marty beamed when he read it. To him what I wrote was complimentary praise, indeed.

## We Move to Nashville

I was without any official company standing. My position in Raleigh no longer existed. Eagle kept me on as a roving chief pilot for some months. I trained the new chief pilots in both New York and Miami and worked for some weeks at both domiciles. But after a few months in this ad hoc position, I was told it couldn't last and the company would soon have to return me to the cockpit, which I wouldn't do.

Some months earlier the RDU Airport Authority Operations Director's position became vacant. I applied and was interviewed by the Airport Director. Through my membership on the Airport Noise Abatement Committee, I had gotten to know and work with several people in the airport authority. But I had never managed an airport, let alone a large, international one, and I wasn't optimistic about my chances. After many weeks I heard nothing. Meanwhile the crash had occurred, the announcement was made that American's and Eagle's RDU hub was closing, and my job was cast into official limbo. That's when the position of Manager of Flight Administration at Eagle's headquarters in Nashville opened. I was offered that job and accepted.

We enjoyed Raleigh and I was tempted to stay there, living off of our Air Force retirement income until some other job came along. But because of the crash and the looming lawsuits I thought it would be wiser to stay attached to AMR Corporation and their lawyers for a while.

So we prepared to move. We put our new home on the market and sold it within the week. On the day the movers arrived, I got a call at home from the RDU Airport Director. It had been several months since I had applied for the Airport Operations Director position. I had given up on it, but to my surprise he offered it to me. With the movers putting our furniture on the van even as we talked, I had to decline.

In Tennessee we bought a two-story house just east of Nashville in the town of Old Hickory. Our house was quite nice, and living there was comfortable. The Cumberland River was to our north, and just to the south was The Hermitage, the historic mansion and estate of Andrew Jackson. Nashville surely is "The Music City." Live music abounded everywhere—good, high-quality, professional music. At Christmastime we went to hear holiday music played by a symphony orchestra with a 300-member chorus. It was spectacular.

I worked in the top floor of a nine-story office building at the Nashville airport. Our headquarters filled that entire floor, and below us on the 7th floor was the FAA. Months later American Airlines decided to close their hub at Nashville and move its assets to the Miami hub. Eagle moved out of the office building and into the vacated AA offices in the terminal building. My new office was immediately overlooking Gate C2; every time a Southwest aircraft pulled on or off the gate, the noise was overwhelming. Nice view, though.

Not long after we moved to Nashville, Eileen's Mom died. As her Mom declined Eileen spent a lot of time in Pennsylvania caring for her. Eileen's Dad died about a year afterward, and Eileen spent considerable time caring for him, too. My Dad wasn't doing well living alone back in North Carolina after Mom's death. We had purposely bought our Nashville home with space and a floor plan to accommodate any one of our parents who might come to live with us. We invited Dad, and so he came.

I was at work one day when an intense storm developed. A tornado dropped down out and hit Nashville to the east of the airport. I was just leaving work for the day and I caught it all on the news. The tornado was headed for Old Hickory. As I approached the town I saw police cars with lights flashing, directing traffic to detour. Trees and telephone poles were down, and debris was scattered everywhere. I became really worried for Eileen and Dad at home. I followed the detour, expecting the worst. When I turned into our housing development, I was relieved to see little damage. In our yard a small tree had blown over. Eileen and Dad were safe.

## New Job in Nashville

I was one of seven headquarters managers who ran flight operations. As Manager of Flight Administration I supervised our Manager of Crew Scheduling in Dallas. That meant spending about one of every five weekends there.

My Manager of Crew Scheduling was a former Eastern Airlines flight attendant who had survived the crash of Eastern Flight 401 in the Florida Everglades. She had been traumatized by that crash and found solace by visiting other airlines and speaking to flight attendant training classes about the lessons to be learned from her experience.

But she carried a lot of mental baggage for years after the crash, and she was not performing well for us. Eagle fired her (a decision made at the VP level), and she sued the company.

I flew to Dallas as the company representative to witness her deposition. She really botched it, essentially blaming herself for the very matters that caused Eagle to fire her and admitting she had refused to abide by the advice of her own psychiatrist. I liked her, and it was a sad thing to witness. She was a troubled lady.

After the deposition her lawyer was left alone with us, regretfully shaking his head. He said they would be dropping her lawsuit.

258

Afterward I went to lunch with our company's lawyers. There's some humor in that—I seemed to be spending an inordinate amount of time with lawyers of late.

These three were labor lawyers, and they could hardly wait to pump me about our pilot labor agreement. They all had many years' experience in labor law but had never worked with an airline pilot contract before. They asked me if ours was a typical pilot agreement, and I said that it was. They were amazed by its immense size and detail—it was fully four times bigger than any other they had worked with. I remarked dryly that they should experience the pleasures of dealing with it daily like I did.

Our pilot labor agreement required binding arbitration to resolve implacable differences. The arbitration panel judging that proceeding consists of an appointed professional arbitrator, a company rep, and a union rep. I've been the company representative on arbitration boards occasionally.

One case involved a female pilot who was fired for not coming to work. She had been granted a leave of absence but didn't come back to work afterward as she was supposed to. She finally returned only when the union told her to, under management pressure.

The case seemed open and shut, but things didn't work that way. Her union lawyer presented some really, really feeble excuses for her absenteeism, complete with assumptions and extraneous hypothetical suppositions straight out of Disneyworld. The union's intent was to draw the arbitration out to ridiculous extremes, hoping the company would cave and reinstate her on a trial basis. The appointed arbitrator was from a different planet and didn't know boo about pilots, flying safety, airline operations, crew rest, or anything else regarding the danger of placing an unreliable pilot in the cockpit. As a result, the arbitration dragged on for weeks, and it was finally decided to bring her back to work under probation. Soon afterward she got fired again for more absenteeism. The union didn't contest it.

Another manager in flight operations made a big mistake and was fired for it. While still working at Eagle, he and some partners started a small airline in eastern Tennessee. When it was discovered he was

259

apparently borrowing Eagle's proprietary information, he was summarily dismissed. He was promptly marched out of the building carrying only a few private possessions. I went down to say good-bye to him in the parking lot. He was crying.

Promotion Denied, Sort of . . .

American Eagle in Nashville—Nashville Eagle—was having maintenance problems, and the VP of Maintenance was let go. Our Director of Operations was promoted to become the new Vice President of Maintenance. (Poor Kevin inherited a mess and was in a "vice" in more ways than one.) Our VP of Flight Operations, Ed Criner, wanted to appoint me as the new Director of Operations, but first I had to be approved by the FAA. The FAA is approval authority for an airline's top flight operations managers. The FAA declined to approve me because I had never been a captain.

So I had reached my "glass ceiling" in the airline business. I was barred from further promotion in flight operations. It made no difference that I had been a domicile chief pilot supervising hundreds of captains. It made no difference that I had trained our other domicile chief pilots. My many years as an Air Force Command Pilot—the equivalent of captain—also meant nothing. Likewise, it made no difference that I had held Air Force equivalent jobs of Director of Operations, CEO, and more.

I thought it was strangely hypocritical that the FAA regulates airlines to promote safety but yet they give credence to a unionized system that promotes first officers to captain based on a seniority number, not individual merit.

So Ed simply had me assume the Director's responsibilities with no job title. No raise, either.

No More Lawyers!

Four years after the Raleigh crash I flew from Nashville to Dallas for yet another meeting with lawyers in preparation for the upcoming trial. The legal firm had plush offices on the umpteenth floor of an office building in the heart of Dallas. While five of us conferred in a huge conference room, a secretary entered and announced a phone call for the lead lawyer. He left the room, and when he returned he simply said, "Art, you're done." The judge had thrown out the negligence charges that had involved me, and just like that my four-year escapade was over. It happened so suddenly that I was stunned. I simply shook hands and left, meeting the rest of them later that night for dinner.

Throughout the legal ordeal I had been repeatedly told, "Art, this isn't about you. It's a normal legal process to get more money." But I had no context to put that in. I had been told that nothing would come of the negligence portion of the case, which was apparently pro forma for aircraft accidents. But how was I to know for sure? Nothing in my life prepared me for the strange world of accident litigation. For four long years I was entirely at the mercy of a hoard of lawyers. They were nice guys, and I particularly liked the two lawyers in North Carolina. But what was routine business for them was torturous for me.

After all was over I felt bruised by the entire experience, and it took quite some time for my emotions to subside. I was resentful that I had been used as a legal punching bag. Others didn't have the emotional entanglement I did and were able to view it more objectively. I was alone in my dismay.

No one in the company ever asked me how I felt as the legal process transpired. Everyday work at Eagle went on as if nothing had ever happened. I led a dual life: while I dangled in a legal spotlight, Eagle promoted and advanced me several times as if nothing had happened. To everyone except me it was just part of the airline business.

But I had tasted enough. Now that I was no longer meat on the table for lawyers, I decided I would leave Eagle when the right opportunity came along. This airline business—fraught with its legal jeopardies, unionization "uber alles" atmosphere, stodgy regulatory oversight, and dog-eat-dog competitive tensions—was unpalatable to me. I missed the honor and sensibility of the Air Force. I wanted out.

## The Merger

AMR Corporation, the parent of American Airlines, was making some very consequential business decisions. American had bought Eastern's Miami assets in order to expand its hub operation there. The growing hub-and-spoke airline model major airlines used depended on employing regional airlines to feed passengers to the major airline's hubs. AMR Corporation decided to incorporate and wholly own its regional airline and increase its capacity to feed American Airlines.

The decision was made to merge all four Eagle companies into one and consolidate all their operations from west to east coast and into Puerto Rico, the Bahamas, and Mexico. When four airlines merge, essentially that means that about three of every four upper management positions are eliminated. I was facing the probability of being without a job again.

But even as managerial jobs were being cut, a new Manager of Crew Resources position was created for the merged company, and the job was offered to me. I accepted. The new American Eagle Airlines, Inc., office was established in Dallas, so Eileen, Dad, and I moved again.

## The First Consolidated Bid

The first step in the four-airline merger was mine, and it was a critical one. It was up to me to consolidate all the pilots from the four airlines and assign them new positions and domiciles. That had to happen before the rest of the merger could begin.

The timing was important, and the President and VPs were anxious. I periodically briefed upper management on my progress. I

262

was given ultimate resources and support to pull it off, including the able help of Sam Mann. Sam was an AA manager who was brought over to work with Eagle, and he was one of the few people who could coordinate essential AA support to help us with American's computer interfaces.

To make it work I had to design a consolidated bidding award and placement system using the consolidated seniority list and the domiciles and aircraft types from all four companies. I had hoped American Airlines had a bidding system I might use and adapt, but no such luck—when I visited them I found their system was surprisingly primitive, and besides they were having problems with it.

So I had to build one based on what I had designed for Nashville Eagle. Once I came up with something, Sam worked the computer interface—the Sabre System—that allowed pilots to enter their bids on their domicile's computers and let us capture the data. We trial-tested my system several times, and it looked like it would work.

With everything set up I announced the bid and its dates. The bidding began and closed, and we collected the results from Sabre. So far, so good.

The second part of my system sorted the bids and awarded pilot assignments. I assembled my team and union observers in a room, and for the first time awarded 2,300 pilots positions and new domiciles for the new American Eagle. The bid awarding took four days that first time but it worked with scarcely a hitch. No one was more surprised than I—unless it was Sam.

In one unfortunate case a new, young first officer bid himself from his domicile in middle America to Puerto Rico by mistake. He called his chief pilot literally in tears because of his error—he was a newlywed with a pregnant wife and simply couldn't afford the move or Puerto Rico's high cost of living. In one of the few instances of actual company-union collaboration, the union agreed to look the other way while I "fixed" the bid to leave the pilot where he was. When I phoned him, he was so grateful I thought he'd kiss me if he could. I sternly warned him he damn well better not tell anyone of the fix or he'd find himself in Puerto Rico in a heartbeat. After I hung up I felt really good

263

that we did something for the poor guy and his wife—and that we had found a brief, fleeting moment of cooperation with the union.

## Manager of Crew Resources

I designed the new bidding and placement system using interlaced Excel spreadsheets—big, complex spreadsheets with lots of formulas. While I was still developing the system, the company hired a Ph.D. from a software company to look over my shoulder and design sophisticated software intended to eventually replace my spreadsheets. I worked with him for hours, but he had trouble grasping the bidding mechanisms. His first trial piece of software was so useless that he was fired on the spot.

About a year later we tried again. We put out a request for proposal to software companies to design an integrated bidding and placement software suite, but the low bid (from a Pakistani company) came in at a cool one million dollars. We gulped at that and kept on with what I had implemented. Several years after leaving Eagle I learned that my "temporary" system had become permanent.

A year after that first bid I was tasked with performing a company review to resolve all the union "Presidential" grievances that had ensued. There were around 160 grievances to be settled—pilots claiming they had received the wrong bid award, went to training out of seniority order, were moved out of sequence, etc.

I began to parse and resolve all those grievances for the company. The union was expected to challenge our position, of course. At first it looked like there would be a lot of blood-letting with the union leaders. I was promised the assistance of union reps to help with the dirty work, but they never showed up—I had to do it alone. But as I got into it I found that almost all those grievances didn't hold water. Most were easily explained or resolved.

A meeting was convened with company management and union leaders, and I presented my results. I had determined there were only about a dozen legitimate grievances and only three of those warranted

264

compensation. To my surprise and delight, no one disagreed with my results, and the entire meeting was over in 30 minutes. Not bad.

Within the next year our company incorporated yet another regional airline. With the additional merger of Boston's Business Express, American Eagle grew to 2,700 pilots and roughly half that number of flight attendants. American Eagle had become the world's largest regional airline with revenues that categorized us as a major airline.

Eagle's Director of Inflight Operations (flight attendants) was having problems managing her increased number of FAs following the merger, and staffing shortages were causing numerous flight cancellations. I was asked to help her out. I knew Penny well from our time in Raleigh. I met with her and looked at her staffing methods. I designed a simpler version of my pilot system and applied it to the FAs. Staffing considerations for FAs were somewhat different, (much higher FA absenteeism, for instance), but overall it was much easier to manage.

In about three months all was working smoothly, but Penny and her staff had difficulty learning the new system. In frustration she essentially said, "No thanks," and reverted to her old ways, which didn't work. She was fired.

## Enough, Already

In the fall of 1999 Eileen and I took a week's vacation to Arizona. I was fed up with airline work and really needed a break. Every time we got away we cast an eye toward places we thought might become our future retirement location. We thought our likely target would be around San Marcos and the Texas hill country south of Austin, but that wasn't certain.

Our first stop was in Payson. It was nice, but small, so then we went to Prescott. In all my earlier Air Force years living around Tucson and Phoenix, I had never traveled to Prescott. It looked pretty nice. One morning over our hotel breakfast Eileen and I found ourselves thinking alike—that this might be the retirement place for us.

Until this visit I wasn't aware that Embry-Riddle Aeronautical University's western campus was in Prescott. Prior to getting my chief pilot job back in Raleigh, I had considered teaching part-time for ERAU at nearby Seymour-Johnson AFB. Embry-Riddle approved my application, but my new chief pilot job proved too demanding to pursue additional teaching.

So when Eileen and I decided Prescott would become our retirement destination, I decided on the spot to call Prescott's Embry-Riddle campus. I simply told the operator I was in town on vacation and wanted to talk to someone about faculty employment. My call was passed on to several people, and the last person asked if I could come to campus the next day. When I arrived I walked into a room where a search committee had been convened. We had a really nice talk, I explained my background, and I walked away with a job offer as assistant professor of aviation.

I drove back to our hotel to tell Eileen. She agreed to it, and I found myself headed for another career change . . . and another move. I joined the ERAU faculty at the beginning of the new year.

When we returned to Dallas, I walked in to tell my boss that I was leaving the company. As I expected, that didn't go over very well. My boss after the merger was a young-ish Vice President who went by nickname of "J.J." J.J. had been promoted from American Airlines to work as a VP at Eagle. He was a classic workaholic. I'm sure he thought I would be there forever. I might have explained that, unlike him, I didn't anticipate or welcome a long future with American Eagle. I had been there eight years, and that was plenty.

My department was essentially one person deep—me. I had a small staff, but my department revolved around my bidding and placement system and other software tools I had designed to manage crew resources. When AMR Corporation directed management to seek patents for any proprietary property or processes, my bid award system was Eagle's only eligible candidate.

266

J.J. extracted my promise to give him two months to hire and train my replacement. We put our house up for sale and it was quickly bought. Although my time with Eagle was relatively short, I was eligible for retirement, giving us airline travel benefits.

My last day at work was a perfect example of the atmosphere at Eagle. It was all hard-knocks business, all the time.

That morning J.J. told me he was taking me and some other managers to a nearby restaurant for lunch. When I arrived I noticed there was a cardboard box on the floor next to our table. As we finished eating, J.J. reached down to the box and unpacked an alabaster statue of an eagle inscribed to me. We chatted and bantered for a short while, the others wishing me well. And that was that—I hoisted the cardboard box out to my car and we all went back to work, business as usual.

That afternoon was typically intense. We worked a staffing problem of some sort. Late in the day some other problem came up, and I went into J.J.'s office. It was around 5:30. Our president stepped in along with Ed Criner, VP of Ops. The four of us discussed other end-of-day issues as we often did. It was after 6:00 and the discussion was going strong. I was thinking how Eileen, Dad, and I were hitting the road early in the morning, driving two cars and the dog, that dinner was waiting, and I still had packing to do. As the conversation threatened to go on forever, I interrupted and simply said, "Gentlemen, I'm leaving. It was good working with you."

The looks on their faces were of surprise and bewilderment. It was an awkward moment. I truly think they had forgotten I was leaving and were maybe a little perplexed that they hadn't given consideration for my departure. To them it was just another day. It was precisely this lack of concern for the individual—this robotic, mechanical approach to management—that kept me forever apart from liking the airline business.

I received their hasty well-wishes and walked out to the dark, empty parking lot, much relieved. That was the abrupt end of my eight years with Eagle. It was a typical American Eagle performance.

When I was commanding the 17th, the Chief of our Physiological Support Division told me something about himself. Major Bill White had been an Air Force pilot who had left the Air Force some years before for an airline pilot job. Like others, he viewed the airlines as the Golden Goose, offering pilots heaven on earth—plush conditions, luxurious pay, prestige, and other tempting rewards. Instead, he found that the airlines delivered no such green pastures, but quite the opposite. He found that working conditions were poor, and he was laid off a couple of times. He became just another number on the union's seniority list.

Bill realized he had made a mistake. Taking advantage of a special recruiting program, he was hired back into the Air Force at his officer rank, but he had to give up being a pilot. However, Bill had already been to the other side and was simply glad to be back in the Air Force as a physiology specialist.

Bill went on a crusade. He developed a clever presentation that he gave to Air Force pilots, warning them of the pitfalls awaiting those who were naively tempted to fly for the airlines.

Major Bill White was a sharp officer and an excellent public speaker who had experienced first-hand the contrast between airlines and Air Force.

I should have heeded his advice myself.

# Two Careers Down, One to Go

Dad had moved from North Carolina to live with us in Nashville. Within a year we moved again when I was given the Manager of Crew Resources job in Dallas. Now, just eighteen months after the Dallas move, we were moving to Arizona.

Eileen and I were experienced movers, but Dad certainly wasn't accustomed to it, and his age didn't help. It was quite hard on him. Dad was always able to meet tough challenges, and he was a realist.

One day before the move Dad simply asked me to sell his car. He had realized he was losing his ability to drive and find his way. I've often reflected on his remarkable determination to confront life's unpleasantries and make hard choices.

Another surprise: Dad was ready to try living in a senior home. Thanks to Eileen's care, his health had improved considerably since he first came to live with us in Nashville. So in moving to Prescott, he decided he was ready to live more independently again.

Dad stayed with my cousin in the Phoenix area until we got settled. We found a pretty nice senior complex in Prescott, and Dad decided to live there. His new independence and the company of other seniors seemed to work. He did quite well, putting our minds much at ease. But after being there a couple of years he took a fall one night and broke his hip. He was 92 and never recovered. My brother died not long after that, and my branch of the family tree had reached its end.

269

We arrived in Prescott in late December of 1999 and rented a townhouse. We purchased property and designed and built a home on a mountainside. It had a spectacular, panoramic view of the entire Prescott Valley. Our builder was a no-good scammer, but we still got a good house out of it. It was beautiful to be on the mountainside, 5700 feet high. Deer, javelina, bobcats, foxes—they all visited. We lived on the edge of the Prescott National Forest, the world's largest stand of Ponderosa pine trees.

It was great to be in Arizona, in Prescott, and teaching at the Embry-Riddle campus. On my first day driving to the campus I saw a double rainbow in the morning sun—a fine omen for sure. After eight years in the airline pressure cooker, the freedom, friendship, and relaxation of campus life was refreshing and stimulating. I relished the opportunity to be an instructor and professor of aviation to eager, young, upcoming pilots.

I taught eight years at ERAU, and it was the most rewarding way I can imagine to cap my aviation career.

## Embry-Riddle

Embry-Riddle Aeronautical University consisted of the main academic campus and also a campus at the airport where students flew and took flight-related classes. It followed the same concept as Air Force Undergraduate Pilot Training. Small cluster buildings dotted the main campus, giving it a relaxed, quiet, western atmosphere in the shadow of nearby Granite Mountain.

When I first walked into the Aviation Department it was like joining an Air Force flying squadron all over again. The faculty were mostly retired military officers and pilots about my age. I immediately met an old friend. Bob and I had worked together back at Sheppard AFB teaching the Vietnamese. And Randy had been an F-105 pilot who supervised NASA's U-2 (ER-1) operations and knew

270

some of my old U-2 friends. Fred and Nick had been stationed with me at Da Nang in Vietnam. We all had so much in common.

There's a certain trust and camaraderie that's found among pilots and military members, and that's what I found at the Embry-Riddle campus. Everyone in the department worked hard and willingly as a team.

My office was in one of the small, brick cluster buildings that dotted the campus. It was pretty tight in there. Cozy, actually. There were four tiny faculty offices for Dave Viger, Dave Branstein, Ron Frola, and me. Dave Viger kept a hummingbird feeding station outside. At the start of fall semester we'd all dress in our grubbies, push brooms and clean the campus areas. It felt really good to be there.

## Ron

Ron was a Marine. I say that affectionately, of course. I tried to convert him to the Air Force way, but it was too late. You know, "Once a Marine, always a Marine." Hoo-rah.

Ron Frola was a retired colonel—a former pilot and commander who flew F-8 Crusaders. We became lasting good friends—the best. We worked side by side for eight years and retired about the same time. Work and life were more interesting with Ron around. I think everyone felt that way about him. He had a giving personality—he truly cared about others.

Ron was a unique guy. There are few people endowed with his likable personality and talent. He and Charlotte made a wonderful pair. Eileen and I considered Charlotte and Ron as our favorite people. We had good times together.

Ron contracted blood diseases and was given just a few years to live. Like a true Marine officer as well as a giving husband and father, he bore his illness quietly and bravely. When countless blood transfusions no longer worked, he died peacefully. Through all of his

271

travails we saw the same, stalwart bravery in Charlotte—and still do. I feel the loss of Ron as I would a member of my family.

## Teaching Again

My years in academics paid off, allowing me to step into my new position easily. I was an assistant professor, and most of the others were, too. I certainly didn't have ambitions for any higher status than that. But someone up the university hierarchy decided we ex-military aviators should get doctorates for promotions and tenure and began pushing us to do so. I and others felt that at this stage of our careers we weren't reaching for the stars anymore, and we resisted. When the University president got wind of the push, he agreed with us and put a stop to it.

My first semester was the spring semester of 2000. My first courses began just a few days after we arrived, so for that first semester I stayed very busy both at work and at home preparing for the next day's classes. It was all-day, all-evening work for a while, but I was truly happy at work for the first time in years.

The prior instructor for the first course I inherited didn't do me any favors. I asked for any course materials she might provide, given that I had just arrived and would be teaching "right out of the box." She was reluctant, but then gave me some stuff. I understand her reluctance—the materials she used were pure junk. She was teaching off the cuff, without much teaching experience, having been a former flight attendant with an airline captain husband. She was using her husband's union pamphlet as a textbook. I put an end to that nonsense. I spent long hours throughout that first semester building a rigorous, meaningful academic course.

When the semester was over and final exams had been given, I was faced with a perplexing problem—what do I do with the summer? There was no work from late May until we assembled in August to prepare for fall semester. In my entire career I had never encountered this dilemma—weeks of free time. I locked my office until I returned in the fall. It felt so strange to have the summer off. I actually felt uncomfortable about it—briefly.

I began teaching a senior-level course about the techniques of flying high performance airplanes. It was juicy aviation stuff, talking to seniors about the fascinating aspects of flying fast and large airplanes as many were soon to do. I also taught a course on commuter aviation, something that related well to my experience at Eagle. Later on I taught aircraft systems of the Boeing 747 and a course on airline operations—essentially a business course.

One of the satisfactions of teaching at the university level was having license to tailor courses to fit university and student dynamics. Every course was a work in progress, and that was especially true for aviation courses. Every semester I spent a great deal of time researching and updating my courses. Aviation itself is never stagnant, and aviation courses shouldn't stagnate, either. I really enjoyed my evolving course work.

Over the years I picked up attendant responsibilities and duties. I was appointed as a member of the Academic Dean's Council. I served on the Campus Curriculum Committee and became its chairman for several years. I was an alternate member of the faculty senate and a member of several faculty search committees. When the College of Arts and Sciences instituted a new degree program in Global Security and Intelligence Studies, I agreed to be on their search committee. I ran our department's student internship program and became the department's faculty scheduler. And for two years I was the Campus Grievance Coordinator. Many other projects and involvements occupied my time and gave variety to my job.

Faculty work was both busy and fulfilling, and the best part was that I was mostly my own boss. How I scheduled my time was mostly up to me. We all had a class schedule to follow, but since I was the scheduler, I had control over that, too. Of course there were those incessant faculty meetings—there's no avoiding those. But throughout my years at ERAU there was no boredom. There was work to be done, but it was pleasurable work. The sheer intensity of the airline atmosphere was happily gone, replaced by a more benign environment. I still missed the Air Force, but at Embry-Riddle I had found the next best thing.

## Have a Heart

I arranged my teaching schedule so that I could regularly play handball at an athletic club downtown. It was a short drive from campus, and I would skip food to play. We had a good group of players, and I enjoyed the game as I had for years. But one day as I played I noticed my heart felt strange. That afternoon I stopped by the VA hospital to check out my condition. The nurse listened to my heart and immediately checked me into urgent care. I had a heart rhythm irregularity. I called Eileen and I was hospitalized overnight. That was the beginning of my years-long bout with atrial fibrillation.

Atrial fib is caused by irregular electrical pulses within the heart. It increases the risk of stroke and shortens life span. It's also associated with sleep apnea, and I was diagnosed with that, too. Over time my atrial fib became more irregular and more constant. It caused me to experience times of extreme weakness, and sleep apnea produced continuous fatigue through disturbed sleep. I gained control over my sleep apnea by wearing a mask hooked to a continuous positive air pressure (CPAP) pump at night. Only fifty percent of sleep apnea patients are able to adapt to wearing a CPAP mask and harness, but in flying airplanes I had worn an oxygen mask and helmet for many years. Wearing the CPAP mask was like a walk in the park.

My A-fib grew steadily worse and was unresponsive to heart medications. My doctor was the lone cardiologist at the VA hospital in Prescott, and he hadn't really kept up with current cardiology developments. It became apparent that I needed better treatment than he was providing, so I took myself to the Mayo Clinic a hundred miles away in Phoenix. Drug-resistant atrial fib was a perplexing problem that required surgery. Fortunately I was placed in the hands of the head of Mayo's electrophysiology department, Dr. Srivasthan.

Dr. Sri, as he was called by his staff, was from India and was a miracle worker. In the course of four years he performed three catheter ablation heart surgeries on me. Catheter ablation is a surgical procedure whereby probes are inserted through openings in the jugular and groin and then threaded into the heart. One of the probes has a heating element at the tip to cauterize parts of the heart and use scar tissue "dams" to block extraneous electrical signals. To allow for healing, the operations were performed a year apart. Each of my operations lasted 7-9 hours—very, very hard on Eileen who had to wait all day with the uncertainty. Unfortunately I encountered complications and incurred a week's hospital stay after each surgery. The good doctor persisted, and the third operation was fully successful, and I'm now cured. I'm the only patient Dr. Sri has ever given three catheter ablations. I've always been a little stubborn that way. Interestingly, Srivasthan's next patient was the King of Saudi Arabia.

I really have enjoyed playing handball over the years. Finding a bunch of handball players was another pleasant Prescott surprise. Experts warn that handball is a sport particularly hard on knees, and it certainly did a number on mine. I must be particularly lucky with doctors, though, because I discovered one of the best orthopedic surgeons in the nation right here in Prescott. Dr. Bertrand Kaper has replaced both of my knees—and both of Eileen's, too—most successfully.

## Talk, All Talk

In the late 1970s my first assignment to the Pentagon brought me within an easy drive to visit my parents in Hickory, North Carolina. Dad asked if I'd be willing to talk to his Rotary Club about my U-2 experiences. I hadn't done that before, but I agreed. How would I tell people about the U-2 and its highly classified operations? My audience would likely have no aviation knowledge or frame of reference to relate to the U-2's missions and would be a mix of small town Americans, men and women.

I experimented with different approaches and finally came up with one I hoped would be interesting. I prepared a presentation and gave the talk. Afterward I was showered by questions and handshakes. I was pleasantly surprised how eager everyone was to have learned about that magical airplane.

In time other such opportunities came up, so I refined and developed my presentation to fit various audiences. I augmented my graphics using PowerPoint slides and a projector, added some animation, and included videos of U-2 landings—and crashes. Over the years I've given my talk about 45-50 times. I was invited to speak at the Smithsonian Air and Space Museum's "Airpower" lecture series, but our sudden assignment to Nebraska prevented that appearance. My largest audience was to around 300 attendees at the Arizona Airport Managers' convention held in Prescott. My smallest audience was just a dozen or so at a senior living facility. Size didn't matter— what mattered was audience enthusiasm, and that's never been disappointing. Several times I've been told that my talk was the best their club or organization had ever had. I've even been asked back to give a repeat presentation. That surprised me—why would anyone want to hear the same talk twice?

The fame and aura of the U-2 sustained my presentation for years—decades, actually. I had struck on the perfect subject for an interesting presentation—a guaranteed success every time. Word of my talk got around, and I've been interviewed on radio and TV and for newspaper articles. I've thoroughly enjoyed telling people about the U-2, and the people I've talked to were always enthusiastic.

I've given that presentation long after I left the U-2 and the Air Force. However, I promised myself that I would stop giving my talks when I felt that my U-2 knowledge—or I—were becoming too dated and stale. It's now been two years since my last talk, and I really miss giving it. A video of my talk is archived with Embry-Riddle's Aviation History records.

Many pilots have difficulty when flying isn't part of their lives anymore. Saying good-bye to flying is tough for most—much like post-partum depression.

Returning to the cockpit after Air Force retirement was a mistake. Dialing back the clock to fly again just wasn't satisfying, and airline flying in particular wasn't my cup of tea. When I was the RDU chief pilot I flew moderately with two of my most experienced, trusted captains, but I really had no urge to fly commercially except to escape my office now and then.

Flying high performance Air Force aircraft spoiled me for flying low and slow ever again. Ron Frola and I went up in his Cessna 180 and roamed northern Arizona one morning, flying around the spikes in Monument Valley, down the canyons of Lake Powell, and over the red rocks of Sedona. That was nice flying, but taking the controls didn't really captivate me as much as simply seeing the sights.

Several of us flew to San Antonio and Randolph AFB to evaluate simulators for Embry-Riddle's flight program. Randolph had realistic, three-axis simulators for their new AT-6 Texan turboprop, and we spent some time flying one. The instructor set it up for simulated formation flying, and I took a turn at that. I surprised myself, and apparently the others, too. All my formation flying came back in a flash, and I caught right onto it.

Embry-Riddle's spring commencement was coming up. We held commencements outdoors in Arizona's always-good weather, and the ceremony featured a flyby using three of ERAU's own aircraft, the twin-engine Beechcraft Duchess. Students weren't trained to fly formation, so the flyby pilots were former military pilots from the faculty. Sean, Mike, and Bob regularly filled those roles, but for this particular graduation, Mike was receiving an award and had to be present on the ground. Sean recalled seeing me fly formation in the AT-6 simulator at Randolph and asked me to fill in for Mike. I hadn't flown anything in ten years and didn't have a current physical, so I needed an instructor to fly with me.

We flew one practice flight before doing the real thing. It didn't take me long to get the feel of the Duchess. Time erodes many skills, but apparently not the memories of formation flying.  It all quickly came back, and I soon fell into a comfort zone.  The Duchess was a little underpowered, but no real challenge to fly.  It all went quite well, and after graduation we got compliments for our formation.

That was the last time I ever flew an airplane.  Sure, I miss my lifelong passion, but who gets to fly a three-ship formation flyby on his very last flight?  'Twas nice.

# *I'm Almost Done*

I had been at ERAU for eight years after serving over 26 in the Air Force and eight in the airlines. I had enjoyed a long, productive career in aviation, but I had also slowed incrementally over that time. Workplace dynamics in the Department of Aviation were changing, too, and I sensed it was time to take my third and final retirement.

When I had begun teaching at ERAU in 2000, most of us on the faculty were of the same "vintage," heading toward the last productive years of our working lives. Except for instructing, our aviation experiences were behind us. We were all ripening at about the same rate. Medical and health issues crept into our conversations.

I decided to retire from ERAU when I felt that my aviation experiences and my age might be making me dated and irrelevant. I didn't feel like a fossil; quite the contrary, once my atrial fib was cured and I had two new knees, I felt quite vibrant. Hearing aids and glasses restored my senses (tongue in cheek).

I've seen others cling to employment like there was nothing else left to do. I've seen a longing for productive employment keep people in the teaching game beyond their point of usefulness. It's hard to tell former professional pilots they shouldn't fly anymore, but it's doubly hard to tell those same people they need to retire from even teaching.

In academia it's highly unusual for a professor to get the axe. For many, tenure gives them the right to die and rot in their office chairs. Age is a revered quality among higher education faculty, and few academic leaders have the gumption to tell a fellow professor that he's getting on in years and should quit. The image of an old, doddering professor teaching young students until he keels over is iconic. But I

279

just couldn't stomach the idea that young students would see me as that doddering old professor. I was a pilot before I was a professor, and I've got a pilot's pride.

I've taught young people to fly for many years. I taught them in UPT. I taught young Vietnamese. I taught young cadets in AFROTC. And I taught young students at Embry-Riddle. I'm a true believer that aviation is for youthful people with gobs of vigor.

With that in mind I looked at myself, my age, my circumstances, and decided it was time to retire.

I sought a way to ease out of gear gradually, and so I took a phased retirement from ERAU in my eighth year. I wrote my own contract so I would work just two days of the week, teaching two courses. It was an enjoyable year as I headed for retirement. Yes, I had sadness and regret, but I was ready.

I have few attachments to Embry-Riddle anymore. The Prescott campus is now under the able leadership of the Chancellor, Dr. Frank Ayers, who also happens to be retired Air Force Colonel Frank Ayers. Years ago when I was the SAC Senior Controller, Frank worked at my side as an Operations Officer. He's had quite a career, proving his talents many times over.

Many of our friends are from my teaching days—other faculty and their families who retired about the time I did. A couple of students stayed in touch with me through occasional phone calls; one did that for years.

Eileen and I went out to the campus recently for a friend's retirement party. That party was my first time on campus in years, and I got to see old friends from long ago. I found myself preoccupied with observing how much everyone had aged. It was they who had aged—not me, of course.

Some years earlier Bob and Mike—the flyby pilots—left widows when they collided their sport airplanes while practicing acrobatics for Prescott's air show. It was a tragic, abrupt shock to our clan of aviators, wives, and families. They were respected colleagues and friends, and their loss was palpable to us all. We were all changing with time, and their accident caused time to jump ahead even faster. We were gravitating toward the same eventual demise—had Mike and Bob become too old to fly acrobatics and pull Gs? Did one or both react too slowly?

I remember back when I, stupidly, tried to hop back into the cockpit of an airliner and fly again. The first thing I faced was a cockpit filled with an array of instruments around me, including an overhead instrument panel. Wearing my bifocals, I could read instruments looking down, but when I tried to look up at the overhead panel it was blurred. I was getting too old! I had to get trifocals! If I had been thinking straight, I would have taken that as an unmistakable sign that I shouldn't be in the cockpit anymore.

I believe that Bob and Mike's accident was in some way age-related, but no one will ever know.

After we retired, Ron Frola and I and started meeting regularly for restaurant lunches. As other faculty colleagues retired our lunch bunch grew. Now we have 6-8 of us mostly-retired flyboy-professors meeting for lunch every two weeks. We're all retired military colonels or lieutenant colonels, and we're all pilots—even Nick. Two still teach at ERAU. We're full of half-baked memories and are pretty much tall talk now. We have difficulty staying on any one subject, but we still converse using our hands the way good pilots do. Three of us also meet for an occasional breakfast coffee where we tackle all the world's spillover problems that our lunch bunch didn't get around to. Somehow the problems we fix reappear as soon as we're out the coffee shop's door. We're the last of our tribe.

We're also a very fortunate collection of people. We were all professional military pilots who had our most productive years during the pinnacle era of manned flight. Drones and other pilotless, driverless vehicles are now coming into use, and the era of hands-on piloting is waning. We are relics of the Golden Age of Pilots, drifting into obsolescence, remembering that it had once been a great time to fly.

Aviation is an all-consuming passion. Pilots get old and tired, but they always love the game.

## Pure Politics

I had never "gone political" before, but once fully retired I decided to explore local Republican politics. I had written numerous letters to the local newspaper, but my sense was that words are cheap, and various societal and government problems needed to be addressed by the political party organizations. To that end I decided to become politically involved for the first time.

At a GOP chapter meeting I met a lady who once ran the County's Women's Republican Chapter. I explained my intentions, and Darlene said I needed to become a Precinct Committeeman first of all. I submitted my application and was approved by the County Board of Supervisors. But the job of a PC was to get out the vote by doing legwork, and that's not why I joined.

I had managed enough organizations and people to recognize organizational dysfunction when I see it, and the Yavapai County GOP organization seemed in disarray to me. I wrote a letter to the county GOP Supervisory Committee with my recommendations for organizational improvement. I figured it would be shot down with gusto, but to my surprise it was received with enthusiasm. It was even circulated to our state senator who wrote me a letter of thanks for it. I was invited to attend meetings of the county GOP Executive Committee as an advisor, which I did regularly.

I remained involved for almost two years, but to my disappointment there was little strong leadership to support a reorganization effort. The people who could scream the loudest at rallies dominated, and the party leadership just wasn't populated by many visionaries (Kevin Lane and Mark Sensmeir excepted). I withdrew from my unofficial position at the Executive Committee meetings, ending my attempt at formal political involvement.

## Too Much Travel

Eileen and I have moved so often in our lives that travel and sightseeing offer little pleasure anymore. My family is all gone, but we'd visit our son and Eileen's family every year, most often by sharing a beach rental at the Outer Banks of North Carolina. David isn't healthy and mobile anymore, but when he was we'd take him to the Chesapeake Bay eastern shore to spend time together. But age and everyone's health make all of that a burden now. With my airline retirement we could skip off to just about anywhere flying standby, but standby flying was never very enjoyable before, and it's even worse now. Our airline travel benefits go largely unused.

So travel isn't high on our list of pleasures. Besides, we live in one of the most desirable locations in the US, according to numerous magazines who rate those things. There is a lot to do around here. For many years, for instance, we'd drive off on a September morning and walk the south rim of the Grand Canyon, returning home in time to slap a steak on the grill. Everyday life around here is pretty grand.

We travel shorter distances, often to Nevada for some gaming and a golfing opportunity in Vegas with my old U-2 buddy, Chuck. Occasionally we'll head for a short vacation on the California coast and make day trips to the local attractions of scenic Arizona. But most travel isn't for us.

## Old Hobbies, New Interests

What do people in retirement mostly do?—travel and hobbies. Hobbies are usually just pastimes, but mine became something more than that. Two hobbies occupy my time these days: music and painting watercolors.

My folks entered me in piano lessons at an early age. My piano teacher taught both classical and pop music, splitting each lesson between the two. I learned fundamentals from the classical side and how to put chords and melody together from the popular side. When our family moved to North Carolina in the '50s my lessons stopped, but I had learned enough to keep up my interest. Ever since I've played mostly casual, popular music.

I've owned a succession of pianos over the years, which made my frequent moves more interesting. In Prescott I bought an electronic piano and began to learn all the amazing things I could do by recording and arranging music using my computer for sound engineering. Once retired I devoted more time to arranging and composing.

Acting on a whim I took five of my compositions, put them on a CD, and marched them down to the KAHM Radio station in Prescott. KAHM broadcasts uninterrupted soothing music to much of northern Arizona and Phoenix and also streams it on the Internet. I was prepared for utter rejection, but to my surprise the station's music director called the next day to say she wanted all five.

Over the past five years eleven of my compositions have been broadcast on the airwaves, most of them still being heard. It's really a treat to be listening to famous musicians playing familiar hits on the radio and suddenly hear your own music. Some listeners have even tracked me down and called with their compliments.

I'm fortunate to have another hobby that competes for time with my music. Years ago when I was buried under work at the Pentagon, Eileen gave me a beginner's watercolor set for Christmas. I still don't know what inspired her, but watercolor painting captivated me.

I didn't do much with it for some years. I dabbled, so to speak. Painting is one of those pastimes that is mysteriously inviting but is also quite intimidating when you really don't know how to do it. I could feel quite comfortable flying at the edge of outer space, but there's nothing that put beads of sweat on my brow like hovering over a blank piece of paper with a paint brush in my hand.

When I retired from Embry-Riddle I began to take watercolor painting more seriously. I self-studied and attended a workshop in Sedona given by famed watercolorist Tom Lynch. Tom had been my watercolor hero since he broadcast his television series on PBS. Tom had been the official artist for the Masters Golf Tournament and wore golf sweaters in his instructional videos, so I figured that if a fellow golfer could paint, maybe I could, too. In my skewed way of thinking I thought I might even shave some strokes off my game.

I've made progress and paint decently now. I exhibited fifteen of my paintings at the local library. They required me to put prices on them. I had no idea how to price paintings, and it never crossed my mind that any would sell. To my surprise someone plunked down four hundred for one.

## Some of Us Get Old

Music, watercolors, golf, some local travel through the scenic southwest, good times with good friends—that's enough for me now. I'm on cruise control these days. It's too bad old age has to set in and slow us down. That's the "brakes."

Unfortunately, age-related health issues have crept into our lives. If there's not something affecting us, there's something affecting our friends and family. There's no dodging it—we've got to plan for that next phase of living. The dwindling phase.

We've found our home here. We live comfortably in an area rich in attractions and scenic beauty. Our lives are pleasant, and there's no place else that suits us nearly as well. There's some family separation to deal with, but we're still mobile enough to pay visits back East.

The community surrounding Prescott is relatively small, and we're distant from Arizona's metropolises of Phoenix and Tucson with lots of desert in between. Eileen and I have enjoyed living in and around Prescott—an area that provides so much without being too big. I always looked upon the Air Force as a big family; it wasn't unusual to meet an old friend or acquaintance halfway around the world. In the

Prescott area it's even more that way. I always got a kick out of unexpectedly bumping into friends or my students around town. This place is just like that—small and friendly.

We've traveled extensively, visiting and living in places around the globe and throughout this country, discovering myriad new and interesting things. I've lived and worked more than five years in other countries. Eileen has visited both China and Russia—countries that my security clearances didn't permit me to enter. Here in the US we've lived coast to coast, north to south, residing in fifteen different states. Moving was often a hardship—short notice assignments, finding accommodations, buying/selling homes, leaving behind friends and family, and always costing us money.

Altogether I've made major moves over 35 times during my lifetime—most of them with Eileen—along with many shorter moves too numerous to count. That's over now.


## What Does It All Mean?

I'm not one to dwell on the past much. I'm more apt to stick past events in a reserved corner of my mind and bring them out if I need to. The future has always seemed more important than things behind me.

Although I've been inclined toward adventure, I wouldn't describe myself as an adventurous person. I've always felt restrained by a certain degree of caution. I accommodate measured risks if they have a purpose but avoid wild and crazy antics. Whatever might happen, I prefer to meet it on my terms. I want to have firm control over my life and its circumstances. I ordinarily don't welcome surprises; instead I take pleasure in matters when they turned out as planned.

Having said that, I don't think there's a lot of adventure awaiting me anymore. I'm slowing down, getting weaker. When I drive a golf ball it flies shorter year after year, and so it seems with almost everything I do these days. I think golfers measure life's decline in terms of reduced yardage.

So it's a good time to write memoirs while I cast an eye toward the terminal stage of life. Not that I expect to go out the door anytime soon. There's still a lot more living to do, but I'm simply stating that I expect some of it to become unpleasant.

Now I find myself looking back on times long ago more than ever, and doing that can be quite emotional. Good times, times not so good—they all seem to rise to the surface these days. I find myself pondering my past, trying to put it all in perspective.

My childhood was good, and I was very well cared for by smart, loving, and caring parents. I have fond remembrances of them—still miss them a lot. My varied childhood experiences and good schooling prepared me well for the numerous detours I encountered along the way.

I think back to all those years in aviation with tranquil satisfaction. I've had a rich, fulfilling professional life spiced with escapades and exploration. Life has thrown many challenges my way. I think—I hope—I've measured up to them.

My decisions may not have all been right, but I don't think I made any really bad ones—the kind that leave scars upon me or others. I met adversity head-on when it came, accepted my responsibilities, and tried to grow myself over time.

Flying multi-million dollar airplanes on crucial missions was responsibility enough when I was a young pilot, but in time I learned that having an Air Force commander's responsibility over peoples' lives and livelihoods trumped that. I didn't ponder those responsibilities every day, but in more pensive moments I acknowledged that I was doing things that had importance to the country and others. I realized that in my military work I was protecting the lives of Americans, and I was respectful of that.

I'm a patriot. Mine is a less-corny form of patriotism from that of some others. My patriotism comes from within; it isn't reserved for Fourth of July celebrations or Veterans Day parades. After 26 years of military service, patriotic holidays don't affect me much. My patriotism is more apt to arise when life's little burps and tickles suddenly awaken some past memory of my service career. My sense of country is expressed less in saluting our flag than by a deep feeling that I'm part of that flag.

I once had occasion to speak before a class at the Air Force NCO Academy in England. I spoke candidly and expressed these thoughts of duty and patriotism to them (better than I'm doing right now). I tried to convey the idea that they and I were all doing what we thought was necessary and right; that we had chosen a path that protected others even at our personal risk, and that along the way a piece of what we did was returned to us in the form of personal pride and patriotism.

I went to see the Vietnam Veterans Memorial Wall in Washington when it was first built. Fifty-eight thousand names etched in black. It was too emotional for me, and I vowed never to go there again.

## Frosting on the Cake

So now I look back on life. I write memoirs. Certain recollections bring to the surface feelings of accomplishment while others make me wonder how I didn't get killed for being so stupid. It's with a mixture of these contrary feelings that I recall these highlights of my life . . . .

For sheer enjoyment and wonderment, my year in pilot training stands above any other. I was continuously walking on a cloud—flying on a cloud, actually—over my good fortune. It was surely the springboard to my entire aviation career.

Some of my aerial encounters were quite adventuresome, too. The war supplied plenty of those. But mostly it was flying and operating the U-2 all those years that provided me a lifetime of entertainment— and satisfaction.

If pressed to answer, I could pop my suspenders and tell someone that I had probably been the highest-flying or fastest human on earth at various times. But credentials like that are superficial, relevant only

288

when playing Trivial Pursuit for cash. They were incidental to the job and aren't meaningful.

However, some of my more sublime airborne moments make it to the top of my life's favorites list:

Flying at dawn and dusk in the U-2, I've seen the most spectacular sunrises and sunsets, unblemished by the earth's tainted atmosphere. I vividly recall the first time I witnessed a sunrise flying high in a U-2. It was so surprising, as if someone raised the window shade. Try as I have, I've never been able to adequately describe those scenes to others. I've just never found a word picture that does it justice.

Likewise, I've seen the curvature of the earth and viewed more stars than even the highest mountain climber. On so many U-2 missions I've flown thousands of miles over many, many hours, completely alone in my work and thoughts. I've flown solo across oceans and seas, continent-to-continent, and coast-to-coast across the United States. I've looked down into thunderstorms to see a dazzling array of lightning below. I've seen the earth as a planet and viewed the universe above as no earth-bound person ever has.

These are my fondest memories of flying, and they are always with me.

\* \* \* \* \* \* \* \* \*

My Air Force years were the best. In the Air Force I associated with some of the finest, most caring, most patriotic people this country has produced—people who willingly sacrificed comforts and put themselves at risk so that others never have to. And let's be very clear—military spouses are very much veterans, too.

I've commanded several Air Force units. There is no civilian equivalent to military command, and I've yet to meet the non-veteran civilian who fully comprehends what those command responsibilities entail.

I'm grateful to have received significant awards for performance and achievement in Air Force service. The medals now hang in a beautiful shadow box on my wall, but more important to me is that blue uniform they once adorned.

* * * * * * * *

Seventeen years with the U-2 produced too many significant episodes to catalogue. Unusual events occurred regularly, sometimes with complete surprise and suddenness. Many placed me either in the right place at the right time, or the wrong place at the wrong time, but with enough "wiggle room" to recover. Some such adventures aren't so nice until they're over, but they all ride high in my mind.

* * * * * * * * *

I flew 17 months in combat during four tours of duty in the Vietnam War. Despite close calls, I survived while others I knew didn't. Some of my combat encounters were somewhat more "stimulating" than I preferred them to be, but I got through without physical or mental scars. I'm cautious to say this in the company of those who haven't flown in combat, but I actually regard that first year in the Vietnam War as one of my best. That singular year affected every year of my life ever since—everything I see, do or think.

* * * * * * * * *

I think I made the most of my time at American Eagle, but I sure didn't like it much. I went from lowly first officer to a succession of key management positions in a short while. The airline grew, merged, then grew and merged some more during my eight years there. It was a tumultuous time. I played a significant part in all of that and left behind a legacy improvement to Eagle's operations. Despite the success, I just wish I had done something different.

* * * * * * * * *

I was glad to settle in Prescott. I had experienced enough thrills and didn't relish any more adventure in my life. Aside from occasional vacations, I sure didn't want any more travel.

By the time I came to Embry-Riddle I was finished climbing a career ladder. I had no further interest in job promotion or advancement. I had already been a full professor and department chair elsewhere in academia, and I didn't aspire to do any of that again.

As that general in England once said, "Them who can't, teach." And that's been just fine with me. I've been content to finish my working years as an assistant professor teaching aviation students at Embry-Riddle. It was all good stuff, working with great people I respected and liked.

I've been genuinely happy to have found the capstone of my long aviation career at Embry-Riddle Aeronautical University in Prescott, Arizona.

Frosting on the cake, it is.

This may sound corny, but I believe that one gains new perspective from soaring many miles above the earth, alone—not just physically, but philosophically, too.

When flying a U-2 I could see across the many states below as if I were looking at a roadmap. That physical view made life on earth appear quite finite, fragile, and constrained. From above I saw the works of both nature and human endeavor laid out in a microcosm beneath me.

My sense of this country and its people is mostly shaped from my participation in America's defense for 26 years while living and working around the globe. After you give a sizeable chunk of your life to the national defense, you tend to take the country's peccadilloes more personally.

I was assigned as Senior Controller of the nation's largest nuclear arsenal. I'm likely the only person on earth who has experienced both ends of the nuclear spectrum, having both controlled a nuclear force and also flown within the detritus of a nuclear detonation. I've never looked at this nation and the world the same way since. I know how quickly nuclear war could be upon us, but I'm completely without power to convey that caution to others.

Most people blithely regard nuclear war as but a relic. It's not.

I'm appalled by the utter neglect that has typified our government over recent years for not protecting against the rise of rogue nuclear states. This world cannot stomach pop-up nuclear powers with fragile governments and happy trigger-fingers. You don't make deals with these people, either. You must use every ounce of American power to make it impossible for them to ever go nuclear. Anything less is world suicide.

. . . And don't ever trust nuclear Russia, either.

There is a huge chasm between those who guard our nation and those who extemporize from the sidelines. I'm dismayed to watch the political left wantonly waltz the country down a dangerous path, frittering away our constitutional and legal protections while relegating defense of the nation to an inferior status, perennially neglected and underfunded.

As I've described elsewhere in this missive, fear is a very real, powerful motivator. Americans should rightly fear the repercussions of a socialist nanny-state with weakened foundations. They should fear those among us who have never run a government, but want government to run us.

I really think American society needs to hit the reset button to bring back traditional American values, but I'm afraid time and prosperity have dimmed our memories of historical lessons learned during precarious times, when democracy was more precious.

Perhaps America needs a good war to jar people to their senses.

I'm done now.

# Acknowledgements

I met and married Eileen when I was 38 years old and had pretty much resigned to remain a bachelor. I'm fortunate to have found her. The stars must have been aligned just right.

I'm still amazed at her capacity for handling the many trials we've been through. My career choices led us far from the traditional family life depicted in movies and story books. Eileen has deep, inner courage and salt-of-the-earth qualities that continue to surprise and comfort me. Quite a lady.

\* \* \* \* \* \* \* \* \*

I'd also like to tip my cap to all those in the U-2 program who came before me. Before we sent man into space, we sent him into the upper reaches of the atmosphere. When Wolfe wrote "The Right Stuff," he somehow failed to mention the U-2 program's pioneers. Perhaps he purposely did that because their exploits far overshadow those of the early astronauts.

Out of the original 55 U-2s, 37 were lost to accidents. Seven were shot down. During the first three years of operation, 13 U-2s were lost with 11 pilots killed.

The early astronauts had glory; those early U-2 pilots had the right stuff.